W9-CMF-225

Beyond Binaries in Education Research

Routledge Research in Education

For a full list of titles in this series please visit www.routledge.com

29. Cross-Cultural Perspectives on Policy and Practice
Decolonizing Community Contexts
Edited by Jennifer Lavia and Michele Moore

30. Education and Climate Change
Living and Learning in Interesting Times
Edited by Fumiyo Kagawa and David Selby

31. Education and Poverty in Affluent Countries
Edited by Carlo Raffo, Alan Dyson, Helen Gunter, Dave Hall, Lisa Jones and Afroditi Kalambouka

32. What's So Important About Music Education?
J. Scott Goble

33. Educational Transitions
Moving Stories from Around the World
Edited by Divya Jindal-Snape

34. Globalization, the Nation-State and the Citizen
Dilemmas and Directions for Civics and Citizenship Education
Edited by Alan Reid, Judith Gill and Alan Sears

35. Collaboration in Education
Edited by Judith J. Slater and Ruth Ravid

36. Trust and Betrayal in Educational Administration and Leadership
Edited by Eugenie A. Samier and Michèle Schmidt

37. Teaching and Learning with Technology
Beyond Constructivism
Edited by Concetta M. Stewart, Catherine C. Schifter and Melissa E. Markaridian Selverian

38. Gender Inclusive Engineering Education
Julie Mills, Mary Ayre and Judith Gill

39. Intercultural and Multicultural Education
Enhancing Global Interconnectedness
Edited by Carl A. Grant and Agostino Portera

40. Systemization in Foreign Language Teaching
Monitoring Content Progression
Wilfried Decoo

41. Inclusive Education in the Middle East
Eman Gaad

42. Critical Issues in Peace and Education
Edited by Peter Pericles Trifonas and Bryan Wright

43. Children's Drawing and Writing
The Remarkable in the Unremarkable
Diane Mavers

44. Citizenship, Education and Social Conflict
Israeli Political Education in Global Perspective
Edited by Hanan A. Alexander, Halleli Pinson and Yossi Yonah

45. Emerging Teachers and Globalisation
Gerry Czerniawski

46. Social Studies as New Literacies for Living in a Global Society
Relational Cosmopolitanism in the Classroom
Mark Baildon and James S. Damico

47. Education Policy, Space and the City
Markets and the (In)visibility of Race
Kalervo N. Gulson

48. Memory and Pedagogy
Edited by Claudia Mitchell, Teresa Strong-Wilson, Kathleen Pithouse and Susann Allnutt

49. Universities and Global Diversity
Preparing Educators for Tomorrow
Edited by Beverly Lindsay and Wanda J. Blanchett

50. Equity and Excellence in Education
Towards Maximal Learning Opportunities for All Students
Edited by Kris Van den Branden, Piet Van Avermaet and Mieke Van Houtte

51. Global Pathways to Abolishing Physical Punishment
Realizing Children's Rights
Edited by Joan E. Durrant and Anne B. Smith

52. From Testing to Productive Student Learning
Implementing Formative Assessment in Confucian-Heritage Settings
David Carless

53. Changing Schools in an Era of Globalization
Edited by John C. K. Lee and Brian J. Caldwell

54. Boys and Their Schooling
The Experience of Becoming Someone Else
John Whelen

55. Education and Sustainability
Learning Across the Diaspora, Indigenous, and Minority Divide
Seonaigh MacPherson

56. International Case Studies of Dyslexia
Edited by Peggy L. Anderson and Regine Meier-Hedde

57. Schooling and the Making of Citizens in the Long Nineteenth Century
Comparative Visions
Edited by Daniel Tröhler, Thomas S. Popkewitz and David F. Labaree

58. Islamic Education and Indoctrination
The Case in Indonesia
Charlene Tan

59. Beyond Binaries in Education Research
Edited by Warren Midgley, Mark A. Tyler, Patrick Alan Danaher, and Alison Mander

Beyond Binaries in Education Research

Edited by Warren Midgley,
Mark A. Tyler, Patrick Alan Danaher,
and Alison Mander

Routledge
Taylor & Francis Group
New York   London

First published 2011
by Routledge
711 Third Avenue, New York, NY 10017

Simultaneously published in the UK
by Routledge
2 Park Square, Milton Park, Abingdon, Oxon OX14 4RN

Routledge is an imprint of the Taylor & Francis Group, an informa business

© 2011 Taylor & Francis

Typeset in Sabon by IBT Global.
Printed and bound in the United States of America on acid-free paper by IBT Global.

Library of Congress Cataloging-in-Publication Data
Beyond binaries in education research / edited by Warren Midgley . . . [et al.].
    p. cm. — (Routledge research in education)
    Includes bibliographical references and index.
1. Education—Research—Methodology.   I. Midgley, Warren.
    LB1028.2.B48 2011
    370.72—dc22   2010047158

ISBN13: 978-0-415-88512-6 (hbk)
ISBN13: 978-0-203-81660-8 (ebk)

For those who have helped us move
beyond the binary of me/you with love.

ever thine
ever mine
ever ours
Ludwig van Beethoven, "Immortal Beloved" letter 3

Contents

List of Figures   xiii
List of Tables   xv
Foreword: Renewing the Critical Function of Education Research   xvii
MICHAEL SINGH
Preface   xxi
BRUCE MUIRHEAD AND SAMANTHA DEAN
Acknowledgments   xxiii

1   Constructing and Deconstructing Binaries in
    Education Research   1
    ALISON MANDER, PATRICK ALAN DANAHER, MARK A. TYLER,
    AND WARREN MIDGLEY

PART I
Researching Researchers

    Part I Introduction   15
    WARREN MIDGLEY

2   Methodology, the Western, and Myself ~~The West/Non-West~~
    ~~Binary~~ in a Non-Western Educational Researcher's Pursuit
    of a PhD   17
    AKIHIRO SAITO

3   Determining a Voice to Use in Writing About Mixed Methods
    Research   27
    DINAH R. DOVONA-OPE

4   Beyond *Observer* and *Observed* in Reflexive Analysis   34
    WARREN MIDGLEY

5   Destabilizing Binaries in Early Childhood Education:
    The Possibilities of Pedagogical Documentation   46
    LAURIE KOCHER AND VERONICA PACINI-KETCHABAW

6   Moving Beyond Sedentarism: Conceptual and Empirical
    Developments   60
    PATRICK ALAN DANAHER AND ROBYN HENDERSON

PART II
Privileging Participants

    Part II Introduction   81
    MARK A. TYLER

7   A Tango in VET: Whose Notion of TAFE Teacher Leads?   83
    MARK A. TYLER

8   Beyond the Binaries That Keep Us From Writing With and
    Like Children   100
    SHELLEY KINASH AND KIRSTEN KINASH

9   Burying the Binaries: Getting Discourses to Converge in a
    Program for First-Year University Students   119
    ROBYN HENDERSON AND KAREN NOBLE

10 Not Education Research Binaries—Just Parts of a Whole   131
    LINDY ABAWI

11 Beyond the Binary of Researcher/Researched: The Complexities
    of Participatory Action Research   147
    KAREN HAWKINS

12 Understanding Cultural Differences Between Western and
    Confucian Teaching and Learning   161
    PENG ZHOU AND CEC PEDERSEN

PART III
Considering Contexts

Part III Introduction   179
ALISON MANDER

13 From Maintaining to Sustaining: Moving Beyond Binaries
    Toward a Framework for Cultural Sustainability
    in Higher Education   181
    SARA HAMMER, JILL LAWRENCE, AND HENK HUIJSER

14 Exposing Bush Binaries: Using the Media to Problematize
    Gender   195
    SHERILYN LENNON

15 Expectations of Ability and Disability at University:
    The Fine Art of Managing Lives, Perceptions, and Curricula   211
    SARA HAMMER, SHALENE WERTH, PETER DUNN, KYM LAWSON,
    AND DANIELLE D'ABADIE

16 Formal, Informal, and Incidental Learning: How Recreational-
    Diving Instructors Achieve Competency   221
    KEITH CARDWELL

17 Limited-Term Contracts and Tenure: The Case of Foreign-
    Language Teachers in a Japanese University   232
    SEAN MEHMET

18 Beyond Educator/Practitioner Binaries: Overcoming Barriers
    to Cooperation Using Professional Cultural Axes   242
    R. TODD HARTLE, ROSEMARY J. SMITH, STEPHEN ADKISON, DJ WILLIAMS,
    AND PAUL BEARDSLEY

Respondent's Text   259
MÁIRÍN KENNY

Contributors   265
Index   273

Figures

4.1   Reflexivity as looking in a mirror.   35

4.2   Reflexivity as me looking at you looking at me.   37

4.3   "Looking at me . . . looking at you . . . looking at me."   38

10.1 The 'helixical' relationship built a closely entwined
      thread of understanding.   138

11.1 Different aspects of the PAR process are fluidly interwoven
      with one another.   152

12.1 A conceptual framework to illustrate cultural differences
      between the Western and the Confucian traditions of
      teaching and learning.   163

13.1 Operationalizing cultural sustainability.   186

Tables

7.1   A Synthesis of Kat's Position as Obtained From the
      Analysis of Her Interview   96

8.1   The Characteristics of Adult, Controlled, and Empowered
      Child Authorship   114

9.1   Margaret and Erin's Interview   125

10.1 The Researcher/Teacher Binary From My Perspective
      in 2003   139

10.2 The Researcher/Teacher Binary From My Perspective
      in 2007   139

13.1 Preliminary Differences Between Concepts   185

Foreword
Renewing the Critical Function of Education Research

Michael Singh

The either/or logic of binaries means that one part of a binary is positioned as being normal, while the other part of the binary is constructed as deviant or deficient. There is a hierarchical relationship in a binary where one part of the either/or pair is superior and powerful, while the other part is weak and submissive. For instance, those in the powerless position are seen as having all the faults, rather than the dominant interests being questioned because they render the former's claims to intellectual equality invisible. The challenge is in understanding and questioning the role educational research plays in reproducing such a position, despite claims to the contrary. Such binaries impact on the ways in which education researchers perceive relationships, such as between the hierarchical ordering of inequitable power relations and people's acting as equals. They also impact on how we relate to other people, mostly by forestalling conceptual advances in education research and thus being complicit in sociocultural marginalization. For example, the focus on the theory/practice binary privileges education researchers as theorists and teachers as practitioners, forestalling any prospects of engaging the divisions in different forms of knowledge produced by researchers and teachers under different conditions of labor. The theory/practice binary ignores the different time frames driving the knowledge of education researchers and teachers, and the divisions this creates in the types of knowledge they engage. Engaging the theory/practice binary means understanding the difference associated with the transfer, translation, and transformation of knowledge arising from the expectation of short-term effectiveness and influence as opposed to operating within a longer time perspective.

There are multiple ways of conceptualizing binaries as suggested by the range of terms that resonate with this concept: bifurcation, dichotomy, dualism, opposition, polarization, and schism. This terminological complexity points to the challenges of providing a widely acceptable, unambiguous, or canonical definition of ways of moving beyond binaries in and through education research. However, binaries provide an important focus for critique in education research, even while such research is implicated in perpetuating binaries. An important contribution of the education research in this book is in the identification, construction, and analysis of binaries, and, in some instances, in their disruption rather than reproduction.

Education researchers have various strategies for critiquing the hierarchical power relations evident in binaries in order to engage and perhaps move beyond them. A familiar strategy entails rendering binaries as necessarily and inescapably persistent—reproducing them in spite of an expressed desire to do otherwise. Education research can propagate an affirmative disposition toward the existing hierarchical ordering of binaries: justifying rather than challenging the binaries. Much education research is conservative and immunizes against possibilities for changing binaries, neutralizing alternative ways of conceptualizing education and research. An alternative strategy is to reverse the binary oppositions, for instance, by education researchers creating spaces for worker-intellectuals to make their knowledge claims known. At least where binary categories are contested by being inverted they are shown not to be innocent.

The accounts in this book provide variegated insights into the divergent and even contradictory strategies education researchers use to trouble particular binaries. Indicating a multiplicity of strategies, these studies consider the contradictions, possibilities, and limitations of moving beyond binaries.

Through deconstruction it is possible to shake loose the static positioning of the either/or logic that constrains thought and action. The critical analysis and interrogation of binaries can lead to efforts to disrupt the marginalization of what is presumed to be the weaker member of the pair. Analyses of constructions of otherness provide the potential for disrupting binaries. Redefining the relationship between the pairs that constitute the binary can see them as being in contact rather than oppositional, thereby enlarging understanding of both as mutually constituted. This brings to light the complexity and contingency of the binary relationships, showing that the two entities are more interdependent and mutually influential than oppositional and antithetical. Detecting similarities, in spite of striking differences, between binaries enables the rejection of binary ways of thinking and the foreclosing of understanding. This opens up spaces for new interests, understandings, and translations, catalyzing the potential for rediscovery. The emphasis here is on the fluidity and permeability of the boundaries beyond both halves of the binary so as to reconstruct these relations positively.

Education researchers have another strategy for engaging and moving beyond binaries, namely whereby the subjects are positioned as knowing agents confronting the ways in which normal/deficient are researched, and reshape the ways in which the superior/submissive are studied. Education research that seeks to undo binaries is not concerned with the dominated being given fair treatment by dominant interests, because this encourages them to focus passively on what they can expect from the dominant. The undoing of the binaries is attempted through acting together based on the presupposition that the dominated are as intelligent as the dominant, even if the latter do not recognize or acknowledge that intellectual equality.

The accounts in this book pose insightful new questions about the complicated task of moving beyond binaries in and through education research. The focus can be on developing unambiguous prescriptions for use of the terms involved in binaries by arguing for conceptual clarity. The emphasis here is on conceptual abstractions that tend to be vague and lack any empirical reference. A shift to emphasize consistency in reasoning through the logical analysis of binaries offers insights into the contradictory framing of education researchers' thinking. The irony in the strategy of questioning the uses of binaries by authoritative sources carries with it a necessary presumption of an authoritative stance on the part of education researchers, opening such critiques to being domesticated or neutralized. Critiques of the binaries built into the educational structures they uphold have proven precarious strategies, offering few convincing procedures for transcending these binaries.

The efforts at moving beyond binaries in education research represented by the accounts in this book reaffirm and review the critical function of education research through reexamining the concepts and methods for challenging binaries. Together they point to the scope and limits of efforts to move beyond binaries as an objective and a method of education research that takes as its aims the rejection of subservience to sociopolitical domination or unquestioning acquiescence to intellectual authority, and creating new modes of education research and knowledge production.

Preface

Bruce Muirhead and Samantha Dean

The intellectual and academic structuralist movement swept through France and Europe during the mid twentieth century, knocking existentialism off its avant-garde pedestal and radically redefining theoretical approaches and critiques of culture, research, and philosophy. Frequently cited as the founder of the movement is French structural anthropologist Claude Lévi-Strauss, who grounded his work in a view of myths as a record of the true history of the principal philosophical endeavor of mankind.

According to Lévi-Strauss, there existed major oppositions among the mythical archetypes of certain animals. Each mythic creature represented a particular meaning and set of associations and from this Lévi-Strauss argued for a general rule: that a pair of antagonists was the primary element of all mythical narratives and, further, that this was a broader symptom of the way in which the human mind operates.

Structuralism thus positions human behavior as guided by an unconscious gravitation toward organizing concepts into binary opposites (male/female, public/private, good/evil, academia/pop culture). Conceptualizations of binary opposites have proved an enduring feature of critical analysis, weathering poststructuralist and postmodernist deconstruction and assault, to the point where poststructuralism is often described as a mere 'theoretical hangover' following the structural revolution. In an academic sense, the intellectual marshlands of postmodernism (difficult to emerge from, once one begins to struggle and resist) have widened the goal posts on the playing field in an analysis of binary opposites within a wide range of academic contexts.

Beyond Binaries in Education Research goes one step further, examining the prevalence of binary opposites within the research process itself, focusing its lenses on education research in recognition of existing and prevalent dualisms within the sector: ability/disability, academic/vocational, adult/child, West-East. It is logical that the contributors to this collection have found ample subject matter on which to reflect and contribute given that education and teaching represent the transference of knowledge in its purest and most direct form.

The most basic cultural binary opposition, the male/female gender divide, is a dualism which is drummed into us at an early age (Blue nursery walls or pink? Tea-parties or trucks?). Sherilyn Lennon discusses this in Chapter 14, *Exposing Bush Binaries: Using the Media to Problematize Gender,* providing a mode for disrupting gender beliefs and practices that can work to inhibit students' schooling and life performances. Similarly, Patrick Alan Danaher and Robyn Henderson speak of constructive ways of disrupting sedentarism (the binary in the Western world which positions fixed residence as the sociocultural norm against which mobility is positioned as a pathology) in formal education in Chapter 6, *Moving Beyond Sedentarism: Conceptual and Empirical Developments.*

Constructive disruption may seem like a paradox, but it is an important concept in terms of moving beyond narrow conceptions of education, teaching, and learning patterns at all stages of development, early-years through to early-years career researcher. In the coming decades our emerging knowledge economy will position research, learning, and education as a commodity of escalating value and importance.

During the 1970s author, poet, and inventor Jacob Bronowski spoke of students approaching their studies with a certain "ragamuffin, barefoot, irreverence", the point of learning not being to worship what is known, but to question it.

Beyond Binaries in Education Research skillfully adheres to this worthy ideal, questioning why binaries continue to operate in education research and the ways in which this conceptual, physical, and/or methodological space can be maneuvred to obtain positive synergies rather than positive–negative binaries.

Acknowledgments

The editors record their gratitude to the many individuals without whom this book would not have been published. Particular thanks are extended to the following people:

- Mr. Max Novick and Ms. Jennifer Morrow, respectively Commissioning Editor and Senior Editorial Assistant at Routledge, for their unfailing commitment and professionalism
- Ms. Eleanor Chan and her colleagues at IBT Global for typesetting and copyediting the volume
- The participants in the 2008 research symposium of the University of Southern Queensland Postgraduate and Early Career Researcher group where the idea for the book was formed
- The chapter authors for their respective chapters and their contributions to the writing workshops that facilitated the composition of those chapters
- Professor Michael Singh for writing the Foreword
- Professor Bruce Muirhead and Ms. Samantha Dean for writing the Preface
- Dr. Máirín Kenny for writing the Respondent's Text
- Ing. Emilio A. Anteliz and Mrs. Phyllida Coombes for assisting with proofreading
- The colleagues who reviewed anonymised versions of the submitted chapters:
    - Professor Vanessa Andreotti, University of Oulu, Finland
    - Dr. Llandis Barratt-Pugh, Edith Cowan University, Australia
    - Mr. Martin Bauch, Chemnitz University of Technology, Germany
    - Mrs. Phyllida Coombes, Independent Scholar, Bundaberg, Australia
    - Dr. Geoff Danaher, CQUniversity, Australia
    - Dr. Mike Danaher, CQUniversity, Australia
    - Dr. Ann Dashwood, University of Southern Queensland, Australia

- Professor Judith Gouwens, Roosevelt University, USA
- Associate Professor Anne Jasman, University of Southern Queensland, Australia
- Dr. Devon Jensen, University of Calgary, Canada
- Dr. Geri Pancini, Victoria University, Australia
- Dr. Helena Pettersson, Umeå University, Sweden
- Dr. Leonie Rowan, Griffith University, Australia
- Dr. Dina Strong, University of Latvia, Latvia
- Dr. Donna Velliaris, University of Adelaide, Australia
- Mr. Richard Warner, University of Adelaide, Australia
- Mr. Robert White, University of the Sunshine Coast, Australia
- Dr. Viv Wilson, Canterbury Christ Church University, UK

- Our colleagues in the Faculty of Education at the University of Southern Queensland, Australia for their support and encouragement
- Our families and friends for their unfailing love and interest

1 Constructing and Deconstructing Binaries in Education Research

Alison Mander, Patrick Alan Danaher,
Mark A. Tyler, and Warren Midgley

ABSTRACT

This chapter interrogates the concept of the binary—a representation based on an either/or logic—in relation to contemporary education research. Discussion focuses on multiple definitions and conceptualizations of binaries and diverse examples of their role in constructing educational experiences and outcomes. That diversity is matched by heterogeneous positions about what deconstructing and moving *beyond binaries* might entail. From this discussion the authors elicit a list of questions that helps to frame the succeeding chapters' constructions and deconstructions of binaries and to highlight their contributions to helping to move beyond those binaries.

INTRODUCTION

This chapter and the book that it introduces are founded on the proposition that binaries are alive and well in contemporary social life and hence in education research in the early 21st century. This is because we see education research as inextricably linked with that social life and therefore centrally positioned to replicate and/or to transform it. This proposition is outlined in this chapter and demonstrated in successive chapters from a diversity of theoretically framed and empirically grounded perspectives.

The corollary of this proposition that we also articulate here is both the possibility and the desirability of moving *beyond binaries* in educational policymaking and provision. We acknowledge that binary relations are not always and automatically destructive and negative, and that they can lead to effective and productive relationships. At the same time, there is considerable historical and current evidence that many binaries generate situations in which one member of the binary pair is positioned as being more appropriate, normal, and powerful than the other, which by contrast is constructed as being deficient, disadvantaged, and even deviant (see also Danaher, Coombes, & Kiddle, 2007). In such situations, "'the other' ends up being designated as the one who is non-normative in a given context, non-predominant, different, and outside" (Cyss-Wittenstein, 2003, n.p.).

Our focus in this chapter is therefore on the constructions and deconstructions of binaries in education research—on what they are, how they are constituted, and the diverse ways in which we can engage with them. The chapter consists of the following three sections:

- Defining, conceptualizing, and constructing binaries
- Deconstructing and moving beyond binaries
- Outlining the book's organizing questions, structure, and intended contributions to moving beyond binaries in education research.

DEFINING, CONCEPTUALIZING, AND CONSTRUCTING BINARIES

Binaries are a complex phenomenon that continues to be defined, conceptualized, and constructed from multiple and heterogeneous perspectives. Terms such as *dichotomy* (Chen, 2010, p. 15) and *dualism* are sometimes deployed to help in explaining the meaning of binary, with Stephens (2004) employing the even more overtly value-laden word *schism* (p. 88), and Chen and Derewianka (2009) referring to "entrenched polarisations" (p. 223) and to "stark oppositions" (p. 242), although these words are not necessarily synonymous with one another and display different nuances of understanding. According to Coe, Domke, Graham, Lockett John, and Pickard (2004), "Binary communications represent the world as a place of polar opposites" (p. 234). Chen (2010) observed how in a binary one part of the pair "gets an upper hand in a hierarchical relationship" (p. v). Gibson-Graham (2002) noted that, in "any such binary formulation within Western knowledge systems, superior power is already distributed to the primary or master term" (p. 29), a point that was illustrated with regard to the global/local binary:

> [W]e find 'global' and 'local' positioned in a familiar hierarchy wherein each derives meaning from the other. The global is represented as sufficient, whole, powerful, and transformative in relation to which the local is deficient, fragmented, weak, and acted upon. (p. 30)

Binaries have been closely associated with structuralism (Rogers, Malancharuvil-Berkes, Mosley, Hui, & O'Garro Joseph, 2005), "in which society is recast as a language or linguistic process" (Elliott, 2009, p. 5) that has a profound and continuing impact on the ways that individuals perceive the world and their relations with it. In particular, human relationships that are commonly identified as binaries in structuralist theory and that exhibit multiple contemporary and popular manifestations range from gender (Graham Davies, 2010; Haynes & McKenna, 2001; Nestle, Howell, & Wilchins, 2002) to multiculturalism (Powell, 1999a) to relations between Europe and/or the West on the one hand and Asia and/or the East on the other (Lieberman, 1999).

A wide array of binaries has been identified in addition to the sociocultural dichotomies identified above. These have included "Global vs. Local" (Gibson-Graham, 2002, p. 25) and "oppositional and zero-sum relationships between areas of knowledge, such as the distinction between policy and practice, which are better represented by a continuous or holistic relationship" (Sands & Nuccio, 2008, p. 467). Chen (2010) noted how in travel literature often "peoples and cultures are defined within conveniently maintained boundaries between home and abroad, West and non-West" (p. v), and furthermore how "the binary oppositions of the traveller and the traveled, mobility and stasis, the native and the diasporic, home and abroad" (p. v) are constructed. Del Casino and Hanna (2006) drew on their cartographic interests in seeking to "interrogate the binaries of representation/practice, production/consumption, conceptualization/interpretation, and corporeality/sociality upon which so much analysis is based" (p. 35). Stephens (2004) named several variations on the same fundamental binary forestalling conceptual and policy advances in relation to motherhood research: "the work/home split" (p. 88), "between public and private" (p. 88), "in the notion of the 'good mother' and that of the 'working mother'" (p. 88), and "work/family" (p. 90). In discussing current approaches to literacy education in Australia, the United States, and the United Kingdom, Chen and Derewianka (2009) referred to "the traditional/progressive pendulum" (p. 242), and to distinctions between:

> the horizontal discourse of children's personal experience and the more vertical discourse of educational knowledge, between the strong framing of direct teacher input when appropriate to the weaker framing of [student] group activity, between the formative evaluation of learner competence during the unit to a summative assessment of performance at the end. (p. 242)

Debate continues about whether binaries are inherently marginalizing. Wetherell and Potter (1998) thought not, contending that "binaries are made sexist or progressive in the context of specific ideological practices" (p. 377). By contrast, Lorber (1996) appeared to regard sociological categories as at least implicitly complicit with sociocultural marginalization: "Data that undermine the supposed natural dichotomies on which the social orders of most modern societies are still based could radically alter political discourses that valorize biological causes, essential heterosexuality, and traditional gender roles in families and workplaces" (p. 143).

A crucial element of binaries—and hence of the potential for disrupting them—is their integral connection with constructions of the other and of otherness. For example, Chen (2010) referred explicitly to "the binary logic of self and other" (p. 9), and contended that "encoded dichotomies" position "the traveller as" separate from and immune to "the influence of the other" (p. 21), even though such a separation and immunity are subverted by constructions of "the transcultural subject" (p. 21). Chen also acknowledged "the static, binary representation of [the] self–other relationship predicated on racial category" (p. 168). Likewise, Powell (1999b) decried the "binary form of analysis that collapses a myriad of distinct culture voices into the overly simplistic category of 'Other' defined in relation to a European 'Self' [as being] theoretically problematic" (p. 1).

Given our proposition of the integral connections between education and other dimensions of contemporary social life, it is inevitable that the complexity and diversity attending definitions, conceptualizations, and constructions of binaries are reflected in the educational manifestations and effects of such binaries. Broader binaries such as those related to gender, ethnicity, and socioeconomic status are clearly represented in education research (Asher, 2007; Kitching, 2010; Ladson-Billings, 2005; Martino, Lingard, & Mills, 2004). More specific binaries that take up the particularities of educational practice are also evident. For example, the experiential learning approach that underpins much contemporary outdoor adventure education has been critiqued for constructing binaries between experience and reflection and between learners and situations (Brown, 2009). Similarly, the distinctions between developed and underdeveloped countries and between the North and the South have been linked with certain educational practices that in turn have been posited as helping to create new socioeconomic inequities (Tikly, 2004). Likewise, educational binaries often take on additional power when they are appropriated by political leaders and deployed in media discourses for particular purposes (Coe et al., 2004).

This section of the chapter has noted the difficulty of providing universally accepted and clear-cut definitions of binaries, while also recording something of the complexity of their contemporary conceptualizations and constructions. We have also explored some of the educational manifestations of current binaries. We turn now to identify a number of strategies that have been elicited for deconstructing such binaries, and associated efforts to move beyond them to more enabling understandings and enactments of sociocultural relations.

DECONSTRUCTING AND MOVING BEYOND BINARIES

Several scholars have sought to identify ways in which binaries can be deconstructed, disrupted, and even transformed. For example, Morehead (2001, as cited in Stephens, 2004) contended that homes and workplaces are not necessarily "temporally bounded" (p. 91), and that working mothers are often able to complete several tasks simultaneously, thereby enacting a kind of *synchronous time*. In other words, for Morehead, contesting the supposed fixity of space and time can be effective in challenging the foundation of the work/home and worker/mother binaries. Gibson-Graham (2002) also identified "two strategies for challenging the power" (p. 30) of binaries:

> The first involves the tools of deconstruction, the theoretical intervention that has been so effective in shaking loose static identities that constrain thought and politics. . . . The other involves practices of re-subjectivation, a set of embodied interventions that attempt to confront and reshape the ways in which we live and enact the power of the [binary]. (p. 30)

Similarly, Chen and Derewianka (2009) highlighted the necessity of contextually nuanced and fluid approaches to literacy education by all groups of stakeholders to challenge the binaries that they identified as suffusing that field:

> This requires teachers with high levels of specialist knowledge to inform their decision-making, policy-makers who are open to intricacy rather than the simple quick fixes required by political expediency, and researchers who are able to provide useful evidence not only of 'what works' but [also] why and under what conditions and in which contexts for which students. (p. 242)

Likewise, Chen (2010) eschewed "those postcolonialist readings that render these [binary] hierarchies hopelessly pervasive and inviolate" (p. 28), and also rejected "the same binary logic . . . which simply reverses the oppositions" (p. 28). Instead, she argued that "the binaries such as self and other, home and abroad, should be conceived on a relational rather than hierarchical plane where the power relations can never remain stable" (p. 16). Indeed, Chen insisted that embracing otherness, whose construction was identified above as crucial to the creation of binaries, is equally vital to moving beyond such binaries: in the case of a traveler's engaging with a new country, for instance, it is important to establish a

> contact zone as an in-between space where the self–other binary can seldom hold stable, a space where the old, coherent sense of self is disrupted and a new self emerges with an 'enlarged' understanding of self and other, and home and away. (p. 22)

For Chen (2010), this contact zone functioned as an evocative metaphor for transcultural understanding, which "brings to light the complexity and contingency of the self–other relationship, showing that the two entities are more interdependent and mutually influential than oppositional and antithetical" (p. 24). Elsewhere, this understanding was expressed in terms of "detecting similarities underneath striking differences between cultures, and . . . a nuanced vision of both home and the visited place that rejects a binary and categorical way of thinking which forecloses understanding of the foreign" (p. 106). Transcultural understanding was also held to "[open] up space for the traveller's sustained interest to understand and translate otherness, which in turn catalyzes the constant rediscovery and translation of the travelling self" (p. 146).

Chen (2010) elaborated this sophisticated theoretical development explicitly in terms of being "an answer to the call of the critical debate within the field of travel literature studies" (p. 231):

> This debate revolves around different approaches to the self–other binary in travel writing. On the one hand, it highlights and critiques the hierarchical power relations between the traveller and the native. And, on the other hand, it counteracts this very hierarchy by illustrating how the power relations can only be symbolic and never remain stable. To enter into this scholarly conversation, my thesis acknowledges the contribution of both sides of the debate; while the first approach enhances our critical consciousness of the imperialist ideology of the genre, the second one reminds us of the complexity of the representation of the self–other interaction in the contact zone. The critical approach I propose is to attend to the contact zone as the zone of *interculturality*; instead of reading the travelling self and the native as two different, unrelated entities trapped within a power-based relationship, I examine the dynamics of their communication and the consequences of their cross-cultural contact. . . . So, it is the process of cultural translation and the transformative nature of that very process that I investigate in this project. This critical approach brings to the forefront a complicated rapport between self and other, and home and abroad, a relationship that is not only different and oppositional but also interdependent and mutually transformative. (pp. 231–232)

Chen's (2010) approach was worthwhile citing in detail because it encapsulated many of the key elements of moving beyond binaries that have been identified less comprehensively by a number of other scholars, and that are taken up in greater depth in the succeeding chapters. These elements include refusing to accept the power-laden and hierarchical logic of the binary category, seeing the boundary between the halves of the binary as fluid and permeable, and reconstructing the relations between those halves in more positive and sustainable ways than the binary construction has previously allowed. Powell (1999b) interpreted this move as being:

> to help implement this new phase of "cultural reconstruction" by self-consciously moving beyond binary forms of analysis and inventing new critical paradigms that will help scholars to theorize the fluidity,

multiplicity, and intricate contradictions that characterize all forms of cultural identity. (p. 2)

and as being:

> to reconstruct cultural identity in the midst of a *multiplicity* of cultures, in a theoretical matrix where there are no centers and no margins—a critical paradigm that will allow scholars to study the polyvalent nature of lived cultural identity. (p. 5)

Similar ideas about potential strategies for deconstructing binaries are evident in contemporary education research. For example, Crozet, Liddicoat, and Lo Bianco (1999) suggested the need to "negotiate comfortable third places between *the self* and the *other/the foreign*" (p. 1) in foreign-language teaching. Davis and Sumara (2010) drew on complexity theory and the notion of nested learning systems to suggest ways of addressing current dichotomies in educational practice. Brown (2009) recommended "[m]oving beyond conceptions of the learner as an autonomous 'processor' of experiences" (p. 3) toward more accurate and nuanced understandings of students' engagements with outdoor adventure education. Lather (2006) promoted the concepts of *paradigm proliferation* and *coloring epistemologies* with their emphasis on multiple understandings and multifaceted perspectives as effective means of resisting "a resurgent positivism and governmental imposition of experimental design as the gold standard in research methods" (p. 35) in education. Bolton and English (2010) claimed that their research contributed to dissolving "the traditional bifurcation of logic and emotion in the preparation of educational leaders" (p. 561), and that this finding "restores to decision-making preparation a more 'real world' perspective" (p. 561).

This section of the chapter has outlined several posited strategies for deconstructing and, in some cases, subverting contemporary binaries, including those experienced in educational contexts. Those strategies clearly reflect broader and deeper assumptions about the character of social life and education's multiple places within it. There are also divergences, even contradictions, evident among some of the proposed engagements with particular binaries. At the same time, each suggested approach constitutes a potential means for moving beyond binaries toward more positive and transformative ways of conceptualizing and enacting human relations, including in relation to education.

OUTLINING THE BOOK'S ORGANIZING QUESTIONS, STRUCTURE, AND INTENDED CONTRIBUTIONS TO MOVING BEYOND BINARIES IN EDUCATION RESEARCH

Clearly, what we have outlined to this point in the chapter is at once a variegated landscape and a troubling terrain (Henderson & Danaher, 2008).

The sociocultural and educational binaries identified above are deeply embedded in human interactions and have operated powerfully for millennia across multiple contexts and locations. Indeed, as several of the succeeding chapters demonstrate, there is compelling evidence that formal education and education research are integrally implicated in disseminating and perpetuating binaries and in contributing to the continued existence of the resultant socioeconomic inequities.

Yet, as we presented in the previous section of this chapter, education researchers do have access to a range of conceptual, methodological, and other resources that can be deployed to challenge the hegemony of binaries. This book is intended to contribute to that deployment and to helping to demonstrate ways for moving beyond binaries and for creating new forms of educational provision and education research.

With that project to the forefront of our thinking, we have articulated the following organizing questions for the book:

- What binaries continue to operate in education research?
- How and why do they continue to operate?
- How can binaries in education research be made transparent?
- What are the ethical, methodological, and social-justice implications of binaries?
- In what ways might conceptual, physical, and/or methodological space be maneuvered to obtain positive synergies rather than positive–negative binaries?
- What conceptual models might help to work within binaries?
- What conceptual models might help move beyond binaries?
- What might education research beyond binaries look like?

These questions both derive from the preceding accounts of binaries and their disruptions, and are designed to frame the subsequent discussion in the succeeding chapters in the book. None of the chapters is able to engage comprehensively with all these questions, and their take-up of particular questions is sometimes implicit rather than explicit. Nevertheless, all the chapters are concerned with identifying particular binaries, elaborating how those binaries are manifested in particular educational contexts, and outlining ways in which educational providers, policymakers, and/or researchers are able to move beyond them.

The book has been structured around the following three parts:

- Researching researchers
- Privileging participants
- Considering contexts

As the part introductions make clear, the chapters in each part exhibit considerable diversity in how they engage with the respective section theme. On the other hand, each theme enhances the coherence and focus of the chapters in that part, and in combination the three themes constitute something of a microcosm of the "risky business" (Midgley & Danaher, 2010) that is contemporary education research. That is, researchers need to display heightened reflexivity about their own assumptions and activities; they are required to demonstrate appropriate attentiveness and respect to research participants; and they must recognize the crucial roles played by specific contexts in framing and constraining the possibilities and limitations of research outcomes.

While we acknowledge that all engagements with binaries and moving beyond them are inevitably limited and partial, the chapters in this book are intended to contribute to extending current understandings of such binaries and to mobilizing strategies for helping to move beyond them. In particular, we see that contribution as being clustered around the following foci:

- The range of countries traversed (Australia, Canada, China, Japan, Papua New Guinea, and the United States)
- The array of binaries discussed (settled/itinerant, observer/observed, new vocationalism/professional identities, adult/child, researcher/teacher, ability/disability, educator/practitioner, among several others)
- The diversity of conceptual and methodological resources deployed both to explain particular binaries and to identify ways of moving beyond them
- The three part themes as sites of cohesion enhancing focus in an otherwise highly differentiated landscape.

Thus we envisage the book as both linking with and extending from the scholarly literature surveyed above. We look forward to maintaining the conversations and enlarging our collective understandings as we continue to engage with the character and complexities of binaries in contemporary education research.

CONCLUSION

Atkinson (2003) noted with approbation "the postmodern resistance to binary oppositions, and to certainties regarding identity, position or fixed residence" (pp. 35–36). She identified one of the "characteristic features" of postmodernism as being the "disruption of binaries which define things as either/or" (p. 36). And she sought "to demonstrate that a postmodern approach to research in education and the social sciences cannot deliver specified outcomes or lead to predetermined goals, but that its effect on ways of thinking, seeing and doing may nevertheless change the world" (pp. 46–47).

Atkinson (2003) acknowledged the necessity to avoid "making post-modernism into another Grand Narrative" (p. 47), and certainly several theoretical resources as well as those of postmodernism have been deployed in the succeeding chapters of this book. At the same time, Atkinson's statements in the previous paragraph encapsulate the book's focus and intended contributions to existing knowledge. Our hope is that the several demonstrations of constructing and deconstructing specific binaries in contemporary education research will alert all of us to possible strategies for helping to move beyond those binaries and thereby to "change the world" (p. 47) as that world is currently constituted, understood, and practiced.

ACKNOWLEDGMENTS

The authors are grateful for the research findings of the contributors to this volume that have extended their understandings of binaries in contemporary education research. They acknowledge also the continuing influence of the theorists mobilized by these contributors whose work identifies ways of moving beyond those binaries.

REFERENCES

Asher, N. (2007). Made in the (multicultural) U.S.A.: Unpacking tensions of race, culture, gender, and sexuality in education. *Educational Researcher, 36*(2), 65–73.

Atkinson, E. (2003). The postmodern prism: Fracturing certainty in educational research. In J. Swann & J. Pratt (Eds.), *Educational research in practice: Making sense of methodology* (pp. 35–50). London: Continuum.

Bolton, C. L., & English, F. W. (2010). De-constructing the logic/emotion binary in educational leadership preparation and practice. *Journal of Educational Administration, 48*(5), 561–578.

Brown, M. (2009). Reconceptualising outdoor adventure education: Activity in search of an appropriate theory. *Australian Journal of Outdoor Education, 13*(2), 3–13.

Chen, H., & Derewianka, B. (2009). Binaries and beyond: A Bernsteinian perspective on change in literacy education. *Research Papers in Education, 24*(2), 223–245.

Chen, L. (2010). *The question of cross-cultural understanding in the transcultural travel narratives about post-1949 China* (unpublished doctoral dissertation). University of Alberta, Edmonton, AB.

Coe, K., Domke, D., Graham, E. S., Lockett John, S., & Pickard, V. W. (2004). No shades of gray: The binary discourse of George W. Bush and an echoing press. *Journal of Communication, 54*(2), 234–252.

Crozet, C., Liddicoat, A. J., & Lo Bianco, J. (1999). Intercultural competence: From language policy to language education. In C. Crozet, A. J. Liddicoat, & J. Lo Bianco (Eds.), *Striving for the third place: Intercultural competence through language education* (pp. 1–22). Melbourne, Australia: Language Australia.

Cyss-Wittenstein, C. (2003, November 22). *Layers of outsidedness: Dialoguing with the dialogue between Jesus and the Samaritan woman (John 4:1–43).*

Paper presented at the annual meeting of the Society of Biblical Literature, Atlanta, GA. Retrieved from http://home.nwciowa.edu/wacome/cysswittenstein2003.html

Danaher, P. A., Coombes, P. N., & Kiddle, C. (2007). *Teaching Traveller children: Maximising learning outcomes.* Stoke on Trent, UK: Trentham Books.

Davis, B., & Sumara, D. (2010). "If things were simple . . .": Complexity in education. *Journal of Evaluation in Clinical Practice, 16*(4), 856–860.

Del Casino, V. J., & Hanna, S. P. (2006). Beyond the 'binaries': A methodological intervention for interrogating maps as representational practices. *ACME: An International E-Journal for Critical Geographies, 4*(1), 34–45.

Elliott, A. (2009). *Contemporary social theory: An introduction.* London: Routledge.

Gibson-Graham, J. K. (2002). Beyond global vs. local: Economic politics outside the binary frame. In A. Herod & M. W. Wright (Eds.), *Geographies of power: Placing scale* (pp. 25–60). Malden, MA: Blackwell.

Graham Davies, S. (2010). *Gender diversity in Indonesia: Sexuality, Islam and queer selves (Asian Studies Association of Australia Women in Asia series).* London: Routledge.

Haynes, F., & McKenna, T. (Eds.). (2001). *Unseen genders: Beyond the binaries.* New York: Peter Lang.

Henderson, R., & Danaher, P. A. (Eds.). (2008). *Troubling terrains: Tactics for traversing and transforming contemporary educational research.* Teneriffe, Australia: Post Pressed.

Kitching, K. (2010). An excavation of the racialised politics of viability underpinning education policy in Ireland. *Irish Educational Studies, 29*(3), 213–229.

Ladson-Billings, G. (2005). The evolving role of critical race theory in educational scholarship. *Race Ethnicity and Education, 8*(1), 115–119.

Lather, P. (2006). Paradigm proliferation as a good thing to think with: Teaching research in education as a wild profusion. *International Journal of Qualitative Studies in Education, 19*(1), 35–57.

Lieberman, V. (Ed.). (1999). *Beyond binary histories: Re-imagining Eurasia to c. 1830.* Ann Arbor, MI: University of Michigan Press.

Lorber, J. (1996). Beyond the binaries: Depolarizing the categories of sex, sexuality, and gender. *Sociological Inquiry, 66*(2), 143–159.

Martino, W., Lingard, B., & Mills, M. (2004). Issues in boys' education: A question of teacher threshold knowledges? *Gender and Education, 16*(4), 435–454.

Midgley, W., & Danaher, P. A. (2010). Risky business: Capacity-building in collaborative research. In C. H. Arden, P. A. Danaher, L. R. De George-Walker, R. Henderson, W. Midgley, K. Noble, & M. A. Tyler (Eds.), *Sustaining synergies: Collaborative research and researching collaboration* (pp. 25–36). Mount Gravatt, Australia: Post Pressed.

Nestle, J., Howell, C., & Wilchins, R. (Eds.). (2002). *GenderQueer: Voices from beyond the sexual binary.* Los Angeles, CA: Alyson Books.

Powell, T. B. (Ed.). (1999a). *Beyond the binary: Reconstructing cultural identity in a multicultural context.* New Brunswick, NJ: Rutgers University Press.

Powell, T. B. (1999b). Introduction: Re-thinking cultural identity. In T. B. Powell (Ed.), *Beyond the binary: Reconstructing cultural identity in a multicultural context* (pp. 1–13). New Brunswick, NJ: Rutgers University Press.

Rogers, R., Malancharuvil-Berkes, E., Mosley, M., Hui, D., & O'Garro Joseph, G. (2005). Critical Discourse Analysis in education: A review of the literature. *Review of Educational Research, 75*(3), 365–416.

Sands, R. G., & Nuccio, K. (2008). Postmodern feminist theory and social work. In R. A. Cnaan, M. E. Dichter, & J. Draine (Eds.), *A century of social work and social welfare at Penn* (pp. 466–476). Philadelphia, PA: University of Pennsylvania Press.

Stephens, J. (2004). Beyond binaries in motherhood research. *Family Matters, 69,* 88–93.

Tikly, L. (2004). Education and the new imperialism. *Comparative Education, 40*(2), 173–198.

Wetherell, M., & Potter, J. (1998). *Discourse and social psychology*—silencing binaries. *Theory & Psychology, 8*(3), 377–388.

Part I
Researching Researchers

Part I Introduction

Warren Midgley

Whilst it is not possible to completely extract researchers from their relationships with the participants and contexts of their research, in this book we have decided to group chapters around the focal points of *researchers, participants*, and *contexts*. Many of the chapters in this book could be equally well placed in more than one part; the selections we have made are based on the synergies we, the editors, found in our reading of and reflection on the chapters.

In the chapters in this first part, *Researching Researchers*, authors explore how a variety of binary constructions can impact upon researchers and the work that they do, offering suggestions for ways of productively engaging with those binaries. Saito (Chapter 2) explores the West/non-West binary from the perspective of a Japanese researcher who learnt research methodology in Australia. Dovona-Ope (Chapter 3) investigates cultural binaries from the perspective of a Papua New Guinean woman from a matriarchal society conducting research in (amongst other sites) a patriarchal society. Her particular focus is trying to resolve the complex issue of selecting an appropriate voice when reporting on research. Midgley (Chapter 4) writes from the position of a Westerner involved in cross-cultural research, highlighting the impact that binary understandings can have on reflexive research, and suggesting an approach to try to move beyond the possible limitations of a binary approach.

Chapters 5 and 6 present conceptual frameworks for moving beyond binaries in conceptualizing research in two different contexts. Kocher and Pacini-Ketchabaw (Chapter 5) discuss Pedagogical Documentation as a tool for destabilizing binaries in Early Childhood Education, and Danaher and Henderson (Chapter 6) explore conceptual and empirical developments in seeking to overcome binaries associated with education for people who are not from sedentary communities. We have placed these two chapters in this first part because the conceptual frameworks discussed seem to us to have significant implications for the work of researchers. This placement also serves as a useful segue into the following part on *Privileging Participants*.

2 Methodology, the Western, and Myself[1] ~~The West/Non-West Binary~~ in a Non-Western Educational Researcher's Pursuit of a PhD

Akihiro Saito

ABSTRACT

Contemporary education research, like other social science disciplines, is embedded in Western intellectual traditions. Such is a reiterated motif in non-Western academia as well as cross-cultural research. Where methods and methodologies invented in one geographical place are deemed as foreign, there arises a suspicion: "Are those foreign methods and methodologies valid in our local context?" Although this question appears to posit a valuable, thought-provoking vantage point for a non-Western researcher, there seems to lurk a dualism that perpetuates the binary relationship of West versus non-West. This chapter depicts how the author as a non-Western education researcher sought to reconcile this binary through an ongoing dialogue with his inner self as a non-Westerner about the identity formation of himself, of the founders of methods and methodologies, and of non-Western academia. The chapter is structured through four stages. First, I lay a backdrop to the chapter in which I retrospect on my experience that gave rise to and guided my reflection on the binary. Second, I tell a narrative of the nation to which I (am purported to) belong so as to restore historicity that recontextualizes the binary. Third, I seek to unfix the subject positions that conform to the binary discourse in the context of performance and performativity. Fourth, I identify the way a dualism operates behind the suspicion. I argue the validity of methodologies cannot be dismissed on the mere basis of the dualism undergirded in the use of essentialist categories revolving around the discourse of binary: the foreign as other versus the local as self. Such a methodological distrust seems to be valuable, but in reality it is circular and limiting. It fails to be reflexive about its own dichotomous assumptions.

INTRODUCTION

Designing a research methodology needs to be fine-tuned in order for it to suit its research context. Apart from identifying a researchable problem, the decisions to be made in this process range from a choice of paradigms and theories, through means of sampling, data collection, and analysis, to ethical and political considerations (Silverman & Marvasti, 2008). Although this applies in any research context, there are times when a binary confronts a researcher when the methodology is applied beyond its Western historico-cultural roots to a non-Western research context. There a binary emerges between the *west/self* as gazer and the *non-west/other* as gazed-at (Smith, 1999). By contrast, this chapter addresses a similar but distinct sort of binary that I as a non-Westerner encountered during my doctoral candidacy at a non-Western institution. This binary, which I refer to as *West/Non-West*, revolves around the cultural roots of both the practice of doing research and research methodologies. The West/Non-West binary emerges when the practice of doing research is seen by non-Westerners. Thus this chapter is positioned in the methodological landscape as seen from the other side of the binary. From that perspective the practice of doing research ceases to be the sole property of the center and is handed down to the periphery, to constitute a foreign practice. Methods and theoretical perspectives interwoven in methodologies represent organic artifacts of Western intellectual history. The suspicion arises: Do Western methods and methodologies work properly in this non-Western context? In what follows, I depict how I as a non-Westerner conducting his PhD study in language education sought to resolve the West/Non-West binary.

METHODOLOGY

As the method of this chapter, I draw upon a retrospective and introspective depiction of my personal experience of the phenomenon of West/Non-West. Specifically, the method is situated in the context of (performance of) autoethnography and personal narrative[2] (Corey, 1998; Ellis & Bochner, 2000; Langellier, 1999). The personal narrative "tell[s] about personal, lived experience in a way that assists in the construction of identity, reinforces or challenges private and public belief systems and values, and either resists or reinforces the dominant cultural practices of the community in which the narrative event occurs" (Corey, 1998, p. 250). In this sense, autoethnography and personal narrative work as a method to explore moves "from what some might presume to be an insular engagement of personal reflection, to a complex process that implicates the performative nature of cultural identity" (Alexander, 2008, p. 92). In this methodological context[3], I seek to retell, recontextualize, interrogate, and transform subjective positions as discursive artifacts surrounding the binary construct of West/Non-West through a dialogue with "history, social structure, and culture, which themselves are dialectically revealed through action, feeling, thought, and language" (Ellis & Bochner, 2000, p. 739). Thus the personal narrative stands vis-à-vis the master narrative (or dominant discourse)—*West/Non-West* in this chapter—that often dictates collective identities, reflects culture and one's relation to culture, and mirrors and excavates the cultural contexts that give rise to experience (Alexander, 2008, p. 92).

THE RETROSPECTION: THE SUSPICION THAT CLOUDED MY VISION

After I completed my master's thesis in Australia, I enrolled in a doctoral program in my home country of Japan. Shortly after enrolment, I had an occasion to present the initial outline of my proposed study in the presence of attendees from the university. The method that I intended to use was a mixed-methods design (Creswell, 2003)—a combination of grounded theory and hypothetico-deductive psychometric approaches—that I had been introduced to during my master's study in Australia. I intended to investigate how children of transient laborers whose ancestors once emigrated from Japan to South America (de Carvalho, 2003; Ishi, 2008) might best adjust to mainstream Japanese schooling.

In a postpresentation informal briefing, one of the attendees at the session questioned whether and how I would be able to justify that all these foreign research methods would work in the local research site. Without prior thought, I was unable to formulate a response. I felt as if I had been silenced into the margins of the dominant local academic culture. The methodology I presented might have looked new or unfamiliar. This unfamiliarity might have been intermingled with the fact that I was a student having returned from a Western institution. Yet in turn that question triggered for me some responses that provoked a further thought. One was related to the historicity of the practice of doing research: Wasn't the practice itself Western in origin? The other was related to the relevance of that question: How should I respond to this question? I was unable to answer either of these questions, nor could I start my doctoral project at that time.

Today I find myself immersed in this inherently Western practice of doing research at an Australian university. Thinking back on the above scene, I ask myself, what has been and continues to be practiced in contemporary Japanese academia? Is that practice still deemed foreign? No. Rather, in my eyes, the institution dwells in that society as if it were there ahistorically. I pose yet another question to myself: What induced that attendee to raise that question? A series of these questionings guided me to the site of identity formation: of myself, of the founders (and practitioners) of methodologies, and of the academe in my home country.

THE INTROSPECTION: UNFIXING DISCURSIVE SUBJECT POSITIONS IN THE PERFORMATIVE

The origin of the practice of doing research in contemporary Japan dates back to the latter half of the 19th century, when modern science was massively imported from the Western powers (Bartholomew, 1989). This nation's memory that I was taught in the not-so-distant past is the one which I believed was true. As the memory of the nation can only be narrated (Anderson, 2006, p. 204), I as a member of the nation called Japan[4]— the community that exists insofar as people believe—re-create a version of narrative, using somewhat hesitantly the first-person plural pronoun *we* to represent an identity of mine apropos this fictitious community.

> *In the face of Western pressure, we opened up our doors, striving to transform ourselves to be accepted into a community of modern nation states. We appropriated from the West a means of building a nation state. Public education, and science and technology, were among the significant elements in this endeavour. We built the arsenals by virtue of the sophisticated Western technology to defend our sovereignty against Western imperialism. We tailored Western-style capitalism to aim for economic excellence over the Western powers. It was this way we learnt to share a sense of being a nation.*

The above narrative retelling represents no more than one version amid other thousands iterated (Smith, 1980). Narratives of this sort have been and will be reconstituted with a certain degree of variability in detail, whenever the remembering of the origin of Western artifacts in the community is made possible. Thus, the truthfulness of the narrative is not as much at issue. Rather, it is from this default discursive position, in which narratives of this community are constructed, that the nation's memory is recalled with verisimilitude. By invoking the nation's memory in this narrative reconstruction, I am seeking to restore historicity in this text, such that it creates a discursive site where subjectivities and identities can be visualized and narrated, to constitute a backdrop to the text.[5]

In the meantime, by retelling this historical narrative, crude as it is, I run the danger of reifying and homogenizing the essences of discursive objects. I confine in *us* the people(s) on the archipelago of Japan; I depict *them*—the people who came ashore—as reducible in *the West(ern)*[6]; the reaction that the community at the time took in relation to the West is as if *collective*. Thereby a binary is constructed: us the self (i.e., Japanese) and them the other (i.e., the West). Thus, the memory serves as the venue for memory and identity transmission, operating simultaneously and competitively with history (Crane, 1997, p. 1372). Therefore, it turns out that the binary, in this narrative reconstruction of mine too, is not something pregiven but is discursively constructed in conceptual domains that embrace historicity. As I put things into essentialist categories, these opposing words in the depiction conjure boundaries that delimit modes of thought.

By extension, this discursive context conspires to represent one theme of this chapter—the practice of doing research too—as an imported foreign fabrication. It is against this geographical backdrop that the methodological suspicion was formulated. However, there is yet another condition for this particular suspicion to have been formulated, which was utterly forgotten[7] or discursively concealed. Research as practiced in Japan, in which all academics and researchers immerse themselves, is also an artifact which is and has been *foreign* in origin (Bartholomew, 1989). The methodological suspicion is articulated by this unwitting (or deliberate?) oversight. The foreignness of my methodology came to the forefront, whereas that of the practice of doing research remained hidden behind the scene. What allowed this forgetting to occur? I pause to consider. I delve into this question, disturbing the unacknowledged axiom of the methodological suspicion.

I argue that the suspicion cast upon the validity of foreign methodologies is based upon a particular perspective of identity. Classic sociolinguistics contends that how you speak depends on who you are (Cameron, 1995). The suspicion questions the methodological validity on the assumption that who the *othered* founders of methods and inventors of methodologies are and where they come from prescribe the way they see and understand the world; thus their methodologies are likely to produce others' invalid accounts of the phenomenon under investigation. Cameron (1997) argues that, "while sociolinguistics traditionally assumed that people talk the way they do because of who they (already) are, the postmodernist approach suggests that people are who they are because of (among other things) the way they talk" (p. 49). This argument ties in with the poststructuralist theory of performativity (Pennycook, 2007). Pennycook states, as it unfolds in his discussion of performance and performativity, that performativity is "the way in which we perform acts of identity as an ongoing series of social and cultural performances rather than as the expression of a prior identity" (p. 69). Thus, according to this concept of performativity, the (trans)formation of identity is viewed in the doing.[8]

The performative identity transformation through sedimentation can be compared with the post-Meiji modernization process of Japan and its consequences. As thematized in the literature (e.g., Fu & Heine, 1995; Miyoshi & Harootunian, 1989), its postwar economic miracle, advanced capitalism, and highly technological society mark Japan's symbolic entry into the West (Burman, 2007, p. 182), whereas the Westernized *and* culturally intact self of Japan signals the end of the Westernization of the world (Laïdi, 1998, p. 123). Similarly, the way *Japan* is discursively thematized in this way can be compared with the "sedimentation of acts repeated over time within regulated contexts" (Pennycook, 2007, p. 72). Whether Japan belongs to West or East is not in question. What is important is that behind this discursive representation of Japan's identity is a series of persistent endeavors as represented in the narrative that I retold. Among these endeavors is the appropriation of the practice of doing research. The view of sedimentation links to the backdrop to the methodological suspicion. The suspicion was articulated where the acts of doing research had been repeated within regulated contexts *to the extent that research as a foreign institution is no longer deemed foreign.*

The understandings of performativity and sedimentation warrant a fresh look at the identity issue apropos contemporary Japanese academia. Importation and borrowings of concepts, theories, and applications from the Western academia were not just random attempts at repetitions of a fixed practice and identity, but these have also been performed and adjusted in Japanese contexts with the semblance of new cultural meanings and identities. Unfamiliar methodologies that were once imported from overseas have assumed familiar appearances through the performative. In this sedimentation effect that enabled the methodological suspicion to be stated, with the Western roots of the practice of doing research forgotten. With this, it is at one's discretion to *other* the methods and methodologies as Western artifacts. It is this way one can posit that the way *they* understand (i.e., theories, methods, and methodologies) is different from the way *we* do, but not that what *they* understand is invalid (i.e., interpretations/findings). Within this discourse, the methodology embraces the ways of understanding the object as practiced in the observing community (i.e., the West as the subject), whereas I use it as a member of the observed community (i.e., the non-West as the object). Hereby a dualism is reified.

As such, the methodological suspicion is based on the dualism of self and other, which is an unacknowledged axiom in its own right (Heywood & Stronach, 2005). Because of this dualism, the suspicion is circular. It suggests that the researcher interprets, or the methodology concludes, the phenomenon under study to be X (which is inferred to be "wrong") because they belong to the other. The fact that the researcher interprets and concludes this way proves that the researcher is a member of, or the methodology is an artifact of, the other, which is the unacknowledged starting point of this logic. Thus, operative behind the suspicion is a transcendental appeal to hidden grounds in order to justify itself (Heywood & Stronach, 2005, p. 114).

CONCLUSION

I explored the methodological landscape as seen from the other side of the binary, problematizing the discursive backdrop to the suspicion posed about my methodology. I sought to interrogate and decipher the tangled web of discursive representations and embodiments that constitute the West/non-West binary that I had encountered at the liminal stage of my doctoral candidacy, resorting to some poststructuralist theories. I acknowledge that the methodological suspicion, if based on the dualism, works as a cue for the researcher's exercising reflexivity on the workability of the methodology. However, once this reflexive stance takes hold, the suspicion turns out to have no more than the effect of reflexivity that is generally required to construct any research methodology in any research context in any *socio-historico-cultural* milieu. It follows that any researcher, positioned on whichever side of the binary, needs to ensure methodological congruence[9] (Richards & Morse, 2007) and pay due attention to ethics and trustworthiness (Rallis & Rossman, 2009). The researcher maintains ways to enhance his or her study's credibility, such as prolonged engagement, triangulation, and participant validation (Rallis & Rossman, 2009). I get back to these basics.

In the meantime, the unfamiliar semblance of methods and methodologies takes on a familiar look in practice, within a rigidly regulated frame. The semblance is one thing; the methodological validity is another. I continue to *perform* methods and methodologies, however new and unfamiliar they may be perceived to be in some contexts, until my repeated acts of doing research in a rigid regulatory manner with these unfamiliar methods and methodologies accumulates into the semblance of familiarity. I wonder how I would respond if the same question was raised again. The importation and appropriation of Western artifacts in the narrative that I told represent both resistance of and accommodation to the Western hegemony. The practice of research must be seen in this historico-cultural context. To this one may be tempted to add that the methodological suspicion was part of such resistance, whereas my text in this chapter is that of accommodation. But more importantly the suspicion that once clouded my methodological vision serves the production and reproduction of fixed identities and experiences. Based on this fixity of subject positions, the suspicion interrupts one's pursuit of understanding. It potentially limits the hope and possibility to create understanding among those who are sifted into discursive categories in conflict. The dualistic discourse, on the one hand, succeeds in celebrating the endeavors that the nation undertook, and the subjectivities reified thereof, to represent resistance. On the other, it incessantly stands as a pessimistic vision for understanding. I believe a pursuit of understanding outweighs resistance.

CODA

In embarking on this writing, I worried that I might end up with the monolithicity of the binary, re-creating foundationalist images of West and East as Said's (1978) thesis was once (constructively) criticized as doing. In a post hoc reflection, the binary has served as an intermediary heuristic device in a way that is particular to me. By trying to unravel the conditions for the binary, I have developed my own understanding of this phenomenon. In this sense, my reflection in this chapter cannot simply be generalized to other researchers' contexts. It remains personal. However, I hope to have articulated and shed light on what might otherwise have got lost in anecdotes, suggesting one among many other avenues for someone researching across cultures to navigate him or her through an unfamiliar binary terrain. Here, the binary completes its role in my reflection.

ACKNOWLEDGMENTS

I thank two anonymous reviewers for their careful reading and invaluable feedback on my manuscript. My special thanks go to Dr Warren Midgley for his encouragement and guidance in adding the final touches on this chapter.

NOTES

1. This title is inspired by Japanese novelist Oe Kenzaburo's Nobel Lecture (1994) entitled "Japan, the ambiguous, and myself," rather than by Yasanuri Kawabata's (1968) "Japan, the beautiful, and myself."
2. "The personal" as in personal narrative "implies a performative struggle for agency rather than the expressive act of a pre-existing, autonomous, fixed, unified, or stable self which serves as the origin or accomplishment of experience (Smith)" (Langellier, 1999, p. 129).
3. See Ellis and Bochner (2000) for verisimilitude, and reliability and generalizability checks, in autoethnography (pp. 750–755).
4. My dependency on my Japanese passport identifies me as an insider in this community.
5. Memories are constructed by societies and individuals to serve their own purposes (Shudson, 1995).
6. Japan's European contacts in the 19th century included those with the Portuguese, the Spanish, and the Dutch as well as Germans, Russians, the British, and Americans (e.g., Loveday, 1996, Chapter 3).
7. "Forgetting, rather than remembering, is what takes work in the form of repression and the substitution of 'screen' memories that block access to more disturbing ones" (Olick, 1999, p. 335).
8. In so arguing, Pennycook underscores, citing Butler (1990), that "[t]his process of self-production is by no means a question of free-willed choice to take up some form of identity or another but rather occurs within a 'highly rigid regulatory frame'" (Pennycook, 2007, p. 70).
9. This refers to fit between the research problem and questions, fit between the questions and methods, and fit among all these, the data and the theories (Richards & Morse, 2007).

REFERENCES

Alexander, B. K. (2008). Performance ethnography: The reenacting and inciting of culture. In N. K. Denzin & Y. S. Lincoln (Eds.), *Strategies of qualitative inquiry* (3rd ed., pp. 75–117). London: Sage.

Anderson, B. R. (2006). *Imagined communities: Reflections on the origin and spread of nationalism* (rev. ed.). London: Verso.

Bartholomew, J. R. (1989). *The formation of science in Japan: Building a research tradition.* London: Yale University Press.

Burman, E. (2007). Between orientalism and normalization: Cross-cultural lessons from Japan for a critical history of psychology. *History of Psychology, 10*(2), 179–198.

Butler, J. (1990). *Gender trouble: Feminism and the subversion of identity.* New York: Routledge.

Cameron, D. (1995). *Verbal hygiene.* London: Routledge.

Cameron, D. (1997). Performing gender identity: Young men's talk and the construction of heterosexual masculinity. In S. Johnson & U. H. Meinhof (Eds.), *Language and masculinity* (pp. 47–64). Oxford, UK: Blackwell.

Corey, F. C. (1998). The personal: Against the master narrative. In S. J. Dailey (Ed.), *The future of performance studies: Visions and revisions* (pp. 249–253). Annandale, VA: National Communication Association.

Crane, S. A. (1997). Writing the individual back into collective memory. *American Historical Review, 102*(5), 1372–1385.

Creswell, J. W. (2003). *Research design: Qualitative, quantitative, and mixed methods approaches* (2nd ed.). Thousand Oaks, CA: Sage.

de Carvalho, D. (2003). *Migrants and identity in Japan and Brazil: The Nikkeijin.* London: Routledge.

Ellis, C., & Bochner, A. P. (2000). Autoethnography, personal narrative, reflexivity: Researcher as subject. In N. K. Denzin & Y. S. Lincoln (Eds.), *Handbook of qualitative research* (pp. 733–768). Thousand Oaks, CA: Sage.

Fu, C. W.-H., & Heine, S. (1995). Introduction: From "The Beautiful" to "The Dubious": Japanese traditionalism, modernism, postmodernism. In C. W.-H. Fu & S. Heine (Eds.), *Japan in traditional and postmodern perspectives* (pp. vii–xxi). Albany, NY: State University of New York Press.

Heywood, D., & Stronach, I. (2005). Philosophy and hermeneutics. In B. Somekh & C. Lewin (Eds.), *Research methods in the social sciences* (pp. 114–120). London: Sage.

Ishi, A. A. (2008). Between privilege and prejudice: Japanese–Brazilian migrants in "the land of yen and the ancestors." In D. B. Willis & S. Murphy-Shigematsu (Eds.), *Transcultural Japan: At the borderlands of race, gender, and identity* (pp. 113–134). Abingdon, UK: Routledge.

Kawabata, Y. (1968). Japan, the beautiful, and myself. Retrieved from http://nobelprize.org/nobel_prizes/literature/laureates/1968/kawabata-lecture-e.html

Laïdi, Z. (1998). *A world without meaning: The crisis of meaning in international politics* (J. Burnham & J. Coulon, Trans.). London: Routledge. (Original work published in 1994)

Langellier, K. M. (1999). Personal narrative, performance, performativity: Two or three things I know for sure. *Text and Performance Quarterly, 19*, 125–144.

Loveday, L. J. (1996). *Language contact in Japan: A socio-linguistic history.* New York: Oxford University Press.

Miyoshi, M., & Harootunian, H. D. (1989). Introduction. In M. Miyoshi & H. D. Harootunian (Eds.), *Postmodernism and Japan* (pp. vii–xix). Durham, NC: Duke University Press.

Oe, K. (1994). Japan, the ambiguous, and myself. Retrieved from http://nobelprize.org/nobel_prizes/literature/laureates/1994/oe-lecture.html

Olick, J. K. (1999). Collective memory: The two cultures. *Sociological Theory, 17*(3), 333–348.

Pennycook, A. (2007). *Global Englishes and transcultural flows.* London: Routledge.

Rallis, S. F., & Rossman, G. B. (2009). Ethics and trustworthiness. In J. Heigham & R. A. Croker (Eds.), *Qualitative research in applied linguistics: A practical introduction* (pp. 263–287). Basingstoke, UK: Palgrave Macmillan.

Richards, L., & Morse, J. M. (2007). *Read me first for a user's guide to qualitative methods* (2nd ed.). Thousand Oaks, CA: Sage.

Said, E. W. (1978). *Orientalism.* New York: Pantheon.

Shudson, M. (1995). Dynamics of distortion in collective memory. In D. L. Schacter & J. T. Coyle (Eds.), *Memory distortion: How minds, brains, and societies reconstruct the past* (pp. 346–364). Cambridge, MA: Harvard University Press.

Silverman, D., & Marvasti, A. (2008). *Doing qualitative research: A comprehensive guide.* Thousand Oaks, CA: Sage.

Smith, B. H. (1980). Narrative versions, narrative theories. *Critical Inquiry, 7*(1), 213–236.

Smith, L. T. (1999). *Decolonizing methodologies: Research and indigenous people.* Dunedin, New Zealand: University of Otago Press.

3 Determining a Voice to Use in Writing About Mixed Methods Research

Dinah R. Dovona-Ope

ABSTRACT

Education researchers conducting mixed methods research in cross-cultural contexts can be confronted with a number of binaries through which they need to weave their way. I am an example of an education researcher who has made serious considerations in undertaking a triangulation mixed methods research in a cross-cultural context. A key issue which has challenged me has been the determination of an appropriate voice in crafting the writing of my research report. Although authorities in mixed methods research suggest considering methodological underpinnings guiding the study and/or considering the audience the research targets in determining an appropriate voice to employ, it has not been that simple for me. Consequently, I have considered three key areas to assist me in determining the voice in writing my research report. These have been (1) the methodological underpinnings guiding my mixed methods research in a highly complex sociocultural context; (2) the sociocultural context of my target audience; (3) my social status as a female researcher from a matrilineal context and the strong influence of that culture.

These highlight the importance for education researchers not only to consider the theoretical assumptions guiding the educational research and the target audience in determining the voice. Education researchers also need to consider the sociocultural dimension as well as values that they, as researchers, bring to research, particularly when conducting research in complex sociocultural contexts.

INTRODUCTION

Determining the voice to employ when crafting the write-ups of research reports is one of the major considerations a researcher must make. It is naturally linked to the underlying theoretical underpinnings and values guiding the research (Creswell & Plano Clark, 2007; Wiersma & Jurs, 2005). Although determination of the voice may appear a minor issue in research for some, it has become a major challenge and/or a quandary for me. The challenge and/or quandary has been related to the consideration and determination of the most appropriate tone of voice that truly represents me and my personal values. At the same time, I needed to be culturally competent and sensitive to the population being studied without disconnecting from the underlying theoretical assumptions (King, Sims, & Osher, 2007; Martin & Vaughn, 2007; Mays, De Leon Siantz, & Viehweg, 2002; Wittmer, 1992). This has been compounded by the employment of mixed methods research design (Mertens, 2005) in my study in one of the world's most socioculturally complex contexts, Papua New Guinea (PNG). In this chapter I present the key considerations that I have made in determining the voice that truly represents me, my personal values, and the values of the population I have studied in crafting my research report.

VOICE IN MIXED METHODS RESEARCH

An immediate binary in studies employing a mixed methods research design exists in the fact that they combine quantitative and qualitative research designs in a single study or series of studies (Creswell, 2009; Creswell & Plano Clark, 2007; Wiersma & Jurs, 2005). Creswell and Plano Clark (2007) clearly point out that mixed methods research is:

> a research design with philosophical assumptions as well as methods of inquiry. As a methodology, it involves philosophical assumptions that guide the direction of the collection and analysis of data and the mixture of qualitative and quantitative approaches. As a method, it focuses on collecting, analysing, and mixing both quantitative and qualitative data in a single study or series of studies. (p. 5)

Quantitative studies have traditionally involved quantification of data which are often reported in an impersonal or passive voice, whereas with qualitative studies researchers have traditionally had the benefit of personal engagement in the whole research process by employing personal or active voice (Creswell, 2009). However, in combining quantitative and qualitative research methods through mixed methods research, particularly through triangulation mixed methods which give equal status to quantitative and qualitative data collection, the researcher needs to determine an appropriate voice to employ in crafting the research report. Hence, this has been a quandary I have confronted in my study. Having collected both quantitative and qualitative data, what voice do I use in presenting my research report? Do I use personal or impersonal voice or a collective voice?

Hertz (1997, as cited in Graue, 2006) acknowledges that authors differ on their views about the type of voice to use depending on the methodological and theoretical traditions they employ. These include impersonal voice, which allows for communicating authority but removing themselves from text; first-person-plural voice, utilizing a convention that homogenizes all the authors into a collective authorial voice; and transformative intellectual voice from an advocacy or activist platform.

Sandelowski (2003, as cited in Plano Clark & Creswell, 2008), points out that crafting write-ups mixed of methods studies entails understanding several key areas, one of which is the recognition of research write-up as rhetoric through which information is powerfully disseminated. According to Creswell and Plano Clark (2007), in mixed methods research several options including the use of personal and impersonal voices may be used. Personal voice may be used in the qualitative phase of mixed methods research and an impersonal voice in the quantitative phase. Alternatively, weighting given to qualitative and quantitative components can determine the type of voice to be used. If research is heavily weighted as qualitative research, personal voice should be used, and, if it is heavily weighted on quantitative study, impersonal voice should be used. However, it becomes more complex when quantitative and qualitative components are given equal weighting as in triangulation. Creswell and Plano Clark (2007) advise that in such circumstances the audience to whom the study is directed should be considered a high priority.

Despite the suggestions presented by authorities in mixed methods research design about the use of voice, it hasn't been that easy for me to accept the voice they propose. This has been complicated by an additional dimension, the cross-cultural considerations pertaining to my cultural philosophies and my consideration of cultural competence and sensitivity in my research. Hence, for me, these factors have had a much greater influence in determining the voice that I have used than mere methodological or theoretical underpinnings that have guided my research.

For me, to use a personal voice in reporting qualitative findings and impersonal voice for quantitative findings would have made my research report appear inconsistent and disjointed. To use an impersonal voice would have denied the power and depth of information and the values contained in my personal voice. Simply to consider the audience to whom the study was directed and use impersonal voice would have been to deny my philosophy as a researcher and become insensitive to the importance of voice in my cultural context. Rather, I felt compelled to be guided by my personal values which are embedded in my culture and which are greatly influenced by my social status as a female and a researcher doing research in the PNG sociocultural context and the sociocultural contexts of my audience. The details of these are presented in the following sections.

KEY CONSIDERATIONS IN DETERMINING MY VOICE

Determining an appropriate voice for writing the report of my mixed methods research has involved a consideration of issues beyond just the theoretical underpinnings that guided my study and the audience as suggested by Hertz (1997, as cited in Grave 2006) and Creswell and Plano Clark (2007). To ensure that I have used a voice that has truly represented my philosophy as a researcher, a critical analysis of the use of voice in the PNG culturally diverse context, including my own cultural context and practices relating to utilization of voice, has been conducted. This involved delving into three key areas of consideration.

1. The Methodological Underpinnings Guiding my Mixed Methods Research in a Highly Complex Sociocultural Context

In developing a research design, consideration of its appropriateness within the cross-cultural context and methodological assumptions guiding the study are vital. My decision to employ this research design has been in consideration of the purpose of the study and the complexity presented by the nature of the sociocultural context of the research site, PNG. PNG is one of the most highly complex contexts in the world, as represented by more than 860 distinct languages spoken by people located within the varying geographical locations. Despite such complexities, I decided that triangulation mixed methods research would be the most suitable design for the collection of data that could generate both generalizable and in-depth data in a cross-cultural context.

As the purpose of my study has been to provide an advocacy platform for the marginalized and/or the under-represented population in the PNG context, I decided that mixed methods research design guided by the transformative-emancipatory paradigm was most appropriate. This has enabled me to collect and analyze the values and viewpoints of the underpresented population in the area of academic achievement of female students. Mixed methods research within a transformative-emancipatory framework emphasizes the importance of research for promoting social change by addressing issues of empowerment and other concerns affecting marginalized and underrepresented groups such as women and people with disability (Creswell, 2005; Creswell & Plano Clark, 2007; Mertens, 2005). My mixed methods study has focused on the viewpoints of an under-represented population: the female secondary school leavers and Grade 12 female students.

2. The Sociocultural Context of My Audience

I felt that a simple consideration of my audience to determine my voice in writing my research report would have been inadequate. Hence, a reflection on and an evaluation of my own social status and my values embedded within the two sociocultural contexts I represent—the broader PNG sociocultural context and the Nasioi context of Kieta in Bougainville—have been necessary in determining my voice in crafting a research report for triangulation mixed methods research.

The general PNG sociocultural context I represent is predominantly male dominated and comprises many patrilineal cultures. Most Papua New Guinean communities, particularly in the mainland of New Guinea, are predominantly organized along patrilineal kinship systems. As pointed out by McElhanon and Whiteman (1984, as cited in Flaherty, 1998), in patrilineal cultures lineage is traced through a common male ancestor and land is held in common and often kinship groups live and till the land together. Male dominance is evident in most, if not all, aspects of culture, and women generally have lower status in patrilineal cultures and their voices are often silent as they play subservient roles to male kinship members within their communities.

As a woman in a male-dominated culture, I do not have equal status to male counterparts. However, as an educated woman, I may gain some recognition. In this sociocultural context, I also need to be careful about the voice I can use in disseminating information from my research work, particularly when it is from an advocacy platform. The nature of voice commonly used in this context is collective, comprising the use of words such as *we*, *us*, and *ours*. For example, *"It is our responsibility to ensure that our children are safe between home and school."*

By contrast, cultures in a number of coastal areas of the New Guinea mainland and most islands are organized along matrilineal kinships. Cultures in Milne Bay, Bougainville, East New Britain, and parts of West New Britain and New Ireland are predominantly matrilineal. In matrilineal cultures, lineage is traced through a common female ancestress through successive generations of women. Women in matrilineal cultures also receive rights of descent as well as rights to land whilst in some areas rights to land are passed through maternal uncles (Dovona-Ope, 2010; McElhanon & Whiteman, 1984, as cited in Flaherty, 1998). Owing to the high social status that women of these areas occupy, whether as head of clans (referred to as *hedmeri* in Bougainville) or families, or taking the lead in village economic activities, they have a powerful voice of influence. I have conducted my research project at two sites, one that is predominantly patrilineal and one that is predominantly matrilineal. Hence, it has been important to be culturally competent and sensitive to the participants and use appropriate voice.

3. My Social Status as a Female Researcher in a Matrilineal Cultural Context

I am a woman and the eldest daughter in a family from a strong matrilineal culture of the Nasioi people in Kieta, Central Bougainville. As a woman, my cultural society accords me a significant political and social status. I also come from a culture which has clearly defined rules about relationships and the voices to be used in communication within the contexts of those relationships. There are three key rules concerning voice that I must adhere to in any communication in my matrilineal context: (1) "ee da'," as in reference to a single person when communicating with my friend, my maternal uncle, or my sister; (2) "ee dee'," as in reference to two people when communicating with my brothers, my brothers-in-law, and sisters-in-law,; and (3) "ee dii'," as in reference to many people when communicating with sons-in-law, daughters-in-law, and parents-in-law. Hence, these are not mere impersonal or personal voices; they are linked to respect in various kin relationships and are the core values strongly upheld by members of my society.

As a female researcher, a highly educated woman, and a woman who has performed family obligations with feasts that result in lifting personal sociocultural profiles, I am also mindful that I occupy a higher social position accorded to only a few people, including women, as *ovongtung* (the chiefs) in the Kieta society of Bougainville. In such a position, I am referred to as two people, or many people, particularly by my own male kinship members. Additionally, the protocol of my traditional culture permits me (my voice) to be represented by my brothers or maternal cousin's brothers or uncles on important clan issues and decisions unless none of them are available. When my brothers, in particular, represent me, I am not supposedly referred to by my name or in the first person but as two people with the use of words equivalent to the English form of "they," "them," or using nicknames or as the *"mother of . . ."* (the name of my eldest child). In return I have to relate and communicate with my brothers in the same way as they do. For example, when I invite my brother for dinner, I have to say, *"You two people have dinner with us tonight."* This, in no way, is inviting two people but only one person. When my brother is in a position of telling someone about my instruction to prepare dinner, he has to say, *"Those two people want you to prepare dinner."* Such a representation as two people by no means indicates any weakness, or my kin overriding my status, but is a token of respect accorded to me and, in the same way, reciprocated. Hence, in the matrilineal context, my brothers are given an opportunity to become excellent orators whilst I continue to use them as I exert my power and influence from behind the scenes. Therefore, in my position within my cultural context, I am always mindful and careful of my voice, and I have to know with whom I am communicating.

It is evident from the key considerations I have made that there are complexities involved in determining an appropriate voice for use in writing research reports, particularly when sociocultural perspectives are considered and when one has strong connections to a sociocultural context. However, as I have not been writing my mixed methods research report for my brothers or my in-laws or an audience that comprises my Kieta people, I have felt compelled and satisfied to have reached a compromise. Hence, I have chosen to place myself in the background, giving priority to the stakeholders and the audience in general whom this project targets. Therefore, I have chosen to use an impersonal voice in writing my research report.

CONCLUSION

The content in this chapter indicates that, when writing a research report for a triangulation mixed methods research, if conducted in a highly cross-cultural context, it is important that a researcher not only considers the theoretical assumptions guiding the study in determining the voice. A researcher also needs to be culturally competent and sensitive to the contexts of those being researched, and consider the personal philosophies and practices which he/she brings to education research.

REFERENCES

Creswell, J. W. (2005). *Educational research: Planning, conducting, and evaluating quantitative and qualitative research.* Thousand Oaks, CA: Sage.

Creswell, J. W. (2009). *Research design: Qualitative, quantitative, and mixed methods approaches.* Los Angeles, CA: Sage.

Creswell, J. W., & Plano Clark, V. L. (2007). *Designing and conducting mixed methods research.* Thousand Oaks, CA: Sage.

Dovona-Ope, D. R. (2010). *Female students' attributions for academic achievement in secondary schools in Papua New Guinea* (unpublished doctoral dissertation). University of Southern Queensland, Australia.

Flaherty, T. A. (1998). *The women's voices in education: Identity and participation in a changing Papua New Guinea.* Goroka, Papua New Guinea: Melanesian Institute.

Graue, B. (2006). Introductory essay: Challenges in writing, voice, and dissemination of research. In C. Conrad & R. C. Serlin (Eds.), *The Sage handbook for research in education: Engaging ideas and enriching inquiry* (pp. 511–514). Thousand Oaks, CA: Sage.

King, M. A., Sims, A., & Osher, D. (2007). *How is cultural competence integrated in education?* Retrieved from http://cecp.air.org/cultural/Q_integrated.htm

Martin, M., & Vaughn, B. (2007). Cultural competence: The nuts & bolts of diversity & inclusion. *Strategic Diversity & Inclusion Management Magazine,* 31–38.

Mays, R. M., De Leon Siantz, M. L., & Viehweg, S. A. (2002). Assessing cultural competence of policy organizations. *Journal of Transcultural Nursing, 13*(2), 139–144.

Mertens, D. M. (2005). *Research and evaluation in education and psychology: Integrating diversity with quantitative, qualitative, and mixed methods* (2nd ed.). Thousand Oaks, CA: Sage.

Plano Clark, V. L., & Creswell, J. W. (2008). *The mixed methods reader.* Thousand Oaks, CA: Sage.

Wiersma, W., & Jurs, S. G. (2005). *Research methods in education: An introduction.* Boston, MA: Pearson Allyn & Bacon.

Wittmer, J. (1992). *Valuing diversity in the schools: The counselor's role.* Retrieved from http://www.ericdigests.org/1992-3/diversity.htm

4   Beyond *Observer* and *Observed* in Reflexive Analysis

Warren Midgley

ABSTRACT

This chapter outlines a framework for reflexive analysis which seeks to move beyond the binary conceptualization of *observer* and *observed* (even when what I am observing is myself and my work) in reflexive analysis to explore the notion of "me looking at you looking at me looking at you . . ." The chapter draws on the theories of *surplus of seeing* and *transgredience* that emerge from the theoretical work of Bakhtin. A larger study exploring the experiences of male Saudi Arabian nursing students at an Australian university is analyzed using this framework to demonstrate its potential to uncover layers of meaning that binary observer-looking-in-the-mirror frameworks of reflexive analysis may not have the power to explore.

INTRODUCTION

Reflexive analysis seeks to explore dimensions of research to which other analytical methods may not provide access. By reflecting upon the research process, researchers are able to learn about themselves and the process of research. In this chapter, I argue that some frameworks of reflexive analysis operate upon a binary conceptualization of *observer* and *observed*. In this instance, the observed may be the researcher, the research participants, or the research project as a whole. Whilst this kind of reflexive analysis may lead to useful learning, in the chapter I present a framework which seeks to move beyond a binary conceptualization of reflexive analysis, in order to explore new areas of understanding. This analytical framework I have called a bakhtinian reflexive analysis, drawing on the theories of *surplus of seeing* and *transgredience*, which are originally derived from the writings of M. M. Bakhtin (1981, 1986). After discussing the theoretical foundations for this approach, I present an example of how I have employed it in analyzing a larger study in which I was seeking to explore the experiences of male Saudi Arabian nursing students at an Australian university.

BAKHTINIAN REFLEXIVE ANALYSIS

Reflexive analysis can be seen as the researcher examining him- or herself as though in a mirror (see Figure 4.1); indeed, some papers on reflexivity in research actually employ the metaphor of a mirror (e.g., Kenny, Styles, & Zariski, 2004). I would agree with Smith (2006) that such a conceptualization of research can sometimes be unhelpfully solipsistic. I am not opposed to autoethnographic work, and have published some myself (Midgley, 2008b). I believe that this kind of study is useful in understanding the inner world of academia and the inner lives of academics. However, I am not fully convinced that autoethnography in the purely reflective model can help us learn a lot about the world outside the academy. In order for a nonacademic person to conduct a critical autoethnographic study, he or she would first need to be trained as an academic, which would seem to defeat the purpose of the exercise in terms of seeking to access the knowledge, understanding, and insight of an outsider to the academy. In this sense, reflexive work that is simply looking at the self as in a mirror can be seen to be limited in the scope of its application.

Another kind of reflexive work which is similarly limited is the kind that I believe Walford (1998) had in mind when he frankly admitted, "I find navel-gazing accounts from doctoral students that record every detail of their own learning process very boring to read, and I see them as the worst examples of 'vanity ethnography'" (p. 5). Recording and reflecting upon all the different steps in the process of conducting research may be very helpful

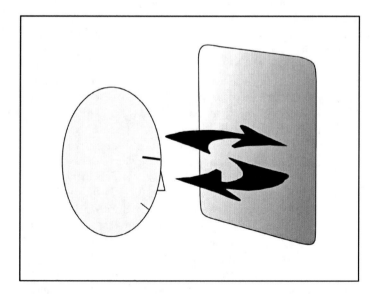

Figure 4.1   Reflexivity as looking in a mirror.

for the researcher's own self-discovery, and it can also be a useful source of knowledge for other research students following along a similar journey. My concept of reflexive analysis, however, goes beyond simply reflecting upon me and my actions.

The framework for reflexivity I have developed draws from the bakhtinian concept of dialogism. I use the word *bakhtinian* with the unorthodox lowercase *b* in order to highlight the philosophical perspective from which I approach the theories and writings of M. M. Bakhtin (especially Bakhtin, 1981, 1986). Rather than engage with the debate over what Bakhtin intended to mean (see, e.g., Matusov, 2007), I have appropriated (in the bakhtinian sense) words and concepts from the writings of Bakhtin, and those who have developed theories based on his writings (e.g., Ball & Freedman, 2004; Gardiner, 1992; Hirschkop & Shepherd, 1989; Holquist, 2002; Makhlin, 2000; Matusov, 2007; Min, 2001; Morson & Emerson, 1990; Todorov, 1984). I have adopted, adapted, or applied the words and ideas to a different context. Thus, bakhtinian with a lowercase *b* refers not to theories *of Bakhtin* but rather theories inspired by the writings of Bakhtin and also secondary works that draw upon them.

In this bakhtinian understanding of dialogism, when two people engage dialogically, centripetal forces operate to polarize self and other as *you* and *me*, whilst at the same time centrifugal forces bring the two together as *you-and-me* within the chronotope (or time-space event) of the particular dialogic engagement. To reflect in this way, I am looking at *me* as separate to *you,* but I am also reflecting upon the *me* in *you-and-me*. Both of those *me*s are contextually and contingently situated within that dialogic encounter. This dialogic perspective on reflexivity, therefore, encompasses more than just a mere reflection of what I see when I look at the research.

The other important bakhtinian concepts which inform the framework for reflexive analysis I have developed here are the overlapping theories of transgredience and surplus of seeing. The surplus of seeing theory posits that, when two people come together in dialogic engagement, the distance between them creates opportunities for both people to learn something new. Transgredience refers to the theory that, because two people engaged in dialogue are not the same as each other, they have the potential to transfer to each other some aspects of themselves, which brings some kind of "illumination" (Morson & Emerson, 1990, p. 185). Jabri (2004) refers to this as a surplus of meaning. In both of these closely related theories, the outsideness of people in a dialogic encounter is an essential feature of coming to see or know something new. According to these theories, I am not reflecting upon an image of myself, but rather I am learning from looking at *you* looking at *me*. The opportunity for seeing different perspectives on *me* and *you* and *you-and-me* arises from the distance that is created when self and other (*you* and *me*) engage in dialogue. The infinite possibilities of this cyclic process—me looking at you looking at me looking at you looking at me and so on (see Figure 4.2)—make this analytical approach a potentially rich source of insight that goes beyond the simple binary of me–you.

An example of the richness of potentiality within this bakhtinian reflexive analytical method is well captured, I believe, in the beautiful and evocative photograph by Jo Fedora entitled *Looking at me looking at you looking at me* (Figure 4.3). In a purely reflective model, I would look at what I see—an old man sitting on a bench. I might try to describe what I see (his clothing, the color of his hair) and I might think about his circumstances (is he poor, frail, lost?).

In the bakhtinian reflexive framework I am describing here, I look at the old man sitting on the bench, and notice that he appears to be looking at me. I wonder what he is thinking when he looks at me. How does he interpret my appearance and my presence in his world? Is he curious, angry, confused, frustrated? Does he see me as a stranger, a threat, or a potential friend? Does he want to engage with me, or avoid me? This line of thinking helps me to see myself through different eyes (surplus of seeing) and creates the potentiality of learning something new about myself.

As I engage in this process of trying to conceive of what the old man might be thinking about me, I also begin to see him differently. He is no longer just an old man on a bench; I begin to see him as an old man with a history, with thoughts and feelings, perhaps with concerns and worries, perhaps with cherished hopes or shattered dreams. I no longer try to describe him; rather, I try to understand him, and (even though I am only

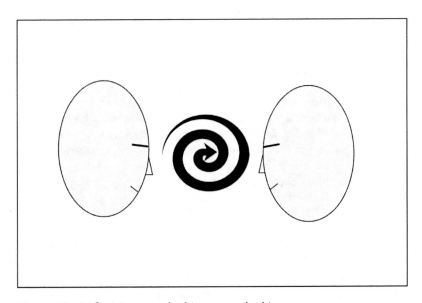

Figure 4.2   Reflexivity as me looking at you looking at me.

Figure 4.3 "Looking at me . . . looking at you . . . looking at me." (Image retrieved from http://www.redbubble.com. Copyright ©2009 by Jo Fedora. Used with permission.)

looking at a photographic image) I begin to feel strangely moved. I feel a sense of compassion, a sense of respect, a sense of goodwill, and many other things that I struggle to find words for. I want to say, "Hello." I want to say something that might make him smile.

Where do these feelings come from? I believe this is an example of the mysterious work of transgredience—somehow something has been transmitted from this old man to me, through the looking at the man looking at me looking at him, and then reflecting upon that. In this way, I come to know something else about myself, something else about the old man (at the very least, something about the way he has impacted my life), something else about the context in which our eyes met, and something else about the power of this kind of reflexive analysis for moving beyond the binary concepts of *me* and *you* as *self* and *other*.

This is the framework of bakhtinian reflexive analysis that I am presenting in this chapter. To demonstrate one of the ways in which I think it can be employed, I have applied this reflexive framework to a larger research project in which I was seeking to explore the experiences of male Saudi nursing students at an Australian university. In that research project, I met with groups of two or three Saudi students for open-ended discussions on their experiences as students at an Australian university. Some of the Saudi participants were friends I had known for several years. Others were introduced to me by friends. The discussions were open and friendly, lasting for between 45 minutes and 2 hours each.

In the analysis that follows, I do not attempt to describe what I did in that research, but rather I seek to reflect upon several interrelated layers on dialogic engagement, including: what I did in the light of the fact that I did it with Saudi participants; what I saw the Saudi participants do, in the light of the fact that they did it with me; what they might have thought that I might have been thinking; and what I might have thought that they might have been thinking, and so on.

This kind of approach may be criticized as being so open-ended that nothing can be validated (see, e.g., Wengraf, 2004, for this kind of criticism). However, the philosophical foundations of my study did not seek to validate findings, but rather to explore important issues. My discussion below outlines two of the many issues that arose as I engaged in a bakhtinian reflexive analysis of the larger research project, specifically with an aim to explore ethical and methodological issues relating to research in cross-cultural contexts.

REFLEXIVE ANALYSIS

The Role of Serendipity

For the purposes of my study, I developed a method of data production which I called narrative discussion groups (see Midgley, 2010). The inspiration for this design arose from two events that occurred on consecutive days about six months into my PhD study. My research journal records that on the 17th of August 2007 a Saudi student came to ask me for help with an essay he was writing for one of his classes. After I helped him with some of his grammar, he asked me how my study was going. In the context of that discussion, he mentioned that Saudis like to get together to tell stories, and therefore it might be good to arrange for groups of Saudis to get together to share their experiences.

The following day, August 18th, 2007, I attended an Open Day at the Islamic Centre on the campus of my university, at the invitation of several of my Saudi friends. On that day I was fortunate enough to be able to participate in one of these Saudi-style conversations, with the accompanying spiced coffee and dates. The conversation on the 17th was not planned by me. The Open Day event was planned some weeks in advance, but I had no idea what was going to happen there. Both of these events, occurring on consecutive days, gave me ideas that I later developed into the concept of narrative discussion groups as a means of data production. I wonder whether I would have taken this approach had I not had these experiences.

Reflecting upon this led me to contemplate the role of serendipity more generally on the design, progress, and outcomes of my research. For example,

I had originally intended to focus on Japanese sojourners for my doctoral dissertation. However, I changed my research proposal after I met some Saudi students, and noticed that some English teachers were struggling to identify how best to support their learning. Thus, by chance I came upon a need which for me also became an opportunity. I also recalled encounters with books, articles, scholars, and ideas which both informed my study and, I believe, greatly enhanced my work. Whilst I did diligently perform literature searches, some of the most challenging and inspiring concepts came from sources I accessed out of general interest, rather than focused reviewing. The opportunity to teach a research methodology course part way through my candidature greatly enhanced my conceptualization of my own methodological approach. These and other experiences that were not planned by me are all instances that might be labeled as serendipitous.

The problem of the role of serendipity in research is that it challenges the notion of research as a professional activity. Marcus (2001), commenting on his reading of recent doctoral theses in anthropology, noted that many anthropology students struggle with this:

> Yet, aside from the accounts of serendipity, of happenstance opportunity, of circumstantial muddling through response, which indeed constitute the dominant rhetoric by which mostly established scholars explain their interesting and creative divergences from traditional fieldwork practice, there is as yet no alternative modality of method or articulation of a set of regulative ideals governing fieldwork that gives professional legitimacy to what is in fact happening to fieldwork. For students, this is a real problem, because in achieving professional status and credentials through their initial work of ethnography, the rhetoric of serendipity is simply not appropriate for them as it is for the established scholar. (p. 527)

Indeed, had I not had a research question specifically focused on exploring the ethical and methodological issues of cross-cultural research, there would have been no place within my research outcomes to discuss the role of serendipity.

There are several important reasons why I think serendipity needs to be discussed. Firstly, it is an important element of transparency in reporting on research. I have worked hard on my thesis, but the findings I have published based on that research are not only the result of hard work; I owe some of the most interesting findings to good fortune. In what ways might this observation reflect upon the quality of my scholarship? I find myself in agreement with Stronach, Garratt, Pearce, and Piper (2007):

> We would rather regard reflexivity as an event in which we somewhat intentionally participate, but nevertheless acknowledge inescapable remainders of the unconscious and the unintended. (p. 198)

At another level, acknowledging the important role that serendipity has played in my own research provides a critical response to Marshall and Rossman (2006), who suggest that serendipity is a problem that can threaten a research project, and must therefore be kept in check by striking a balance between "efficiency and flexibility" (p. 154). I would argue that, if a researcher discovers something that is completely outside the scope of the original research design, then it should not simply be balanced out of the study. If there is not space or time to explore it fully, it should at least be noted for further study. I have demonstrated elsewhere (Midgley, 2008a) how what appears to be a completely unsuccessful research project can still provide useful insights. Subedi (2007) has done likewise.

Whose Data?

On another level, my bakhtinian reflexive analysis has led me to ask questions about the ethical connotations of referring to this study as my research. During the data production phase, I had the opportunity to discuss some of the preliminary findings with a lecturer interested in providing better support to Saudi students. In asking me to share my preliminary findings, she made a point of insisting that she would not use any information I gave her without acknowledging it as my work. This comment, which I acknowledge as both professional and gracious, nevertheless caused me to wonder to what extent this research (and its findings) belonged to me. Upon what grounds could I make a claim of ownership? I might claim the words I am writing here as my own creative labor, but can I legitimately claim discoveries that I came upon by chance? Is there a way of distinguishing between that which is the product of a scholar's labor and that which is good fortune? These are ethical questions that I believe need to be raised, even though I have no definitive answer to them.

Following the same line of reasoning, I am also led to think about the complexity of the role that the Saudi participants played in this research project. Can I claim as my data the things that these men told me during our recorded discussions? Does the signing of a consent form equate to the signing over of rights? Do I now own their words? This is a view that I find difficult to accept. My perspective finds resonance with postcolonial writings, including seminal works by Said (1978) and Spivak (1988), and with respect to research by Smith (1999). This stream of thought highlights the way in which Western perspectives on research and reporting on people from non-Western backgrounds can serve to reinforce Western hegemonic domination over them.

The legal and ethical questions relating to control and ownership of cultural knowledges have been explored in depth by many conducting research with Indigenous, First Nations, and Aboriginal people (e.g., Darou, Kurtness & Hum, 1993; Schnarch, 2004; Sommer, 1999). However, my research was not with an Indigenous community. I was not exploring cultural knowledges, but rather trying to understand the everyday experiences of Saudi students at an Australian university. Nevertheless, I have gained a personal benefit from the things that the Saudi students told me. I have published several chapters and articles, and won a bursary to present a paper at an international conference about my research. These are all positive gains in terms of my career as a researcher. Had the Saudi students not told me anything, I would not have achieved these benefits. In this sense, even seemingly mundane data can become a commodity. They may not be of value to the other participants, but they are of value to me as a researcher. Can I claim ownership over the data simply because they are not of any foreseeable use to the other participants?

In reflecting on this issue further, I turned to the literature referring to my own local context of Indigenous studies, namely the complex issues relating to research involving Aboriginal and Torres Strait Islander communities in Australia. Abdullah and Stringer (1997) drew the distinction between Aboriginal Terms of Reference (ATR), which guide decisions about what kinds of knowledge are valued from Indigenous Australian perspectives, and Academic Terms of Reference (AcTR), which are the criteria that Western academia would use to evaluate research. This perspective caused me to wonder whether I had any idea at all about what Saudi Terms of Reference might be.

THE DISTINCTIVENESS OF THIS APPROACH

By applying a bakhtinian reflexive lens to the research project, I was drawn to ask myself questions about what the Saudi participants might think about what I am doing. The standard response to this kind of question would be to ask the participants themselves. In qualitative research, this is sometimes referred to as verifying the data (Creswell, 2005) or member checking (Cohen, Manion, & Morrison, 2007). This may indeed be a fruitful line of investigation; however, the epistemological framework I have adopted in my study argues against this as a conclusive solution. I can ask the Saudi participants what they think about my research, but ultimately what they say will be influenced by the context of the question, and the fact that I am the one asking it. In other words, their response to my questioning will be influenced by their perspective on what it is they think I want them to say, or what they think is important in Western research, rather than a reified and static perspective on what is true.

If I were to take my findings to my Saudi participants and ask them to confirm them through member checking, according to traditional methods of qualitative research, I may find that the Saudi participants tell me that they agree that the findings are a true representation of their thoughts, feelings, and beliefs. I could then publish my findings not simply as what I think the Saudis think, feel, and believe but as the reality or facts about what Saudis think, feel, and believe. Any alternative perspectives, which might be suppressed by the presence of a Western academic such as myself, risk becoming silenced. Western academia, through me, would therefore have exerted its authority over the Saudis, a little like achieving a confession under duress.

Nevertheless, I believe it is important to demonstrate the attempt to maintain some kind of quality standards in qualitative research. Using reflexive analysis is one way to do this. Adopting a more reflective framework, I might have thought about what I had done in the light of my knowledge and understanding as a Western researcher, making reference to the experiences of those who have gone before. Using a bakhtinian reflexive approach, I have thought about what I have done in the light of what the Saudi participants might have thought about what I have done, based on what I had experienced in dialogic engagement with them. This attempt to try to see me and my work through the eyes of the Saudi participants (accessing the surplus of seeing) at times caused me to think differently about my research. I turned to questions which I might not normally have considered, and this in turn has given me some further insight into myself, my role as a researcher, and the way in which my backgrounds and beliefs have influenced my research, as well as research more generally. Unless I had adopted this approach, I doubt that I would have come to ask myself such challenging questions such as "What is the role of serendipity?" and "Whose data are these?"

CONCLUSION

The bakhtinian reflexive analytical framework opens up avenues for exploration that might be not so easily identified by other reflective approaches that conceptualize reflexive analysis in terms of a binary relationship between the *observer* and *observed*. This binary approach focuses on the researcher end of the relationship; that is to say, the researcher observes on the basis of what he or she already knows. In the bakhtinian reflexive framework I have outlined, the researcher is seeking to learn through the surplus of seeing that develops through engagement in dialogue with other participants.

As this analytical framework is reflexive, it cannot make claims to generate conclusive or generalizable findings. Consequently, the credibility of this method of research may also be called into question, particularly from those working within postpositivist research paradigms. However, as I have demonstrated above, a framework such as this that seeks to move away from a binary conceptualization of reflexive analysis can highlight important dimensions of research that might not have been examined otherwise. Whilst this may not be the only objective of research, I would argue that it is an important one.

AKNOWLEDGMENTS

I thank the participants in the writing workshops associated with this book's production for their helpful feedback on earlier versions of this chapter, as well as the editors, particularly my chapter editor Professor Patrick Danaher, for their continuing assistance. I appreciate helpful feedback about an earlier version of the chapter by two anonymous peer reviewers. I also acknowledge gratefully the Saudi participants in the research project reported here.

REFERENCES

Abdullah, J., & Stringer, E. T. (1997). *Indigenous knowledge, indigenous learning, indigenous research.* Perth, Australia: Curtin Indigenous Research Centre.

Bakhtin, M. M. (1981). *The dialogic imagination: Four essays* (C. Emerson & M. Holquist, Trans.). Austin: University of Texas Press.

Bakhtin, M. M. (1986). *Speech genres and other late essays* (M. Holquist & C. Emerson, Trans.). Austin: University of Texas Press.

Ball, A. F., & Freedman, S. W. (Eds.). (2004). *Bakhtinian perspectives on language, literacy and learning.* Cambridge, UK: Cambridge University Press.

Cohen, L., Manion, L., & Morrison, K. (2007). *Research methods in education* (6th ed.). Hoboken, NJ: Taylor & Francis.

Creswell, J. W. (2005). *Educational research: Planning, conducting, and evaluating quantitative and qualitative research.* Upper Saddle River, NJ: Pearson Education.

Darou, W., Kurtness, J., & Hum, A. (1993). An investigation of the impact of psychological research on a Native population. *Professional Psychology: Research and Practice, 24,* 325–329.

Gardiner, M. (1992). *The dialogics of critique: M. M. Bakhtin and the theory of ideology.* London: Routledge.

Hirschkop, K., & Shepherd, D. (Eds.). (1989). *Bakhtin and cultural theory.* Manchester, UK: Manchester University Press.

Holquist, M. (2002). *Dialogism: Bakhtin and his world* (2nd ed.). London: Routledge.

Jabri, M. (2004). Change as shifting identities: A dialogic perspective. *Journal of Organizational Change Management, 17*(6), 566–577.

Kenny, M. A., Styles, I., & Zariski, A. (2004). Looking at you looking at me looking at you: Learning through reflection in a law school clinic. *Murdoch University Electronic Journal of Law, 11*(1). Retrieved from http://www.murdoch.edu.au/elaw/issues

Makhlin, V. (2000). Bakhtin and the paradigm shift in the humanities. *Dialogism: An International Journal of Bakhtin Studies, 5/6,* 88–94.

Marcus, G. E. (2001). From rapport under erasure to theaters of complicit reflexivity. *Qualitative Inquiry, 7*(4), 519–528.

Marshall, C., & Rossman, G. B. (2006). *Designing qualitative research.* Thousand Oaks, CA: Sage.

Matusov, E. (2007). Applying Bakhtin scholarship on discourse in education: A critical review essay. *Educational Theory, 57*(2), 215–237.

Midgley, W. (2008a). Finding gems in the mud: An example of critical reflection on research in education. *International Journal of Pedagogies and Learning, 4*(1), 14–24.

Midgley, W. (2008b). Lost in the wilderness: When the search for identity comes up blank. In R. Henderson & P. A. Danaher (Eds.), *Troubling terrains: Tactics for traversing and transforming contemporary educational research* (pp. 183–192). Teneriffe, Australia: Post Pressed.

Midgley, W. (2010). *Seeking to understand 'experiences of different' in discussions with Saudi students at an Australian university* (unpublished doctoral dissertation). University of Southern Queensland, Australia.

Min, E. (2001). Bakhtinian perspectives for the study of intercultural communication. *Journal of Intercultural Studies, 22*(1), 5–18.

Morson, G. S., & Emerson, C. (1990). *Mikhail Bakhtin: Creation of a prosaics.* Stanford, CA: Stanford University Press.

Said, E. W. (1978). *Orientalism.* New York: Pantheon.

Schnarch, B. (2004). Ownership, control, access and possession (OCAP) or self-determination applied to research. *Journal of Aboriginal Health,* 1, 80–95.

Smith, L. T. (1999). *Decolonizing methodologies: Research and indigenous peoples.* London: Zed Books.

Smith, R. (2006). As if by machinery: The levelling of educational research. *Journal of Philosophy of Education, 40*(2), 157–168.

Sommer, R. (1999). Action research: From mental hospital reform in Saskatchewan to community building in California. *Canadian Psychology, 40*(1), 47–55.

Spivak, G. C. (1988). Can the subaltern speak? In C. Nelson & L. Grossberg (Eds.), *Marxism and the interpretation of culture* (pp. 271–313). Basingstoke, UK: Macmillan Education.

Stronach, I., Garratt, D., Pearce, C., & Piper, H. (2007). Reflexivity, the picturing of selves, the forging of method. *Qualitative Inquiry, 13*(2), 179–203.

Subedi, B. (2007). Recognizing respondents' ways of being and knowing: Lessons un/learned in researching Asian immigrant and Asian-American teachers. *International Journal of Qualitative Studies in Education, 20*(1), 51–71.

Todorov, T. (1984). *Mikhail Bakhtin: The dialogical principle.* Minneapolis, MN: University of Minnesota Press.

Walford, G. (1998). *Doing research in education.* London: Falmer Press.

Wengraf, T. (2004). Paradigm wars around interview methodologies: Constructionism and postmodernism "on tap" or "on top". *Forum: Qualitative Social Research, 5*(1), Art. 30. Retrieved from www.qualitative-research.net/fqs/

5 Destabilizing Binaries in Early Childhood Education
The Possibilities of Pedagogical Documentation

Laurie Kocher and
Veronica Pacini-Ketchabaw

> Starting out from documentations of pedagogical processes, they constantly reconstruct and reinvent, through rereading, relistening, revisiting, revisioning, relearning, and reinterpreting. This way of unfolding, taking apart, as well as folding, seems to have been a productive way of transgressing what has been folded over by tradition in the everyday practice of the schools. By fixing meaning provisionally and tentatively through researching, negotiations, and commentaries, they release the possibility of new practices, which have got the possibility of challenging the dualistic and binary thought of mind and body, nature and culture, private and public, etc.
>
> (Dahlberg, 2003, p. 277)

ABSTRACT

This chapter explores the concept of pedagogical documentation. We think of this as a research–practice tool for unpacking and destabilizing persistent binaries that construct the field of early childhood education. Specifically, we show, borrowing from existing literature on pedagogical documentation that draws on aspects of postfoundational (in particular poststructuralist and posthumanist) theoretical frameworks, how pedagogical documentation has the potential to create spaces for destabilizing binaries in the very act of practicing/researching. We end the chapter by reflecting on possibilities and challenges for future research–practice directions in pedagogical documentation.

INTRODUCTION

This chapter explores the concept of pedagogical documentation that Dahlberg (2003) refers to above. We think of pedagogical documentation as a research–practice tool for unpacking and destabilizing persistent binaries that construct the field of early childhood education. Specifically, we show, borrowing from existing literature on pedagogical documentation that draws on aspects of postfoundational (in particular, poststructuralist and posthumanist) theoretical frameworks, how pedagogical documentation has the potential to create spaces for destabilizing binaries in the very act of practicing/researching.

In order to make our arguments clear, we begin by explaining how we conceptualize the concept of binaries—in particular, how binaries emerge and are understood within poststructuralist frameworks. Following this discussion, we describe the process of pedagogical documentation in depth, reviewing the various philosophical perspectives in which pedagogical documentation has been situated. We demonstrate, within the context of this review, how pedagogical documentation can become a tool for destabilizing binaries in early childhood education research–practice. We end the chapter by reflecting on possibilities and challenges for future research–practice directions in pedagogical documentation.

MAKING MEANING IN EARLY CHILDHOOD EDUCATION: CONSTRUCTING BINARIES

Meaning making is an important and constant act in early childhood education research and practice. As researchers and educators we are constantly making sense of what we observe, the data we collect, the texts we read. The questions that arise then are: how do we construct meaning(s)? How do we make sense of what happens around us?

Certain themes highlighted within the poststructuralist literature have provided us with conceptual tools to think about these questions. For example, we began reflecting on the idea that there is no possibility of a value-free exploration (Bourdieu, 1994; Corson, 2000). Confusion about what is *the truth* arises partly from the difficulty we have convincing ourselves that reality does not exist independent of the knower and the process of knowing. Rather than our making absolute statements, it is essential to acknowledge the importance of context and values when making decisions. In fact, race, ethnicity, gender, sex, and class are important factors shaping our experiences (Davies, 2000).

We also reflected on the theme that there are no universal principles (Cannella, 1997). Instead of one truth, competing accounts fight for supremacy—many truths relative to a context. Reflecting on this particular theme in relation to young children, we realized that the existence of only one truth with respect to the nature and education of children has been a common belief in early childhood education (Bernhard, 1995; Bernhard, Gonzalez-Mena, Chang, O'Loughlin, Eggers-Pierola, Roberts Fiati, et al., 1998; Cannella, 1997). Several discourses have construed a *true* child. This construction allows people to make sense of what children are, what they should be, and what they need in order to fit into a specific ideal (Burman, 2008; Davies, 2000). One of the problems of universality is its failure to comprehend and accommodate human diversity and complexity.

Another area within the poststructuralist literature that we have found useful is the conceptualization of language. Language can be seen as a discursive system of socially construed signs, a meaning-filled practice, rather than what might be referred to as modernity's instrument for delivering *reality* (Davies & Gannon, 2006). Within this perspective, language does not constitute an absolute representation of reality. Meaning is part of a complex linguistic negotiation among individuals and, as such, it is one of the most important practices through which cultural production and reproduction take place (Corson, 2000). In light of recognizing the discursive nature of language, the term *young children* can be viewed as a social construct with which we infer or build meanings (Cannella, 1997). A universal discourse has been created about children through strategies and techniques of power in accordance with political, social, judicial, and economic conditions of society.

Both historical and power structures in a society determine and legitimize knowledge. Foucault's (1977, 1978) work on power relations has been central in understanding the construction of legitimate knowledge. Foucault argues that knowledge is socially constructed, context-specific, and value-laden. The role of power is key in the organization of knowledge. According to Foucault (1977, 1978), discursive power relations involve the formation and regulation of meanings and understandings, disciplining how people act. This view of power and knowledge challenges the idea that power is a thing to be exercised by powerful people or groups.

Another theme within the poststructuralist literature that we found useful has been the problematization of binary/dualistic thinking (Dahlberg, Moss, & Pence, 2007; Davies, 2000). Oppositions have been framed between the rational and irrational, ordered and unordered, objective and subjective. In early childhood education, we discuss the distinction between included and excluded, empowered and disempowered, and voice and voiceless as being natural (Mac Naughton, 2005). However, these distinctions are contingent upon dualistic conceptions of power struggles and, as such, are problematic. The issue is that systems of knowledge have been taken for granted. Mac Naughton (2005) notes that

> The significance of binary oppositions and their 'other' is that the 'other' is not equal to the main part of the pair. There is a hierarchy of value, set culturally in binaries and dichotomies (Ghandi, 1998). The pairs are always ranked, so one part of the pair always has a higher value in the ranking and is privileged over the 'other'. So using binary oppositions places some meanings in a secondary, subordinate position and often an aberrant position. (p. 83)

Binaries create spaces that make practices and research in early childhood education come to a halt, a standstill space in which possibilities for encountering other ways of seeing and relating or transformations are closed (Dahlberg & Moss, 2005; Mac Naughton, 2005). These binaries are packed with certainties, applicable knowledge, and regulated spaces that disempower children and make early childhood educators and researchers the holders of important knowledge.

Because binaries and the hierarchies created through them are not natural but are socially produced, they can be deconstructed or challenged (Lenz Taguchi, 2005b, 2009; Mac Naughton, 2005). We can begin to think and talk about *both/and* rather than *either/or* (Dahlberg, Moss, & Pence, 2007). It is the process of destabilizing binaries that we turn to in the next sections. We use the concept of pedagogical documentation as a tool that provides possibilities.

PEDAGOGICAL DOCUMENTATION

Our argument is that the research–practice of pedagogical documentation presents possibilities, challenging binaries. In this section, borrowing from existing literature, we explain how pedagogical documentation has been employed to unpack binaries, to uncover the hidden meanings of binary thinking in order to consider alternative discourses. In other words, pedagogical documentation has been used to make visible the binaries that are often taken for granted and are rarely contested or resisted by researchers, practitioners, families, or children themselves in early childhood education contexts. Through pedagogical documentation, it is possible to adopt a critical approach to binary thinking by critically evaluating and acting on our omissions/silences/unjust practices by reimagining and reinventing equitable practices, recognizing that practices and choices involve social and political issues. Before we get to this argument, we provide a brief background on pedagogical documentation.

Pedagogical documentation has been conceptualized using poststructuralist perspectives within the context of continental Europe (particularly within the Swedish literature) and, specifically, in early childhood education. Of course we recognize the extensive work done in other parts of the world by scholars working with postfoundational ideas to destabilize binaries in research–practice—although in this chapter we concentrate specifically on pedagogical documentation and early childhood education. Most notably, the work of Bronwyn Davies (Davies, 2000; Davies & Gannon, 2006) in Australia, Ian Stronach and Maggie MacLure (MacLure, 2003; Stronach & MacLure, 1997) in England, and Lynn Mario de Souza and Vanessa Andreotti in Brazil (Andreotti & Souza, 2008; Souza, 2005) has remarkable potential for destabilizing and questioning entrenched binaries in education research–practice. In fact, the work done by these scholars has been inspirational for some of the literature we review below.

ENGAGING IN THE PROCESS OF
PEDAGOGICAL DOCUMENTATION

The term *pedagogical documentation* (Dahlberg, Moss, & Pence, 2007; Fleet, Patterson, & Robertson, 2006; Giudici, Krechevsky, & Rinaldi, 2001; Rinaldi, 1998, 2006) refers to the process of a teacher/researcher's observing, recording, and, individually and collectively with colleagues, interpreting encounters, discoveries, exchanges, and *ordinary moments* selected from classroom practice, including children's conversations, children's own work, and teachers' dialogues with children. Within this framework, early childhood educators see themselves as observers and researchers and the pedagogical documentation they create as a component of their research. They make careful observations and document their observations with notes, photographs, audiotapes, videotapes, diaries, and other narrative forms. The process is ongoing and cyclical, and it is based on the art of critical reflection on the part of a community of learners that includes researchers, educators, children, and their families. The approach to pedagogical documentation assumes children's competence and strengths. Educators are taught to notice children, observe what they are interested in, and how they are learning. After careful observations, educators recognize what the children in their classrooms are exploring, what they are trying to do, and what they are interested in. Following this approach, educators recognize children's ideas as valuable and important contributions to the classroom. The term *pedagogical documentation* was first coined in the city of Reggio Emilia, Italy (Rinaldi, 2006) and extensive work with this practice has been done in Sweden (Dahlberg, Moss, & Pence, 2007), as well as other parts of the world.

Pedagogical documentation, as Swedish scholar Liselott Olsson (2009) explains, "becomes a vital material that can be used as a tool in the process of learning" (p. 113), both to make children's learning visible and to reflect upon the educator's practices. This is indeed a complex process that involves the educator taking on the role of the researcher. Differing theoretical paradigms come into play as historical and cultural issues of children are considered and children's learning processes are analyzed. Ethics and politics and how they fit into the landscape of early childhood education arise (Dahlberg & Moss, 2005). Trying out multiple perspectives and native ways of working can lead to intense discussion amongst educators. The educational environments are frequently invented and reinvented in response to how children and educators explore and interact with materials and ideas. Observation and documentation techniques are developed and refined continually.

What is of interest within the context of this chapter is the interpretative aspect of pedagogical documentation, or, in other words, how we make meanings of the observations collected through the process of pedagogical documentation. It is in this process that we see the potential for educators and researchers to become aware of and to disrupt hegemonies of knowledge such as binary thinking. It is through this process of interpretation that they often come to question the universalistic developmental theories of early childhood. Teachers become aware of some of their implicit assumptions about children by becoming exposed to diverse cultures in a genuine way. Through these and similar interventions, educators come to consider the perspectives of others and enrich their understandings of diverse children's background and cultural capital. Educators learn to ask different questions and consider multiple perspectives on what is observed in the classroom.

Dahlberg, Moss, and Pence (2007) argue that pedagogical documentation is "a vital tool for the creation of a reflective and democratic pedagogical practice" (p. 145), a tool for questioning dominant ideas and taking responsibility for making meanings and decisions in the field of early childhood. They are clear in pointing out that pedagogical documentation is not to be confused with *child observation* as understood as a way to assess children's development in relation to already predetermined categories. In this way they resist the dominant discourse of developmental psychology, insisting that pedagogical documentation, by contrast, "is mainly about trying to see and understand what is going on in the pedagogical work and what the child is capable of without any predetermined framework of expectations and norms" (p. 146).

Dahlberg, Moss, and Pence (2007) develop the theme of how traditions can be transgressed and alternative early childhood practices constituted by forming an active way of opposing regimes of truth which attempt to determine what is true or false, right or wrong. Understood from a modernist perspective, child observation is located within a traditional objectivist view of enquiry, based on the assumption that an objective, external truth can be recorded and represented accurately. From a poststructuralist perspective, however, pedagogical documentation does not make the claim that what is documented is a true account of what has happened. Rather, there is a recognition that documentation can in no way exist apart from our own involvement in the process. We are active subjects and participants as we coconstruct and coproduce the documentation. From this perspective, documentation is understood as a narrative of reflexivity. Being aware that we are not representing reality "makes it easier to critically analyze the constructed character of our documentation and to find methods to counteract and resist the dominant regimes" (Dahlberg, Moss, and Pence, 2007, p. 147).

Pedagogical documentation, therefore, can function as a tool for opening up a critical and reflective practice, challenging dominant discourses and constructing counterdiscourses (Dahlberg, Moss, and Pence, 2007). The educators in Reggio Emilia and Sweden, for example, have been able to use documentation to "create a space where it is possible to attempt to overcome the techniques of normalization" (Dahlberg & Moss, 2005,

p. 109). Through resisting these dominant regimes, they have been able to "refuse to codify children into prefabricated developmental categories, thereby transgressing the idea of a lacking and needy child" (p. 109).

PEDAGOGICAL DOCUMENTATION AND DECONSTRUCTIVE TALK THROUGH AN ETHICS OF RESISTANCE

Lenz Taguchi (2006, 2009) has also contributed to the field by presenting pedagogical documentation as an ethics of resistance. Collecting, reading, and using pedagogical documentation in various ways, educators work toward a transgression of the modernist *theory–practice* binary that dominates early childhood education and teacher education practices, where theory is meant to be applied to practice. Deconstructively *reading the text* of the documents helps to make visible and to tell the story of teachers' daily practice, which, in turn, provides a concrete starting point for thinking deeply about these practices and their philosophical or theoretical underpinnings. Educators can use what Lenz Taguchi (2006, 2009) has conceptualized as deconstructive talks as a way of making visible the dominant discourses of childhood, identity, learning, play, and gender in the performed and documented teaching practices. She explains that "deconstruction is about disruptions, destabilizations, undermining and challenging taken-for-granted notions, values, practices, and pedagogy 'as usual'" (2006, p. 281).

The notion of deconstructive talk is grounded in deconstruction theory as conceptualized by the French philosopher Jacques Derrida in *Of Grammatology* (1976). As Lenz Taguchi (2008) elaborates, "Deconstructive talk involves conversations that disquiet participants, throw them off balance, and toss them from their comfort zones by purposefully challenging familiar ideas and practices" (p. 272). The talking, the purposeful considering and reconsidering of taken-for-granted ideas, is more than an intellectual exercise; it is an exercise in professional ethics. The centrality of ethics in deconstructive talks is emphasized in Lenz Taguchi's use of the term *ethics of resistance*.

As an example of deconstructive talk, Lenz Taguchi (2006, 2009) describes a study which investigated the reconceptualization efforts of three preschool teachers during a series of meetings focusing on selected pieces of documentation, using two interrelated processes: deconstructive talk and an ethic of resistance.

At the time of this study, the children were engaged in a project designed to help them develop spatial knowledge and orientation within their immediate surroundings. The preschool teachers had asked the children to draw maps of whom to change places with at the lunch table after a request from the children to change places during lunch: "Please draw a map of the person you want to change places with. Don't tell anyone who it is while you are working so we can guess later" (Lenz Taguchi, 2009, p. 203). The children happily went along with this request, although, upon revisiting the documentation, teachers recognized that the question was very problematic. Was it actually a map of a person, the table, or the room that was requested of the children?

The children made drawings ranging from the faces of those they wanted to change places with to a variety of aerial maps. The teachers were surprised by the variety of the drawings/maps. One could be easily *read* as a diagram of a child who wanted to exchange places with another on the opposite side of the table, with arrows marked on the map to point where he wished to move. Another was a sketch of the face of the person with whom the child wished to exchange places. And a third drawing showed two empty chairs with hearts hovering over the seats. The deconstructive talk the educators engaged in as they analyzed the documentation was grounded in different theoretical perspectives, including developmental psychology, constructivism, and semiotics (for further detail on this study, see Lenz Taguchi, 2006, 2008, 2009). They scrutinized the various discourses about children, learning, and map drawing that informed their ways of thinking and valuing the children's work. The multiple readings enabled the educators to resist what they might previously have taken for granted, encouraging them to think differently about the drawings and how they understood the work of the children. Recognizing that their initial reading was steeped in the discourse of developmental psychology (i.e., "children of this age can't possibly have an understanding of an aerial perspective"), they sought out further research about children's mapmaking abilities. Upon a first reading of the image of two hearts hovering over the chairs, the teachers thought that perhaps the child had misunderstood the request. After revisiting the documentation and engaging in deconstructive talk, the teachers reconsidered a semiotic reading, recognizing the symbolism inherent in the child's sketch as a much more abstract representation than first understood.

Resistance is understood here not as opposing or simply replacing one understanding with another, but rather as a continuous process of displacement and transformation from within what we already think and do. Such resistance is a professional enactment of ethics.

MOVING BEYOND THE THEORY/PRACTICE DIVIDE
WITH PEDAGOGICAL DOCUMENTATION

In this way, Lenz Taguchi (2009) shows that the methodology of working with pedagogical documentation goes beyond the theory/practice divide in that it embraces the interdependence of thinking and living. Thinking, as Lenz Taguchi describes it, transforms living (practice), and living (practice) transforms thinking (Colebrook, 2002; Deleuze & Guattari, 1980; May,

2005). We often fail to acknowledge the interconnections and interdependencies between the two sides of the theory/practice divide, and thus make visible how theories are based on lived realities and how lived realities can be theorized to be understood in other ways. The resistance and construction of either–or keeps the binaries in place with emerging conflicts between the polarized practices as a result.

A perceived gap between theory and practice constitutes a binary which is contaminated by the imagery of, on the one hand, a visionary, rational and logical, clean and flawless theory—an ideal state or condition; and, on the other hand, a messy, dirty, disorderly practice, in need of being organized, cleaned up, and saturated by the rationales and visions of theory. In line with such imagery, theory is supposed to be applied to practice. But practice is *already* theoretical, as in the mapmaking example described by Lenz Taguchi (2006, 2008, 2009) above. She proposes that "the problem isn't that practice isn't doing what we think it theoretically could be doing, but rather that it is *already* doing educational theories, and much more than that!" (personal communication, July 17, 2010).

Being a professional teacher or researcher is about acknowledging how theory and practice are interdependent, and, in a certain understanding, one and the same (Lenz Taguchi, 2006). So, to continue with Lenz Taguchi's thinking:

> As we perform pedagogical practices, we (unconsciously) theorize them into existence, and, with an awareness of this, we start to reflect upon practice theoretically, and to trouble our own understandings. As we think deeply and critically about how we stage, arrange, do and analyze our pedagogical performances, this deconstructive process becomes part of our professionalism. (personal communication, July 17, 2010)

It is possible to do multiple readings, or repeated analysis, to understand the same situation in many ways. The deconstructive process can thus be understood as "a simultaneous move of tracing and troubling meaning, and an ethical affirmation of renegotiated meanings and values" (Lenz Taguchi, 2007, p. 286). This may encourage teachers to make situated ethical choices about what to do next to challenge the children to be curiously engaged in their learning processes.

An ethic of resistance refers to conscious acts of thinking deeply about the assumptions and taken-for-granted notions we bring with us, often without awareness, as we engage in our daily work with children. As we practice an ethic of resistance, we deconstruct, or take apart, what we know to be true, to reflect on it, analyze it, criticize it, and resist its seductive powers arising from its familiarity. Practicing such an ethic of resistance has the potential to disrupt unequal power relationships hidden in binary constructs, including adult/child, boy/girl, theory/practice, individualized learning/cooperative learning, and learning/play, to name but a few of the dominant power-producing asymmetrical binaries that riddle educational discourse. This kind of analysis, then, becomes a vehicle for negotiating ethically grounded professional choices.

PEDAGOGICAL DOCUMENTATION AS A NOMADIC PRACTICE

Following the reflexive theme of pedagogical documentation, some scholars continue to expand and exemplify the practice of pedagogical documentation (e.g., Lenz Taguchi, 2009; Olsson, 2009; Pacini-Ketchabaw, 2010). Pedagogical documentation as a deconstructive act alone has received some critiques because it could lead to reintegration of the binaries that it is trying to destabilize (Kind, 2010; Lenz Taguchi, 2009; Olsson, 2009; Pacini-Ketchabaw, with Nxumalo, 2010). Much of this work borrows from, in particular, philosopher Gilles Deleuze's challenge to logocentrism and its oppositional, binary thinking.

Olsson (2009) argues that pedagogical documentation allows for new activations, and engages in movements and experimentation to avoid dualistic thinking and the essentialization of children's meanings. She proposes the use of pedagogical documentation as more than a tool for trying to find out what children's dialogues, children's own productions (e.g., a drawing), children's play *mean*, or what the different ways of interpreting them are. Instead, she proposes, we need to ask what children's dialogues, productions, and play *do* and how they connect with other things.

Pedagogical documentation, from this perspective, can then be conceptualized as a nomadic act. Olsson (2009) explains that nomadic thinking "has no sedentary and stable place within which to perform its activity" (p. 25):

This thinking not only deconstructs codes and habits but actually connects them together in new and unexpected ways. However, nomadic thinking is not presented as the simple opposite of sedentary thinking. Rather nomadic thinking recognizes that the act of organizing a place for thinking is a necessity, but this act of laying out the ground or organizing the place where thinking thinks, is seen as a very bold and dangerous act of creation that never stops taking place. (p. 26)

As a nomadic act, pedagogical documentation is then situated within an ontology of *becoming*, rather than an ontology of *being*. While an ontology of being concerns itself with the organized state of things—their unity, identity, essence, structure, discreteness (leading to the construction of binaries)—an ontology of becoming attends to plurality, dissonance, change, transience, and disparity (Chia, 1995). So to overcome binaries the goal of pedagogical documentation is not to find or discover already defined answers about practices and/or about children. Pedagogical documentation as a nomadic practice works with an ontology of becoming emphasizing a transient, ephemeral, and emergent reality. Pedagogical documentation as a nomadic practice does not take any specific interpretation as permanent but rather each interpretation becomes a moment of rest in a continuous journey (Braidotti, 1994; St. Pierre, 1997). Nomadic movements are "discursive escape routes for preserving the radical and the subversive," but at the same time they involve "hopefulness and pleasure" (Hughes, 2002, p. 418). Pedagogical documentation becomes what Hughes calls nomadic moments: these are moments of "joy and excitement that arise from intellectual endeavor. Such moments can be envisaged as spaces of constant and repeated transitions to many and varied forms of knowledge" (p. 418).

TO CONCLUDE . . . AND OPEN NEW DIALOGUES

We have argued that pedagogical documentation, as it is conceptualized within postfoundationalist perspectives, can become a tool for destabilizing binaries in research–practice in early childhood education. Furthermore, although pedagogical documentation has been mostly used in early childhood education, we have great hope that this tool can become a way of working through binaries within other levels of education. However, we want to end this chapter with some observations that attempt to caution somehow our perhaps over–celebratory review of pedagogical documentation. These cautionary observations are consistent with the spirit of our understanding of the risks of working with poststructuralist theories.

Working with poststructuralist perspectives requires that we think critically about a key element of pedagogical documentation, namely reflexive practice. Poststructuralist and feminist scholars have warned us of the dangers of reflexivity as a way of engaging in a process of searching for educators'/researchers' inner feelings (Burman, 2008; Davies & Gannon, 2006). Some reflexive practices, although presented as tools for destabilizing binaries, have become part of neoliberal strategies of government. Fendler (2003) notes that "some reflective practices may simply be exercises in reconfirming, justifying, or rationalizing preconceived ideas" (p. 16). These critiques suggest that, when engaged in reflective practice through pedagogical documentation, educators/researchers perhaps need to remember that the goal is not to find an answer to their everyday practices but rather that reflective practice can be used "to tell a story that is just that: a story, a situated, partial version; not the whole story. Or even to tell lots of stories" (Burman, 2008, p. 148). Reflective practice in pedagogical documentation can become risky business if the historically, socially, and politically implicated discourses are not deconstructed. Critical reflection cannot be about making the self visible, but is about reimagining new subjectivities in relation to different contexts.

The issue of how we use pedagogical documentation in different contexts requires further problematization. In particular, we want to suggest that a critical dialogue around the contextualization of pedagogical documentation within Eurocentric perspectives is required in early childhood education. As our review above shows, pedagogical documentation has been mainly conceptualized using perspectives from European philosophy and fails to go beyond Northern epistemologies (see Moraña, Dussel, & Jáuregui, 2008, Sousa Santos, 2007; for a critique of Eurocentrism). Nelson Maldonado-Torres (2006) posits the following challenges:

> Since the intellectual production of third world peoples and people of color is often approached as if it were an appendix to European philosophy or as a variety of continental philosophy, we should first reflect on some of the pitfalls of continental philosophy. It is generally believed that continental philosophy receives its name because its main contributors happen to be continental Europeans. I have argued elsewhere, however, that the designation captures not only a contingent relation to Europe, but also a certain commitment with European continentality as a project as well as Eurocentric conceptions of space and time. These skewed conceptions of geopolitical temporality and spatiality need to be radically critiqued, or better put, decolonized. Without such decolonization any kind of rapprochement between continental and analytic philosophies will be bound to repeat the problems that they currently have. (p. 1)

The important observations made in this quotation need to be considered in relation to pedagogical documentation: How can pedagogical documentation become more than a Eurocentric critique of Eurocentrism? Some work has been done in early childhood education that explores how educators can begin to address more explicitly the coloniality of power in their multicultural communities (e.g., Pacini-Ketchabaw & Berikoff, 2008; Pacini-Ketchabaw with Nxumalo, 2010); however, much more thinking that takes seriously Madonado-Torres's (2006) challenges is required. We are only beginning to open the dialogue of pedagogical documentation to make other knowledges possible.

Pedagogical documentation, then, cannot be seen as *the* tool that will solve the challenges presented by binary and hegemonic thinking. Rather, pedagogical documentation becomes a possibility that is always to be revised, revisited, and challenged—a practice for questioning assumptions that involves questioning its own assumptions.

REFERENCES

Andreotti, V., & Souza, L. (2008). Translating theory into practice and walking minefields: Lessons from the project "Through Other Eyes." *International Journal of Development Education and Global Learning, 1*(1), 23–36.

Bernhard, J. (1995). Child development, cultural diversity, and the professional training of early childhood educators. *Canadian Journal of Education, 20*(4), 415–436.

Bernhard, J. K., Gonzalez-Mena, J., Chang, H. N., O'Loughlin, M., Eggers-Pierola, C., Roberts Fiati, G., et al. (1998). Recognizing the centrality of cultural diversity and racial equity: Beginning a discussion and critical reflection on Developmentally Appropriate Practice. *Canadian Journal of Research in Early Childhood Education, 7*(1), 81–90.

Bourdieu, P. (1994). Social space and symbolic power. In M. J. Wolfgang (Ed.), *The polity reader in social theory* (pp. 111–120). Cambridge, MA: Polity Press.

Braidotti, R. (1994). *Nomadic subjects. Embodiment and sexual difference in contemporary feminist theory.* New York: Columbia University Press.

Burman, E. (2008). *Deconstructing developmental psychology.* New York: Routledge.

Cannella, G. (1997). *Deconstructing early childhood education: Social justice & revolution.* New York: Peter Lang.

Chia, R. (1995). From modern to postmodern organizational analysis. *Organization Studies, 16*(4), 579, 3–604.

Colebrook, C. (2002). *Gilles Deleuze.* London: Routledge.

Corson, D. (2000). *Language diversity and education.* New York: Lawrence Erlbaum Associates.

Dahlberg, G. (2003). Pedagogy as a loci of ethics. In M. Bloch, K. Holmlund, I. Moqvist, & T. Popkewitz (Eds.), *Governing children, families, and education: Restructuring the welfare state* (pp. 261–286). New York: Palgrave Macmillan.

Dahlberg, G., & Moss, P. (2005). *Ethics and politics in early childhood education.* London: Routledge/Falmer Press.

Dahlberg, G., Moss, P., & Pence, A. (2007). *Beyond quality in early childhood education and care: Languages of evaluation.* London: Routledge/Falmer Press.

Davies, B. (2000). *A body of writing 1990–1999.* New York: Altamira Press.

Davies, B., & Gannon, S. (Eds.). (2006). *Doing collective biographies.* New York: Open University Press.

Deleuze, G., & Guattari, F. (1980). *A thousand plateaus: Capitalism and schizophrenia* (B. Massumi, Trans.). Minneapolis, MN: University of Minnesota Press.

Derrida, J. (1976). *Of grammatology.* Baltimore, MD: Johns Hopkins University Press.

Fendler, L. (2003). Teacher reflection in a hall of mirrors: Historical influences and political reverberations. *Educational Researcher 32*(3), 16–25.

Fleet, A., Patterson, C., & Robertson, J. (Eds.) (2006). *Insights: Behind early childhood pedagogical documentation.* Castle Hill, Australia: Pademelon Press.

Foucault, M. (1977). *Discipline and punish: The birth of the prison.* New York: Vintage.

Foucault, M. (1978). *The history of sexuality: An introduction.* New York: Vintage.

Giudici, C., Krechevsky, M., & Rinaldi, C. (2001). *Making learning visible: Children as individual and group learners.* Reggio Emilia, Italy: Reggio Children.

Hughes, E. (2002). Planning meaningful curriculum: A mini story of children and teachers learning together. *Childhood Education, 78*(3), 134–139.

Kind, S. (2010). Art encounters: Movements in the visual arts and early childhood education. In V. Pacini-Ketchabaw (Ed.), *Flows, rhythms and intensities of early childhood education curriculum* (pp. 113–132). New York: Peter Lang.

Lenz Taguchi, H. (2006). Reconceptualizing early childhood education: Challenging taken-for-granted ideas. In J. Einarsdottir and J. Wagner (Eds.), *Nordic childhoods and early education: Philosophy, research, policy and practice in Denmark, Finland, Iceland, Norway, and Sweden* (pp. 257–287). Greenwich, CT: Information Age Publishing.

Lenz Taguchi, H. (2007). Deconstructing the theory–practice dichotomy in early childhood education. *Educational Philosophy and Theory, 39*(3), 275–290.

Lenz Taguchi, H. (2008). *Doing justice in early childhood education? Justice to whom and to what?* Paper presented at the European Early Childhood Education Research Association conference, Stavanger, Norway.

Lenz Taguchi, H. (2009). An 'ethics of resistance' challenges taken-for-granted ideas in early childhood education. *International Journal of Educational Research, 47*(5), 270–282.

MacLure, M. (2003). *Discourse in educational and social research.* Buckingham, UK: Open University Press.

Mac Naughton, G. (2005). *Doing Foucault in early childhood studies: Applying poststructural ideas.* London: Routledge.

Maldonado-Torres, N. (2006). Post-continental philosophy: Its definitions, contours, and fundamental sources. *Worlds & Knowledges Otherwise, 1*(3), 1–29. Retrieved from http://www.jhfc.duke.edu/wko/index.php

May, T. (2005). *Gilles Deleuze: An introduction.* Cambridge, UK: Cambridge University Press.

Moraña, M., Dussel, E. D., & Jáuregui, C. A. (2008). *Coloniality at large: Latin America and the postcolonial debate: Latin America otherwise.* Durham, NC: Duke University Press.

Olsson, L. (2009). *Movement and experimentation in young children's learning: Deleuze and Guattari in early childhood education.* London: Routledge.

Pacini-Ketchabaw, V. (Ed.). (2010). *Flows, rhythms and intensities of early childhood education curriculum.* New York: Peter Lang.

Pacini-Ketchabaw, V., & Berikoff, A. (2008). The politics of difference and diversity: From young children's violence to creative power expressions. *Contemporary Issues in Early Childhood, 9*(3), 256–264.

Pacini-Ketchabaw, V., with Nxumalo, F. (2010. A curriculum for social change: Experimenting with politics of action or imperceptibility. In V. Pacini-Ketchabaw (Ed.), *Flows, rhythms, and intensities of early childhood education curriculum* (pp. 133–154). New York: Peter Lang.

Rinaldi, C. (1998). Projected curriculum and documentation. In C. Edwards, L. Gandini, & G. Forman (Eds.), *The hundred languages of children: The Reggio Emilia approach* (pp. 113–125). Norwich, CT: Ablex.

Rinaldi, C. (2006). *In dialogue with Reggio Emilia: Listening, researching, and learning.* London: Routledge.

St. Pierre, E. A. (1997). Circling the text: Nomadic writing practices. *Qualitative Inquiry, 3*(4), 403–417.

Souza, L. (2005). The ecology of writing among the Kashinawa: Indigenous multimodality in Brazil. In A. Suresh Canagarajah (Ed.), *Reclaiming the local in language policy and practice* (pp. 73–95). Mahwah, NJ: Lawrence Erlbaum Associates.

Souza Santos, B. (Ed.) (2007). *Another knowledge is possible: Beyond northern epistemologies.* London: Verso.

Stronach, I., & MacLure, M. (1997). *Educational research undone: The postmodern embrace.* Buckingham, UK: Open University Press.

6 Moving Beyond Sedentarism
Conceptual and Empirical Developments

Patrick Alan Danaher
and Robyn Henderson

ABSTRACT

Sedentarism is the binary in the Western, industrialized world that constructs fixed residence as the sociocultural norm from which itinerancy and mobility deviate and are thereby positioned as pathologies. Sedentarism has a long history of marginalization of mobile individuals and communities, and has been complicit with the antipastoralist policies of state development in Asia and Africa as well as with race-based discrimination against Gypsy Travelers and Roma in Europe.

In the domain of formal education, sedentarism has likewise found allies in an industrialized approach to schooling provision that assumes that learners live in fixed locations. This approach creates difficulties for communities whose occupations require families to be temporary visitors to particular locations. As a result, mobile learners tend to be marginalized and families feel obliged to choose between their way of life and their children's educational access.

This chapter explores several dimensions of moving beyond this disabling sedentarism. Drawing on examples from our respective studies of Australian show people and seasonal workers, we argue that sedentarism's resilience as a marginalizing binary will be disrupted only by the effective combination of conceptual and empirical developments that afford new understandings of residence, mobility, and educational provision. More broadly, the chapter considers implications of this argument for the education of nonmobile as well as mobile learners.

INTRODUCTION

The continuing operation of deeply embedded sociocultural binaries constitutes one of the most serious obstacles to new and more transformative experiences of human relationships within communities, in nation-states, and globally. Appropriately, this book contests unexamined assumptions about the character and development of binary thinking and promotes the articulation of alternative understandings of social interactions. This chapter contributes to that laudable goal by simultaneously tracing selected historical antecedents and contemporary manifestations of one particular binary and elaborating some possible evidence-based substitutes to the enactment of that binary.

The binary in question here is sedentarism, or the settled/itinerant binary. As we explain below, this is a particularly insidious and resilient categorization that has functioned for centuries, if not millennia, and it is complicit with race-based policies and practices that have negatively affected the life chances of communities such as Gypsy Travelers, refugees, and asylum seekers (McVeigh, 1997; see also Hayes & Acton, 2007). Sedentarism is additionally implicated with privileging fixed residence as the natural and normal form of provision of formal education and with the concomitant construction of mobile learners as deviating from that norm, with deleterious impact on their educational opportunities and aspirations (Danaher, Kenny, & Remy Leder, 2009; Danaher, Moriarty, & Danaher, 2004, 2009).

The chapter is divided into the following six sections:

• A background overview of our understanding of what a binary is and why it is significant
• Selected elements of the conceptual etiology of the settled/itinerant binary
• Some examples of the empirical implementation of that binary
• Ideas for moving beyond sedentarism conceptually
• Strategies for moving beyond sedentarism empirically
• Suggested broader implications for the contemporary education of mobile and nonmobile learners.

The data deployed to illustrate this discussion derive from our separate research into the education of Australian mobile show people and seasonal workers. We contend that sedentarism provides a particularly clear and vivid example of the close association between the operation of a specific binary on the one hand and highly differentiated educational experiences and outcomes for diverse types of learners on the other. At the same time, we seek to demonstrate that the line of demarcation between the settled and itinerant binary is fluid and permeable rather than fixed and permanent. Moreover, we see the conceptual and empirical developments outlined in the chapter as vital if that binary is to be challenged and if moving beyond sedentarism is to become a real possibility.

BACKGROUND TO A BINARY

Several paradoxes are attached to the binaries encountered in this book, including sedentarism as discussed here. While these binaries are highly diverse, they have a number of common features; while they are predicated on certainty and fixity, they exhibit both uncertainty and ambivalence that their advocates work hard to disguise; while they are seemingly omnipotent and unassailable, they can be contested and disrupted. If it were not so, a book based on the aspiration of moving beyond binaries would be chimerical, even fallacious.

Binaries are amenable to challenge partly because of another paradox attending their construction: their inextricable interdependence even while one half seeks to render the other half null and void. As Ferguson (1990) remarked about another categorization, so too with the settled/itinerant binary: "Margin and center can draw their meanings only from each other. Neither can exist alone" (p. 13). Yet on the other hand:

> When we say marginal, we must always ask, marginal to *what*? But this question is difficult to answer. The place from which power is exercised is often a hidden place. When we try to pin it down, the center always seems to be somewhere else. Yet we know that this phantom center, elusive as it is, exerts a real, undeniable power over the whole social framework of our culture, and over the ways that we think about it. (Ferguson, 1990, p. 9; *emphasis in original*)

From this we can elicit some other key characteristics of binaries. Firstly, they are based on pairs of polarized attributes and values, with the more highly valued denoting what is supposedly good about a particular social category and the less highly valued personifying what is supposedly bad about that category—or what Mercer (1990) tellingly named "a fundamental polarization of human worth," the "bipolar codification of human value," and the "ordering of differences" (p. 249). Secondly, they are fundamentally concerned with the exercise of power and with the associated distribution of or denial of resources. Thirdly, they are ineluctably ideological, framing and constraining crucial elements of individuals' and communities' worldviews about the purposes and effects of specific cultural practices. Fourthly, they tend to be circular, intellectually impoverished, and restrictive of alternative thinking; as Greimas and Rastier (1968, as cited in Clifford, 1990) noted, "any initial binary opposition can, by the operation of negations and the appropriate synthesis, generate a much larger field of terms which, however, all necessarily remain locked in the closure of the initial system" (p. 146).

Although binaries are by no means the only device for the enactment of ideologies, they have demonstrated their long-term resilience and their capacity to be co-opted by particular systems of thought (such as extreme forms of totalitarianism), with varying degrees of effectiveness. While acknowledging the diversity characterizing binaries noted above, we argue that binaries have proven to be adept at othering—at positioning those different from ourselves as not only different but also disadvantaged, deficit, and deviant (see also Danaher, Coombes, & Kiddle, 2007). Thus the less favored part of the binary becomes unavoidably associated with the absence or lack of, or distance or gap from, something that is commonly held to be crucial to being a *good* person or community. Or as Ferguson (1990) explained:

> Audre Lorde calls this center the mythical norm, defined as "white, thin, male, young, heterosexual, Christian and financially secure". Although each of these characteristics carries a somewhat different weight, their combination describes a status with which we are all familiar. It defines the tacit standards from which specific others can then be declared to deviate, and while that myth is perpetuated by those whose interests it serves, it can also be internalized by those who are oppressed by it. (p. 9)

The reference here to a binary's polarized positioning being internalized is a timely reminder of the different mechanisms by which that positioning is implemented. One such mechanism is homogenization (see also Kostogriz & Peeler, 2004; Steingress, 2010), whereby the differences among the inhabitants of the two poles are elided and each is presented as a community with common characteristics, although one is highly valued and the other is not. Those characteristics are in turn essentialized (see also Morrissey, 2004; Vermeersch, 2008; Wagner, Holtz, & Kashima, 2009), or rendered as supposedly fixed and ontologically stable, as well as naturalized (see also Burke, Joseph, Pasick, & Barker, 2009; Holmes, 2007; Vázquez, 2006), or conveyed as occurring naturally and normally rather than as being socioculturally constructed. The cumulative effect of these processes is a narrowing of understandings about the individuals clustered at the less valued part of the binary and a diminishing of empathy toward them. Additionally, individuals who are the focus of such views can internalize or take unto themselves the blame and responsibility for the situation in which they find themselves instantiated.

Finally in this overview of selective features of binaries, it is important to note a couple of specific strategies that flow from the underlying and largely invisible mechanisms that we have identified. One of these strategies is stereotyping: assigning to the less valued and powerful group a set of reductionist and mostly negative characteristics that are then taken up in popular discourse and in media, fictional, and sometimes nonfictional representations (see also Hugenberg & Sacco, 2008; Quadflieg, Turk, Waiter, Mitchell, Jenkins, & Macrae, 2009; Rudman & Fairchild, 2004). Another strategy, also associated with language, is the development of a list of key terms associated with the social category underpinning the binary, with one list having a positive valence and the other a negative valence. At the same time, this strategy of naming (see also Vuolteenaho & Berg, 2009) is the site of potential resistance and recuperation by the less valued part of the binary—for example, when particular ethnic minorities claim back for themselves terms such as *Black*, *Gypsy*, and *Traveler*, when these terms have been devalued and even demonized in other contexts.

So far we have presented our understanding of a binary: what it is, how it comes about, what impact it has, and why it is crucial to interrogate and if possible to disrupt it. This understanding needs to be set beside the other conceptualizations of binaries outlined in the book as well as to be considered against the foundation of readers' respective notions and experiences of binaries. This understanding also constitutes the framework for the focus on sedentarism and ideas for moving beyond it that make up the remainder of the chapter.

THE CONCEPTUAL ETIOLOGY OF THE SETTLED/ITINERANT BINARY

We use the term *etiology* here less to imply some notion of simplified causation of sedentarism—ideologies are too complex and differentiated to admit readily of such a notion—than to denote the settled/itinerant binary's status as a pathology. Indeed, there is considerable evidence of the ancient lineage and the continued longevity of this binary, as well as its widespread application across multiple forms of mobility and in diverse responses to that mobility.

The settled/itinerant binary has been conceptualized in a number of ways. Malkki (1992/2008) identified "[t]he pathologization of uprootedness in the national order of things" (p. 279). McVeigh (1997) sought to engage in what he called "[t]heorising sedentarism," whereby "the roots of anti-nomadism" (p. 7) could be made explicit (see also Danaher, 2001). He defined sedentarism as "that system of ideas and practices which serves to normalise and reproduce sedentary modes of existence and pathologise and repress nomadic modes of existence" (p. 9). He elaborated his definition in terms that resonate strongly with this chapter and this book by countering the binary logic of sedentarism or antinomadism:

> It is wrong to use notions which reproduce the dichotomy between 'good' *T*ravellers (ethnic, exotic, romantic, free) and bad *t*ravellers (non-ethnic, dispossessed and debased sedentaries, subcultures of poverty). In fact, the suggested dichotomy between the construction of the romanticised 'Raggle Taggle Gypsy' and the pathologised 'itinerant' is a false one. Both simultaneously inform contemporary ideas about, and the treatment of, *all* nomadic peoples. (p. 15; *emphasis in original*)

Viewed from that historical and ideological perspective, prior to the neolithic revolution and the associated development of agriculture beginning around 7,000 years ago, nearly all human communities were nomadic. Agricultural practices required permanent settlement for their efficient management and regulation, with thriving towns and cities springing up along coastlines and rivers. This process of fixed residence was considerably exacerbated by the industrial revolution in the 18th and 19th centuries, when machine-based manufacturing led to urbanization. Although these two revolutions occurred millennia apart from each other, their combined impact was to normalize permanent residence and consequently to pathologize mobility (McVeigh, 1997; see also Lentin, 2001; Levinson & Sparkes, 2004; Okely, 2000).

That pathologization has adopted several historical and contemporary guises. Antinomadism continues to be manifested, for example, in discursive constructions of Gypsy and Traveler children in Britain as culturally disadvantaged and deficient. Additionally, their mobility is often constructed as deleterious to their participation and achievement in formal education (Vanderbeck, 2005). Such constructions have also fueled ongoing associations between British Roma, Gypsies, and Travelers and public concerns about criminal justice (Acton, 2007; Clark & Dearling, 1999). These examples attest to the resilience of what Lucassen, Willems, and Cottar (1998) referred to as "the inclination to view itinerant groups predominantly as down and out riff-raff" (p. 2), which they elaborated more broadly in this way:

> Our knowledge has been severely restricted not only because of historical negligence, but also because of two closely connected paradigms, one which views Gypsies and other itinerant groups as criminal, marginal and poor, and another which focuses almost exclusively on their alleged common ethnic identity and origin. (p. 2)

Again we see the processes of essentialization and homogenization in league with the pathologizing effects of sedentarism—a complicity that has been evidenced also in the growth of anti-Semitism through such medieval Christian myths as the Wandering Jew, sometimes called Ahasuerus, who supposedly taunted Christ on the way to the Crucifixion and as a result was cursed to wander the earth until the Second Coming (Rose, 1990, 1992).

In presenting this necessarily selective account of the conceptual etiology of the settled/nomadic binary, we have highlighted the binary's millennia old historical antecedents, its diverse manifestations across multiple forms of contemporary life, and its ongoing effects on individuals and groups who are variously mobile. The binary's theoretical logic depends on the fixity and permanence of the oppositional experiences of *settled* and *unsettled*, an enduringly powerful separation with considerable impact in its empirical implementation.

THE EMPIRICAL IMPLEMENTATION OF
THE SETTLED/ITINERANT BINARY

There is substantial evidence of the settled/itinerant binary at work in previous and current formal educational provision for mobile learners.

Partly the situation is a reflection of the broader social forces noted above that pathologize mobility; educational institutions are often the sites of reinscription of wider prejudices and inequities (Gale & Densmore, 2000, 2003). For example, Jordan (2000) critiqued "[t]he exclusionary comprehensive school system" (p. 253) in Scotland, which she called a "reproductive model [that] offers little hope of any radical change in the foreseeable future" (p. 254) and whereby "the school experience still alienates and diminishes a substantial proportion of pupils" (p. 254). Jordan criticized "the inability of the present construct of schools to support [the] learning out of school" (p. 259) of the Travellers in Scotland, whose mobility derived from ethnicity and/or occupation. She linked those communities with other groups such as chronically ill children, those who are homeless and in care, those who care for dependent adults, and those who are truants and have been excluded from school, all of whom, she argued, "experience serious discontinuity in their learning and can be classed as interrupted learners" (p. 259).

Similarly, Özerk (2009) explained how the ongoing policy of *Norwegianization* has discriminated against the mobile Sami reindeer herders living in Sápmi, an area that traverses Norway and Russia. Ironically, Özerk argued that "[t]he mobility of the Sami today stems less from their nomadic pastoralism than it does from external requirements set by the Norwegian government" (p. 135), with Sami children being required to move away from their families in order to attend public schools, and young adults often needing to move out of Sápmi to obtain more secure work in other parts of Norway. Özerk was particularly concerned about the linguistically assimilationist effect of Norwegianization; although this legislation was subsequently amended, its long-term negative impact continues to be felt.

The state's complicity in constructing and perpetuating the settled/itinerant binary is evident also in India, where the mobility of nomadic pastoralists is positioned as antithetical to government goals for national economic development. Dyer (2009) exemplified this complicity in the following way:

> The nature of schooling provision [in India] means . . . that formal education and transhumant pastoralism are pitted as mutually incompatible, for the former demands sedentarisation, but the latter demands movement. . . . [T]he narrowness of the government's development policies in relation to transhumant pastoralists is a salutary reminder that schools are embedded in a particular hegemony of development that is highly resistant to change. . . . The dominant hegemony of progress . . . continues to marginalise pastoralist knowledge and a life characterised by movement, apparently assuming them to have neither a place in contemporary society nor a contribution to make to the development of the nation state . . . (pp. 186–187)

At a broader level, Souto-Otero (2009) noted that "when an education system separates 'disadvantaged' children from 'advantaged' children, socioeconomic differences are reinforced, and the legal guarantee of quality education for all is not honoured in practice" (p. 175). He elaborated this charge by outlining the interplay between the settled/itinerant binary and another powerful dichotomy: gender. Referring to the situation of the Roma in Spain, he demonstrated significant differences in educational aspirations and achievement between girls and boys (with girls outperforming boys, despite expectations to the contrary). He also quoted a poignant statement by a Roma boy who enjoyed school-based learning and who expressed dismay at being situated in a triple binary. This was on the basis of his status as a Roma male wanting to succeed in formal education against the wishes of some members of his extended family, against the predictions of the settled community, and against the evidence of girls outperforming boys in his community:

> Many of my cousins, family and other people I know have not studied. They come and say: "Why do you keep on studying?" I reply: "Because I like it". And they treat you as a non-Roma person. That is hard too. . . . [They tell you] you should quit[;] you are becoming similar to a non-Roma. (Abajo & Carrasco, 2004, as cited in Souto-Otero, 2009, p. 178)

Turning to Australia, we find several manifestations of the enactment of the settled/itinerant binary as it applies to the formal educational experiences of various mobile groups. For example, a teacher working in an Australian school in a fixed location that saw regular influxes of seasonal farm workers' children deployed a *binary logic* to explain perceived differences in behavior between them and nonmobile children at the school:

> [S]he juxtaposed "our culture" . . . against "their culture" . . . and, by implication, contrasted an unnamed 'us' with 'them', and the way that 'we' do things in school against the way that [itinerant] Tongan parents might do things in the home. (Henderson, 2009, p. 54)

Similarly, Danaher (2001) listed the formal educational options available to Australian show people's children prior to the establishment of the Queensland School for Travelling Show Children in 2000:

- sending their children to local schools along the show circuits
- sending their children to boarding schools
- not sending their children to local or boarding schools but instead teaching them correspondence lessons [while traveling] on the show circuits
- coming off the show circuits and finding alternative employment for the duration of their children's education so that the children could attend local schools

- remaining on the show circuits and sending their children to live with relatives and attend local schools
- not sending their children to school at all. (p. 255)

While each option had particular perceived benefits and limitations, in combination their effect was what we noted above: requiring mobile parents to reach some kind of temporary compromise between pursuing their chosen occupation and accepting less than optimal educational provision for their children. It was precisely this requirement that animated the show parents' determination to lobby for the creation of a separate school, the Queensland School for Travelling Show Children, which travels with the show families from place to place and provides formal schooling for the children (Danaher & Danaher, 2009).

In this section of the chapter, we have presented empirical evidence of the widespread operation of the settled/itinerant binary across a wide range of mobile groups in several different countries. Clearly, schools function as an alien and alienating institution for many members of such groups, and they do so partly because they are often predicated on a form of residence different from that of mobile communities. We turn now to consider ways in which this binary can be displaced and transformed, first conceptually and then empirically.

MOVING BEYOND SEDENTARISM CONCEPTUALLY

It is encouraging to note that several conceptual resources are available to us in seeking to move beyond sedentarism. For example, West (1990) noted that:

> [F]our major historicist forms of theoretical activity provide resources for how we understand, analyze and enact our representational practice: Heideggerian *destruction* of the western metaphysical tradition, Derridean *deconstruction* of the western philosophical tradition, Rortian *demythologization* of the western intellectual tradition and Marxist, Foucaultian, feminist, anti-racist or anti-homophobic *demystification* of western cultural and artistic conventions. (pp. 29–30; *emphasis in original*)

While we are sympathetic to all four of these activities, we are probably closest to the fourth one, demystification, which resonates with our shared interest in poststructuralist theorizing of contemporary cultural practices. We concur largely with West (1990) that:

> Demystification is the most illuminating mode of theoretical inquiry for those who promote the new cultural politics of difference. . . .

Demystification tries to keep track of the complex dynamics of institutional and other related power structures in order to disclose options and alternatives for transformative praxis; it also attempts to grasp the way in which representational strategies are creative responses to novel circumstances and conditions. In this way, the central role of human agency (always enacted under circumstances of one's choosing)—be it the critic, artist or constituency and audience—is accented. (p. 31)

For us, demystification provides a theoretically rigorous and yet practically attuned framework for helping to move beyond sedentarism. It does this by making visible—and hence open to critique and contestation—the otherwise invisible forces that pathologize and demonize mobility. At the same time, demystification assists in highlighting potential openings in usually closed systems of thought and implementation that can give rise to more effective and equitable alternatives to current operations. It also emphasizes the agency needed to conceptualize and give life to these alternatives, a crucial point that resonates strongly with current research into social transformation that affirms the capacity of individuals and groups to resist and change marginalizing binaries in favor of more productive understandings of the sociocultural world (Todd, 2005).

A potentially strong ally of demystification is systems thinking (Capra, 1996). This approach is premised on the notion of interconnectivity, so that, instead of difference being understood as a set of binary opposites, each part is considered in terms of its contribution to a greater whole; consequently "the focus of this thinking and the forms of knowledge that it produces are more concerned with connections and resonances than with discrete parts" (Danaher, Moriarty, & Danaher, 2009, p. 94). We see this premise as an exciting theoretical development that can contribute powerfully to the goal of moving beyond sedentarism conceptually.

As well as theoretical resources, researchers investigating mobility need to be able to draw on methodological approaches that are resistant of, rather than complicit with, the settled/itinerant binary. From that perspective, it is noteworthy that two experienced researchers with Nigerian nomadic pastoralists (Umar & Tahir, 2000) advocated challenging two other binaries that are common in education research. In doing so, they recommended an approach with wider applicability in terms of disrupting binaries:

The position taken here does not entail an "either/or stance," since positivism and naturalism are not mutually exclusive. Neither are they so irreconcilable that the adoption of one implicitly involves the negation of the other. Any dogmatic stance on methodology will impede progress in nomadic education research. Furthermore, treating quantitative and qualitative methods as mutually exclusive will not engender a deeper understanding of the problems of nomadic education or their resolution. What is required is a flexible approach towards both methods, which also recognizes the limitations of each method *vis-à-vis* the *specific research problem at hand*. Either method *on its own* is incapable of facilitating a deep understanding of the complex problems facing nomadism and nomadic education. What needs to be adopted is an approach that synthesizes the strengths of both methods, while avoiding the weakness of each. (pp. 237–238; *emphasis in original*)

Similarly, we endorse the contention by Levitt and Glick Schiller (2004) that "[m]ethodology and theory have an intimate relationship" (p. 1012), and their conviction about the corollary of that contention: "To develop a transnational framework for the study of migration, we need a methodology that allows us to move beyond the binaries, such as homeland/new land, citizen/non-citizen, migrant/nonmigrant, and acculturation/cultural persistence, that have typified migration research in the past" (p. 1012). By the same token, it is vital to recognize Okely's (2000) objection to a nongrounded and nonmaterialistic idealization of movement associated with "what has been named nomadology" and her assertion that "[i]t is extraordinarily ethnocentric to use nomads as the repository of sedentarist fantasies of opposites and inversions" (p. 18).

This is a crucial conceptual and methodological point that links with two wider insights. The first insight is the attribute noted above of demystification, that it has an empirical and material foundation that is needed to be able to give practical effect to any conceptual moves forward. The second insight was the injunction by Remy Leder (2009): "(**Do not romanticize the population under analysis)**" (p. 219; **emphasis in original**), and the corollary assertion: "Travellers are neither more nor less good, just or true than any other population" (p. 219). That is, giving recognition to mobile community members for the full rein of their humanity is a key ingredient both of moving beyond sedentarism and of developing conceptual and methodological approaches by researchers that contribute positively to that process.

A specific application of this approach was demonstrated by Levinson (2009) in his account of the spatial and temporal orientations displayed by young English Gypsy Travelers when they are at school. He noted that these children often exhibit different conceptions of space and time from their nonmobile counterparts, as part of a wider discussion of the disconnections between their home and school lives. At the same time, Levinson warned against the ease with which educators and researchers alike could fall prey to simplistic stereotypes such as "Gypsies show an aversion to fixed time schedules" (p. 62) and "Gypsy use of time connects to the immediate present" (p. 62). As he stated, "Such a stereotype gives a child-like quality to Traveller culture, and tends to consolidate the dichotomy between oral and literate cultures" (p. 62). For Levinson, the only way to counter these tendencies is "to recall the heterogeneous, multifaceted nature of Gypsy society" (p. 62) and to remember "that diverse home contexts are involved" (p. 62).

These and other proposed conceptual developments are indispensable elements of moving beyond sedentarism. The theoretical foundation of the settled/itinerary binary is longstanding and well-established, and so must be challenged as a system of thought with resistant and hopefully transformative alternative thinking. At the same time, these conceptual developments must be accompanied and supported by material and practical changes, and it is to these that we turn to consider now.

MOVING BEYOND SEDENTARISM EMPIRICALLY

The starting point for our examination of current and possible future developments in moving beyond sedentarism empirically is the classification by Danaher, Moriarty, and Danaher (2009) of different forms of educational provision for mobile communities: assimilation, integration, specialization, and lobbying (p. 9). Each form has achieved some gains for mobile learners in particular contexts, and debate continues about the relative merits and effects of specific forms for those learners as well as for nonmobile students (see, e.g., Danaher and Danaher [2009] about the debate between integration and specialization). More broadly, there is no presumption that perceived gains in providing effective and equitable formal education for mobile learners are necessarily automatic or permanent—witness the disestablishment in 2004 of the European Federation for the Education of the Children of Occupational Travellers (Danaher, Moriarty, & Danaher, 2009), which from its creation in 1988 under the auspices of the European Commission achieved significant improvements in policymaking and understanding that are at risk of having been undermined and reversed since its closure.

Nevertheless, it seems reasonable to assert that assimilation is the option least favored by mobile communities and at greatest risk of perpetuating sedentarism. The examples provided by Danaher, Moriarty, and Danaher (2009) of this form of educational provision included the options of Australian show families listed above prior to the establishment of the Queensland School for Travelling Show Children, and "Itinerant farm workers attending a local school in North Queensland for the duration of the fruit picking season" (Henderson, 2005, p. 9). In both these examples, while individual school principals and teachers are often as inclusive and welcoming as they can be, the short duration of the school visits and the limited interactions between the mobile learners and their nonmobile counterparts do little to dispel stereotypical views that each group holds about the other. Furthermore, there is no pressure on or requirement for the school system as a whole to alter its practices to take account of the itinerant children's mobility, which is accordingly prone to be positioned as an exotic oddity rather than as a valid and viable way of life in its own right.

Integration refers to specialized support for mobile learners within a broader framework of mainstream educational provision. Danaher, Moriarty, and Danaher (2009) cited as one instance the English Traveller Support Services, which assist itinerant students with distance education packs when they are traveling in the summer season and liaise with their classroom teachers when they attend regular schools in the winter season (Danaher, Coombes, & Kiddle, 2007). The other illustration presented was the program that the Brisbane School of Distance Education provided for Australian show children between 1989 and 2000: distance learning packs and regular visits while the children visited a series of local schools along the show circuits (Danaher, 1998). While this approach has the advantage of a dedicated support service for mobile learners, it is at the risk of capture and absorption by broader forces of assimilation—a perception that was the driving force behind the Australian show parents' lobbying for the establishment of the Queensland School for Travelling Show Children (Danaher & Danaher, 2009).

Specialization denotes separate educational provision for mobile learners, often in a designated institution. For instance, Danaher, Moriarty, and Danaher (2009) identified as examples of such provision the Queensland School for Travelling Show Children, the Romani School in Adelaide, South Australia, the National Schools for Travellers in Ireland, berth schools for children living on barges in the Netherlands, boarding schools for pastoral nomads in Oman, and the Camel School Programme for nomadic pastoralist children in Kenya. Many of these establishments have demonstrated progress in facilitating educational success by itinerant students. On the other hand, they are often subject to wider political and economic vicissitudes, and they are potentially complicit with segregating mobile communities and with preventing the education system's full recognition of their diversity.

Lobbying is not a form of educational provision in its own right, but the illustrations provided by Danaher, Moriarty, and Danaher (2009) of this activity highlighted considerable enterprise on the part of mobile communities and of the educators and researchers who support them. These instances included the European Federation for the Education of the Children of Occupational Travellers mentioned above, the Gypsy Research Centre in Paris, the National Association of State Directors of Migrant Education in the United States, the National Association of Teachers of Travellers in the United Kingdom, and the Nigerian National Commission for Nomadic Education. As Danaher, Moriarty, and Danaher noted, the inclusion of lobbying in their classification "reflects the ongoing importance of contesting received opinion and conventional wisdom and agitating for new forms of provision that engage with and facilitate the achievement of the specialized educational aspirations and opportunities of mobile and other communities" (p. 10).

Overall, despite the important work and encouraging achievements demonstrated by individuals and groups under each form of educational provision classified by Danaher, Moriarty, and Danaher (2009), it is clear that the ingredients for sustained and transformative improvement in moving beyond sedentarism empirically have not yet been implemented, and perhaps have not yet been identified incontrovertibly. This is hardly surprising: as noted above, the settled/itinerant binary has developed over centuries, even millennia, and cannot be disrupted easily or quickly. As Danaher, Moriarty, and Danaher argued, "In a real sense, the requirement for new educational futures derives in large part from the failure of current mainstream provision to resonate with the specialized circumstances and needs of learners such as members of such groups" (p. 10). Furthermore, "The envisioning and enactment of new educational futures depend on an openness to acknowledge an existing lack of educational fit and a willingness to consider possible alternative approaches" (p. 10).

IMPLICATIONS FOR EDUCATING MOBILE
AND NONMOBILE LEARNERS

In this final section of the chapter, we consider briefly some of the possible implications of the foregoing discussion for educating mobile and nonmobile learners alike. From one perspective, it can be asserted that, while any particular group is served poorly by the educational forms available to it, all participants and stakeholders in formal education are prevented from benefiting from the full potential of such education being attained. Certainly Danaher, Moriarty, and Danaher (2009) linked the requirement for learners to be in the same place most or all of the time to be able to access educational provision "with wider forces of social segmentation and segregation within and across nation states" (p. 10). Those forces are self-evidently powerful and resilient, and have been identified as contributing to several of the binaries critiqued in other chapters in this book. From this perspective, combating one binary is likely to entail similar strategies to those needed to disrupt others, both conceptually and empirically. As Henderson (2009) pointed out, "Teachers need ways of contesting and disrupting deficit thinking as well as opportunities to examine their assumptions about itinerant farm workers' children and their families" (p. 57), a requirement that clearly applies also and equally to all groups of learners.

Furthermore, it might be contended that what counts as effective educational provision for itinerant students is likely to be founded on fundamental principles that should underpin equivalent provision for all types of learners. For example, Danaher and Danaher (2009) saw the debate between inclusion and specialization in relation to the Australian show community's move from the Brisbane School of Distance Education program to the establishment of the Queensland School for Travelling Show Children as "resonat[ing] with contemporary discourses that

emphasise the importance of learner, parental and community involvement and agency in decision-making about educational provision" (p.
210). Moreover, Dyer (2006) contended that a crucial benefit of conducting and publishing rigorous scholarship about nomadic education was
"to provide critical insights into the nature of education as a concept,
and as a practice" (p. 3), an urgent requirement "if we are to understand, and work towards fulfilling, our global commitments to making
good quality education accessible to all people, and achieving meaningful Education for All" (p. 3). Or as Kiddle (1999) pleaded when conclud-
ing her cogent entreaty for recognizing the voices of mobile children in
educational debates:

> I would make the same argument for all children—the necessity for
> parents and teachers to work together to let the children have the
> chance to learn from both and then move on to be truly themselves. I
> would argue for all children that we should listen to what they have to
> say, because they have to deal with a different world from the one their
> parents and teachers grew into. (p. 156)

Thus, rather than nonmobile learners being disadvantaged if itinerant students receive more effective and equitable educational provision, they stand
to gain significantly from such a situation. This is because social justice for
minority and marginalized groups benefits the majority as well, by height-
ening awareness of and attentiveness to formal education's dual roles as
vehicle for marginalization and bridge to transformation. In the words of
Binchy (2009):

> Perhaps it would be useful for those engaged in the debate about the ed-
> ucation of people on the move to invoke the concept of human dignity,
> which is at the heart of contemporary human rights philosophy and
> appears in the leading international human rights instruments. Human
> dignity recognizes the inherent and equal value of every human being;
> it rises above social prejudice and acknowledges the legitimacy of plu-
> ralism in culture. (p. xxiv)

CONCLUSION

Binaries are complex, heterogeneous, and multifaceted phenomena that do
not admit of easy contestation or ready resolution. Instead, they have often
developed over long time periods and their contemporary manifestations tend
to render them invisible and even more powerful because of that invisibility.

That is certainly the case with the settled/itinerant binary articulated
in this chapter. Its conceptual etiology and empirical implementation
reveal it as being evident in every continent and across a diversity of forms

of mobility. Sedentarism constitutes a continuing obstacle to educational access and achievement for millions of mobile learners around the world, despite national and international policies to the contrary—indeed, nation-states' development agenda are often posited on the suppression of mobility as a way of life.

The chapter also outlined ways in which mobile learners and their educators can move beyond sedentarism both conceptually and empirically. Researchers can play a key role here, and have a particular responsibility to deploy theoretical and methodological resources that highlight the deleterious educational and social impact of sedentarism and that identify more productive and sustainable alternative approaches.

More broadly, we argue that sedentarism provides an especially striking illustration of how the functioning of a specific binary can be complicit with highly differentiated educational experiences and outcomes for diverse groups of learners. On the other hand, we hope that we have succeeded in revealing that the line of demarcation between the settled and itinerant binary is fluid and permeable rather than fixed and permanent—otherwise this and other binaries would not be susceptible to challenge and potential transformation. Finally, we consider that the conceptual and empirical developments outlined here are crucial to such challenge and transformation, and vital if moving beyond sedentarism is to become a real possibility.

ACKNOWLEDGMENTS

We thank the participants in the writing workshops associated with the book's production for their timely and helpful feedback on earlier versions of this chapter, as well as the editors, particularly our chapter editor Dr. Warren Midgley, for their continuing assistance. We appreciate helpful feedback about an earlier version of the chapter by an anonymous peer reviewer. We also acknowledge gratefully the participants in and other contributors to our respective research projects reported here.

REFERENCES

Acton, T. (2007). Human rights as a perspective on entitlements: The debate over 'Gypsy fairs' in England. In M. Hayes & T. Acton (Eds.), *Travellers, Gypsies, Roma: The demonisation of difference* (pp. 1–16). Newcastle, UK: Cambridge Scholars.

Binchy, W. (2009). Preface. In P. A. Danaher, M. D. Kenny, & J. Remy Leder (Eds.), *Traveller, nomadic and migrant education* (Routledge Research in Education Vol. 24) (pp. xiii–xiv). New York: Routledge.

Burke, N. J., Joseph, G., Pasick, R. J., & Barker, J. C. (2009). Theorizing social context: Rethinking behavioral theory. *Health Education & Behavior, 36*(5), 55S–70S.

Capra, F. (1996). *The web of life.* London: Flamingo.

Clark, C., & Dearling, A. (1999, December). Romanies, Gypsies, Travellers or nomads—what's in a name? Retrieved from http://www.enablerpublications. co.uk/pages/

Clifford, J. (1990). On collecting art and culture. In R. Ferguson, M. Gever, T. T. Minh-ha, & C. West (Eds.), *Out there: Marginalization and contemporary cultures* (pp. 141–169). New York: The New Museum of Contemporary Art and the MIT Press.

Danaher, G. R., & Danaher, P. A. (2009). Inclusion versus specialisation: Issues in transforming the education of Australian show children. In P. A. Danaher, M. D. Kenny, & J. Remy Leder (Eds.), *Traveller, nomadic and migrant education* (Routledge Research in Education Vol. 24) (pp. 201–213). New York: Routledge.

Danaher, P. A. (Ed.). (1998). *Beyond the Ferris wheel: Educating Queensland show children* (Studies in Open and Distance Learning Number 1). Rockhampton, Australia: Central Queensland University Press.

Danaher, P. A. (2001). *Learning on the run: Traveller education for itinerant show children in coastal and western Queensland* (unpublished doctoral dissertation). Central Queensland University, Australia.

Danaher, P. A., Coombes, P. N., & Kiddle, C. (2007). *Teaching Traveller children: Maximising learning outcomes.* Stoke on Trent, UK: Trentham.

Danaher, P. A., Kenny, M. D., & Remy Leder, J. (Eds.). (2009). *Traveller, nomadic and migrant education* (Routledge Research in Education Vol. 24). New York: Routledge.

Danaher, P. A., Moriarty, B. J., & Danaher, G. R. (2004). Three pedagogies of mobility for Australian show people: Teaching about, through and towards the questioning of sedentarism. *Melbourne Studies in Education, 45*(2), 47–66.

Danaher, P. A., Moriarty, B. J., & Danaher, G. R. (2009). *Mobile learning communities: Creating new educational futures.* New York: Routledge.

Dyer, C. (2006). Introduction: Education for nomadic peoples: An urgent challenge. In C. Dyer (Ed.), *The education of nomadic peoples: Current issues, future prospects* (pp. 1–7). New York: Berghahn Books.

Dyer, C. (2009). Schooling and the Rabaris of Kachchh in India. In P. A. Danaher, M. D. Kenny, & J. Remy Leder (Eds.), *Traveller, nomadic and migrant education* (Routledge Research in Education Vol. 24) (pp. 186–200). New York: Routledge.

Ferguson, R. (1990). Introduction: Invisible center. In R. Ferguson, M. Gever, T. T. Minh-ha, & C. West (Eds.), *Out there: Marginalization and contemporary cultures* (pp. 9–14). New York: The New Museum of Contemporary Art and the MIT Press.

Gale, T. C., & Densmore, K. (2000). *Just schooling: Explorations in the cultural politics of teaching.* Buckingham, UK: Open University Press.

Gale, T. C., & Densmore, K. (2003). *Engaging teachers: Towards a radical democratic agenda for schooling.* Maidenhead, UK: Open University Press.

Hayes, M., & Acton, T. (Eds.). (2007). *Travellers, Gypsies, Roma: The demonisation of difference.* Newcastle, UK: Cambridge Scholars.

Henderson, R. (2005). *The social and discursive construction of itinerant farm workers' children as literacy learners* (unpublished doctoral dissertation). James Cook University, Australia.

Henderson. R. (2009). Itinerant farm workers' children in Australia: Learning from the experiences of one family. In P. A. Danaher, M. D. Kenny, & J. Remy Leder (Eds.), *Traveller, nomadic and migrant education* (Routledge Research in Education Vol. 24) (pp. 47–58). New York: Routledge.

Holmes, S. M. (2007). "Oaxacans like to work bent over": The naturalization of social suffering among berry farm workers. *International Migration, 45*(3), 39–68.

Hugenberg, K., & Sacco, D. F. (2008). Social categorization and stereotyping: How social categorization biases person perception and face memory. *Social and Personality Psychology Compass, 2*(2), 1052–1072.

Jordan, E. S. (2000). The exclusionary comprehensive school system: The experience of showground families in Scotland. *International Journal of Educational Research, 33*(3), 253–263.

Kiddle, C. (1999). *Traveller children: A voice for themselves.* London: Jessica Kingsley.

Kostogriz, A., & Peeler, E. (2004). *Professional identity and pedagogical space: Negotiating difference in teacher workplaces.* Paper presented at the annual conference of the Australian Association for Research in Education, University of Melbourne, Australia.

Lentin, R. (2001). Responding to the racialisation of Irishness: Disavowed multiculturalism and its discontents. *Sociological Research Online, 5*(4). Retrieved from http://www.socresonline.org.uk/5/4/lentin.html

Levinson, M. P. (2009). Cultural difference or subversion among Gypsy Traveller youngsters in schools in England. In P. A. Danaher, M. D. Kenny, & J. Remy Leder (Eds.), *Traveller, nomadic and migrant education* (Routledge Research in Education Vol. 24) (pp. 59–73). New York: Routledge.

Levinson, M. P., & Sparkes, A. C. (2004). Gypsy identity and orientations to space. *Journal of Contemporary Ethnography, 33*(6), 704–734.

Levitt, P., & Glick Schiller, N. (2004). Conceptualizing simultaneity: A transnational social field perspective on society. *International Migration Review, 38*(3), 1002–1039.

Lucassen, L., Willems, W., & Cottar, A. (1998). Introduction. In L. Lucassen, W. Willems, & A. Cottar (Eds.), *Gypsies and other itinerant groups: A sociohistorical approach* (pp. 1–13). Houndmills, UK: Macmillan.

Malkki, L. (1992). National Geographic: The rooting of peoples and the territorialization of national identity among scholars and refugees. *Cultural Anthropology, 7*(1), 24–44. [Reprinted in 2008 in T. S. Oakes & P. L. Price (Eds.), *The cultural geography reader* (pp. 275–282). Abingdon, UK: Routledge.]

McVeigh, R. (1997). Theorising sedentarism: The roots of anti-nomadism. In T. Acton (Ed.), *Gypsy politics and Traveller identity* (pp. 7–25). Hatfield, UK: University of Hertfordshire Press.

Mercer, K. (1990). Black hair/style politics. In R. Ferguson, M. Gever, T. T. Minh-ha, & C. West (Eds.), *Out there: Marginalization and contemporary cultures* (pp. 247–264). New York: The New Museum of Contemporary Art and the MIT Press.

Morrissey, J. (2004). Geography militant: Resistance and the essentialisation of identity in colonial Ireland. *Irish Geography, 37*(2), 166–176. Retrieved from http://www.nuigalway.ie/geography/documents/IG2-Paper.pdf

Okely, J. (2000). Rootlessness against spatial fixing: Gypsies, border intellectuals and 'others.' In R. Bendix & H. Roodenburg (Eds.), *Managing ethnicity: Perspectives from folklore studies, history and anthropology* (pp. 13–39). Amsterdam: Het Spinhuis.

Özerk, K. (2009). The revitalisation of a threatened Indigenous language. In P. A. Danaher, M. D. Kenny, & J. Remy Leder (Eds.), *Traveller, nomadic and migrant education* (Routledge Research in Education Vol. 24) (pp. 132–144). New York: Routledge.

Quadflieg, S., Turk, D. J., Waiter, G. D., Mitchell, J. P., Jenkins, A. D., & Macrae, C. N. (2009). Exploring the neural correlates of social stereotyping. *Journal of Cognitive Neuroscience, 21*(8), 1560–1570.

Remy Leder, J. (2009). Conclusion: Whither changing schools? In P. A. Danaher, M. D. Kenny, & J. Remy Leder (Eds.), *Traveller, nomadic and migrant education* (Routledge Research in Education Vol. 24) (pp. 214–220). New York: Routledge.

Rose, P. L. (1990). *Revolutionary antisemitism in Germany from Kant to Wagner.* Princeton, NJ: Princeton University Press.

Rose, P. L. (1992). *Wagner: Race and revolution.* London: Faber & Faber.

Rudman, L. A., & Fairchild, K. (2004). Reactions to counterstereotypic behavior: The role of backlash in cultural stereotype maintenance. *Journal of Personality and Social Psychology, 87*(2), 157–176.

Souto-Otero, M. (2009). Against the odds: Roma population schooling in Spain. In P. A. Danaher, M. D. Kenny, & J. Remy Leder (Eds.), *Traveller, nomadic and migrant education* (Routledge Research in Education Vol. 24) (pp. 171–185). New York: Routledge.

Steingress, G. (2010). Globalizing cultures: A challenge for contemporary cultural sociology. *Eurasian Journal of Anthropology, 1*(1), 1–10. Retrieved from http://www.eurasianjournals.com/index.php/eja/article/viewFile/326/139

Todd, J. (2005). Social transformation, collective categories, and identity change. *Theory and Society, 34*(4), 429–463.

Umar, A., & Tahir, G. (2000). Researching nomadic education: A Nigerian perspective. *International Journal of Educational Research, 33*(3), 231–240.

Vanderbeck, R. M. (2005). Anti-nomadism, institutions, and the geographies of childhood. *Environment and Planning D: Society and Space, 23*(1), 71–94.

Vázquez, G. P. (2006). The recycling of local discourses in the institutional talk: Naturalization strategies, interactional control, and public local identities. *Estudios de Sociolingüística, 7*(1), 55–82.

Vermeersch, P. (2008). Exhibiting multiculturalism: Politicised representations of the Roma in Poland. *Third Text, 22*(3), 359–371.

Vuolteenaho, J., & Berg, L. D. (2009). Towards critical toponymies. In L. D. Berg & J. Vuolteenaho (Eds.), *Critical toponymies: The contested politics of place naming* (pp. 1–18). Farnham, UK: Ashgate.

Wagner, W., Holtz, P., & Kashima, Y. (2009). Construction and deconstruction of essence in representing social groups: Identity projects, stereotyping, and racism. *Journal for the Theory of Social Behaviour, 39*(3), 363–383.

West, C. (1990). The new cultural politics of difference. In R. Ferguson, M. Gever, T. T. Minh-ha, & C. West (Eds.), *Out there: Marginalization and contemporary cultures* (pp. 19–36). New York: The New Museum of Contemporary Art and the MIT Press.

Part II
Privileging Participants

Part II Introduction

Mark A. Tyler

The theme that influenced the next selection of chapters is *Privileging Participants*. As the title implies, these following chapters put their research participants front and center. These authors derive the essence of their research from the voices of the participants in their research. This encourages the highlighting and promotion of participant potentialities given their positioning within the reported conceptual and contextual binaries, binaries that may have colluded to create marginalized experiences and a constriction of perceived social value. When you read these chapters you will engage with the realities of people participating in their world and experiencing various degrees of affordance offered through these encounters with binaries. These chapters attempt, through elucidation, to leverage and exploit these affordances to a point where the binaries involved have less potency in their impact on actions within individual contexts.

The following chapters depict: Kat's struggle in the space between different discourses and their effects on TAFE teacher identity (Chapter 7); Kirsten's representations as a child author (Chapter 8); novice beginning teachers and their becoming bona fide university students (Chapter 9); the researcher/teacher experience of Lindy (Chapter 10); collaborative researchers' enhanced capacities through participative action research (Chapter 11); and responses to Confucian-heritage students' struggles with an Australian business course (Chapter 12). All offer contextualized examples of the tensions that are experienced in the occupied space between competing binaries. Unique to these chapters are the articulated escape routes and ways forward that announce to all options to contest and weaken the resolve of unproductive binaries.

7 A Tango in VET

Whose Notion of TAFE Teacher Leads?

Mark A. Tyler

ABSTRACT

Some would suggest that, when the pace of change quickens, the pressures on individuals to enact different identities for different times are increased. This appears to be the case for Technical and Further Education (TAFE) teachers in the vocational education and training (VET) sector in Australia. The impact of neoliberalism on this sector has produced the new vocational discourse that positions TAFE teachers as certain kinds of teachers enacting particular teaching and curriculum within an education market. This chapter explores how the new vocational discourse, and reactions to it, have created a binary between itself and TAFE teachers' notions of themselves and their teaching.

In this chapter, the focus is on the personal. One TAFE teacher's experience at this confluence is reported by way of a case study. The chapter explores the terrain where the discourses that shaper her personal subjectivities as a TAFE teacher have been pressured to merge with the discourse of new vocationalism.

INTRODUCTION

The "tango" referred to in the title epitomizes the push-me–pull-me struggle that exists in relation to notions of a *good teacher* and teaching. In this chapter, I explore Kat's struggle to take and keep the lead in relation to the building her own identity as a TAFE teacher and how she constructed an almost moral dualism between the new vocational discourse and a liberal discourse on teacher identities. From her perspective, new vocationalism was considered the malefactor, and a liberal perspective the benefactor, in relation to notions of good teaching and good teacher. This dance was enacted within a context of change that has swept through the Australian VET sector beginning in the early 1990s and continued through to this day.

The impact of economic rationalism, and its collaborator new vocationalism, in manipulating the topography of the VET sector has been significant (Butler, 1997; Chappell, 1998, 1999; Darwin, 2004; Harris, Simons, & Clayton, 2005; Hawke, 1998; Marginson, 1994; Seddon & Marginson, 2001). How TAFE teachers go about dealing with the educational reform of new directions, policies, and curriculum at TAFE level, and how this impacts upon their identity formation, are particularly significant. The scope and depth of these changes, and their impact on the world of TAFE teachers, and the effects of these changes on their personal and professional lives, have been weighty. Harris, Simons, and Clayton (2005) in a major study of VET practitioners, of whom TAFE teachers as a group occupy a majority presence, stated, "[c]hanges to the VET system have required shifts in practitioners' habits, beliefs, values, skills and knowledge" (p. 10). Of note in this study is the authors' reporting that the VET practitioners from public providers, as TAFE teachers are, "all reported negative feelings" (p. 10) toward these sectoral changes. This is also borne out in research carried out by researchers such as Childs (2000), Chappell (1998, 1999), Grabau (1999), and Kronemann (2001a, 2001b), all of whom reported the positions of marginalization experienced by TAFE teachers. Chappell (1999) summed up the context of change that TAFE teachers have been experiencing when he stated that TAFE teachers are being asked "to change their identity" (p. 3), for example, from teachers to entrepreneurs.

As noted in the intentions of a series of forums conducted by McKenna and Mitchell (2006) as a part of the Reframing the Future (Department of Education, Employment, and Workplace Relations, 2008) strategy, aimed at professional development for educational change by capacity building within the VET workforce, the focus was on looking forward toward "strengthen[ing] a sense of professional identity" (p. 2), an aspiration that I share. But, as mentioned, new vocationalism is changing the very terrain of vocational education. Chappell (1998, 1999) took the position that new vocationalism is asking TAFE teachers "to do things differently . . . asking them to become different teachers" (1998, p. 1). Chappell noted the impact of policy discourses in shaping the new day-to-day realities of TAFE teachers. He gave examples of college director talk that reflects new vocationalism—for example, "'Doing more with less', 'Running as a lean machine'" (1998, p. 6)—and TAFE teachers' sometimes critical responses, for example, "'fewer resources' . . . 'less time teaching' . . . '[a] culture of uncertainty and I guess frustration and . . . varying degrees of cynicism'" (1998, p. 7).

In this chapter I extract from a larger research project (Tyler, 2008, 2009a, 2009b) the subjective position that Kat, a TAFE teacher, holds about herself in relation to both personal and professional identities within the context of her world of work. To Kat's subjective position I apply the concept of critical spirit. This encompasses notions of personal traits, character, or ways of being that motivate individuals to avoid "thoughtless intellectual compliance and passivity" (Oxman-Michelli, 1992, p. 1) and consists of the habits of mind that constitute open-mindedness, independence of mind, wholeheartedness, intellectual responsibility, and respect for others (Oxman-Michelli, 1992). It was revealed that critical spirit as a discourse was used by Kat to increase her understandings of herself, as it appeared to increase her agency within the aforementioned sea of change.

I have used the terms *subjectivity* and *identity*, and their plurals, interchangeably throughout the text. The subtle differences in their meaning notwithstanding, I use the words to convey the essence associated with a "sense of a personal identity an individual has of her/his self as distinct from other selves, as occupying a position within society and in relation to other selves, and as being capable of deliberate thought and action" (McCallum, 1999, p. 3). To this position I apply the postmodern notion that identities are constructed through discourses, a position that I elaborate in the next section.

METHODOLOGY AND METHOD

For this research, the methodology and method I deployed was discourse analysis. Discourse, according to Gee (2005), is "[l]anguage as action and affiliation" (p. 1). His theory and method explore "how language gets recruited 'on site' to enact specific social activities and social identities" (p. 1). In relation to social activities, Gee stated that language is always political in the sense that it is used to create a particular perspective on how "*social goods* are thought about, argued over and distributed in society" (p. 2; *emphasis in original*). On how discourse relates to social identities, Gee suggested that it is "through language [that we] enact a specific social identity" (p. 4). His theory emphasized an acknowledgment that language per se (speaking, writing, signing) is not the sole contributor to enactments of human activities and identities and that this "language-in-use" (p. 7) is augmented by other "non-language 'stuff'" (p. 7). Gee describes this amalgamation of *language-in-use* and *non-language stuff* as "a patchwork of thoughts, words, objects, events, actions, and interactions" that "produce, reproduce, sustain and transform" (p. 7). For this chapter, when I use the term *discourse* in relation to Kat I include the conceptualization that it is inclusive of Gee's *stuff*, and that this contributes to her building of certain situated identities. Therefore, by means of discourse analysis (Gee, 2005), this research responded to the contention that new vocationalism with its entrepreneurial and managerial discourses of competition and the bottom line are putting pressure on, and possibly drowning out, the personal and often more traditional discourses around teaching practice and teacher identities.

The data consisted of Kat's voice extracted from the following sources:

1. A case narrative authored by Kat about a critical incident whilst at work
2. My analysis using a critical spirit framework (Tyler, 2008)
3. Kat's reaction to my analysis obtained through a credibility check (Elliott, Fischer, & Rennie, 1999), and
4. A semistructured interview with Kat conducted in August 2008.

In what follows I combine Kat's voice with my analysis and discussion.

KAT—AN OVERVIEW OF HER CASE NARRATIVE

Kat was a registered nurse and a nurse educator at an Indigenous college in the Northern Territory, Australia where she taught remote area nursing, midwifery, and mental health nursing. Kat then took up employment at a regional TAFE college in northern Queensland where she worked as a full-time teacher for three years. During this time Kat taught competencies from the health industry training package. At the time of the interview, Kat had recently left her full-time position at TAFE and was teaching at TAFE on a casual basis.

Kat emphasized that the topic of her narrative was very much "alive" (cn[1]) for her. It related to her starting as a TAFE teacher undertaking the delivery of competencies in the area of nursing. Kat considered herself a knowledgeable practitioner and saw the opportunity of teaching as a way to enhance her own professional development. Kat told how the assumptions that she held about herself as a knowledgeable practitioner were challenged. Shortly after starting, she was given the responsibility for setting up a mental-health-training program for a remote area: "I personally found the experience to be totally overwhelming. I felt as though I had entered a different reality." Kat put her position down to not understanding the jargon and processes of TAFE and the inability to find a senior person who could answer her questions and provide her with guidance and support: "Every time I asked for assistance they delegated responsibility to someone else." Kat's alternative was to persevere: "I pressed on; I reflected on the entire experience, realized that I would have to take control, figured it out for myself. " She reported that her self-confidence was draining away. She concluded that she needed to take control. She did. Three months later, the course was up and running, with positive feedback being received from the stakeholders. Kat did not rest on her success and moved to further action: "Having gone through this experience I decided to take some positive action." Kat lobbied for, produced, and implemented a series of 10-minute induction sessions for new staff. She wrote about what it was that drove her. It was not only her personal experience of inadequacy, but also what she called "an unrealistic perception by management to dangerously assume" that those employed to teach at TAFE can undertake the role with no support. She made a vigorous claim that holding the minimum qualification (Certificate IV Workplace Assessor or Certificate IV in Training and Assessment [TAA][2]) to teach at TAFE is inadequate preparation for "bridging the theory and practice gap . . . for a teacher to be employed in the VET sector."

In Kat's example, the challenge that prompted critical thinking was an affront to her identity as a knowledgeable practitioner. This experience prompted Kat to direct her thinking toward filling the knowledge gap that created her angst. This culminated in the production of a series of staff induction sessions. This instance shows evidence of the elements of critical spirit that align with *intellectual responsibility* and *respect for others.*

KAT—NARRATIVE ANALYSIS AND CREDIBILITY CHECK

The analysis of Kat's case narrative illuminated chunks of discourse (Gee, 2005) that aligned with the majority of the elements of critical spirit (Tyler, 2008). For example:

1. "need to take care to avoid making assumptions about learners"—open-mindedness
2. "I was enthusiastic and passionate about passing on my knowledge"—wholeheartedness, and
3. "the day I stopped teaching hospitality and began helping individuals"—respect for others.

The complete data set derived from my analysis of Kat's case narrative was sent to Kat for comment. She responded with agreement on all the elements of critical spirit. In some of her affirmative responses she added specific comments about herself; for example, in the comments on *wholeheartedness,* Kat stated that she is "passionate about her subject" (cc), and in relation to *intellectual responsibility* that she "believes in keeping current." Kat's comment under *respect for others* is of note. Kat believed that respect for others is a part of "a principle of adult learning." She disclosed that she upheld this principle and applied it to her teaching practice.

Kat's connection of critical spirit with adult learning principles evoked in me Brookfield's (1987) position on the critical thinker. His suggestion that critical thinking is a developmental task necessary for developing into, and throughout, adulthood, and that it exhibits "an acceptance of a diversity of values, behaviours and social structures" (p. 5), again leads me to think of critical spirit as being a visceral embodiment of critical thinking. The other connection that I made was between *respect for others* and *open-mindedness*. With this perspective Kat is enacting *respect for others* by deploying adult learning principles, which include an acceptance of, and accommodation for, diversity.

As part of the credibility check, I asked Kat four questions. Kat's response to these questions and my analysis follow.

> *What did you find out about yourself through the analysis of your narrative using this method?*

"I should not voice my opinions so openly." (cc)

This comment suggested to me that Kat has concerns with the *independence-of-mind* element within critical spirit. It suggested that there was a personal price to pay for articulating one's position openly. (This is a point that I took up with Kat in her interview.)

> *How might this understanding of critical spirit have value to you in understanding your identity as a TAFE teacher?*

"The critical 'spirit' of the TAFE teacher was not valued in this instance." (cc)

Kat's answer was evident by its tone of disappointment. She suggested that she too embodies elements of critical spirit but her current work environment didn't value it. The apparently difficult experience of doing TAFE teaching for TAFE teachers also emerged from these answers.

> *How might you use this concept?*

"I must continue with the spirit in a new environment." (cc)

This statement from Kat attested to the enactment of critical spirit in a new work environment being a possibility. It also acknowledges that she was going to resign from her position at TAFE.

> *What questions came to mind when you engaged with this analysis?*

"Positive change for the way TAFE teachers are valued and their recognition by industry should be regarded more highly than it is." (cc)

In this response Kat appeared to see it as a benchmarking device for TAFE to use in acknowledging the value of TAFE teachers to the TAFE organization, and as contributors to industry, not just as end users of industry perspectives through implementing industry training packages.

In Kat's narrative artifacts, her individual positioning as being a *worthy teacher* or *professional* appeared through chunks articulating a willingness to learn from student engagement—for students and for themselves. For example:

"sometimes it is my students who teach me"

"we need to take care to avoid assumptions," and

"not allow personal bias to interfere" (cc)

Kat positioned herself similarly in relation to elements of critical spirit discourse: *open-mindedness* through an openness to learn; *intellectual responsibility* through enactments of continuous improvement; and *respect for others* through an articulation of her role in the emancipation of others. It is this last point, the emancipation of others, which is significant in relation to Kat's navigations within the two discourses, education for economic imperatives and education for citizenship. It would appear that Kat positioned herself within a discourse that enabled "developing [of] greater vocational attributes, orientations and identity across *all* students [as opposed to] '*new*' vocationalism [and] the talk of 'enterprise'" (Yates, 2004, pp. 3–4; *emphasis in original*).

Kat also signaled individual possibilities around self-emancipation. Kat's "teacher versus bureaucracy" (cn) offered an instance of how the concept of critical spirit might be put to work in order to challenge the perceived organizational status quo that appeared to reduce opportunities for the articulation of teacher voice (Brady, 2003) and to shape organizational perceptions of the worth of TAFE teachers.

KAT—THE INTERVIEW

The interview with Kat was loosely structured around four questions and these are noted below. The interview was conducted over Skype, a person-to-person Internet protocol. Its duration was 1 hour and 20 minutes. For this section, Kat's voice is organized in stanzas and denoted with a *K*. On a number of occasions the reporting of a prompting question was necessary; on these occasions my voice is denoted with an *I* for interviewer.

What Did Kat Construct as Significant in Her Relationship with TAFE?

Significance for Kat lay in her position of exhaustion in relation to her engagement with TAFE. She began to assemble this position from the beginning of the interview and it lurked in the background throughout the interview, as Stanza 1 attests.

Stanza 1

K: That . . . *totally*
K: like . . . *burnt me out* . . .
K: I'm . . . I'm just *pleased* it's OVER.

Kat's experience appeared as an emotionally taxing one, one that had implications and tensions around her sense of agency, and that of TAFE acting as a social agent. Kat gave voice to this apprehensive relationship in Stanzas 2 and 3. In these stanzas, Kat talked about a specific incident, also referred to in her case narrative, where she had been given the responsibility to liaise with the health industry in order to write and "set up" to teach the Certificate IV in Mental Health.

Stanza 2

K: "Okay . . . off *you* go . . .
K: YOU can go do that" . . .
K: . . . with no real direction or terms of reference.

Stanza 3

K: then they put in *rules*
K: one's that . . .
K: *you* don't really *understand* . . .
K: leaves . . . you feeling . . . oh [sigh] . . .
K: really incompetent.

In Stanza 2 Kat built an identity around being a *battler*, left without resources, and left to fend for herself. The dimensions of this building included a reference to the voice of the organization, an uncaring voice that sends *YOU* off to do work without guidance.

Stanza 3 particularly relates to the rules of the Australian Quality Training Framework (AQTF) (Department of Employment and Training, 2007) that prescribed the manner in which VET curriculum should be written. This prescription appeared as another element of new vocational discourse. Of the AQTF, Kat acknowledged that she knew little. Whether Kat held the training qualification of the Certificate IV BSZ or TAA was unclear (these being the sources through which it could be assumed that Kat would attain that knowledge), but this lack of knowledge clearly caused her some distress. Kat told of her unsuccessful attempts to "get informed" by "hierarchy." Kat placed responsibility for her knowing in the hands of the TAFE organization. I wanted to know what kept Kat in the project. Stanza 4 tells of her motivation.

Stanza 4

> I: What kept you going?
> K: Because . . . I . . . made links *with industry.*
> I: So you had that *professional* standing to worry about?
> K: YEAH . . . yeah . . . *that* especially—
> K: *I* might want to get *another* job one day.

One of Kat's motivations was her connection with others, especially in relation to future employment; she wanted be on good terms with these connections. She shaped a professional identity that was seen to keep intact future useful relationships; her means of achieving this was by sticking with the aforementioned curriculum project.

This positioning of a professional identity appeared to have paid off for Kat, for at the time of the interview she was employed elsewhere and had returned to TAFE as a casual employee. Kat's new casual position at TAFE appeared to give her license to disclose an exasperating feature about her relationship with TAFE. Stanza 5 alluded to the degree of tension within this relationship. This tension appeared to be reduced when Kat became a casual teacher. Kat also articulated what she saw as the cause.

Stanza 5

> I: It's a good position to be in as a casual TAFE teacher?
> K: Yeah . . . BECAUSE . . . AH [sigh] . . . it's just . . .
> K: the *bureaucracy* . . .
> K: . . . OH . . . [sigh] . . . you know . . . like nobody communicates . . .
> K: nobody . . . REALLY . . . seems to have a *grip* on . . .
> K: really . . . what's going on.

Kat appeared to struggle to find the words to describe her experience adequately. This struggle built a picture of her experience as one that had created a great deal of stress for her and that eventually played a role in her leaving her full-time teaching position at TAFE.

What Teaching Identities Did Kat Construct?

Kat built a picture of herself as a teacher who was very different from the preconceptions that she held about what TAFE teachers do. These preconceptions involved her specifically in face-to-face teaching a present-day curriculum. This dichotomy is evident in Stanza 6.

Stanza 6

> K: a *broader* focus . . . on contemporary issues *around* health care . . .

K: BUT . . . it felt like I was going back to when I did nursing
   training . . .
K: about *30 years* ago.

In Stanza 6 Kat appeared as a teacher who was straining with her curriculum. She associated herself with contemporary nursing issues and positioned the nursing curriculum that she taught as representing out-of-date
nursing practice. Furthermore, she arranged herself as at odds with the
"person who ran the show," suggesting that engagement with the students
was prescribed and that it had to be: "like . . . [sigh] . . . a rigid and . . . hierarchical *structure.*" In Stanza 7 Kat articulated this as a modus operandi
that she was uncomfortable with.

Stanza 7

K: this is not . . . really . . .
K: it's what I'm *not good* at.

The words *rigid* and *hierarchical structure* also appear to resonate with
new vocational discourse. The seeming rigidity of an outcomes-focused
curriculum (Billett, Kavanagh, Beven, Hayes, Angus, Seddon, et al.,
1998) and the hierarchical notion of a propensity to control and privilege
certain ways of doing (Gouthro, 2002) are in discord with other ways
of engaging with curriculum and other ways of teacher decision making
(Palmer, 1998).

As mentioned above, in Stanza 7, Kat added to her identity through her
acknowledgment of her uncomfortableness with these ways of doing. This
suggested that she was more comfortable with notions of a collaborative
curriculum and inclusive decision-making practices.

In the interview, Kat shaped her identity as a TAFE teacher as being different from what she constructs as the teacher that TAFE wants. In Stanza
8 Kat responded to my question: "What type of teacher do you think TAFE
wants you to be?" and in Stanza 9 she put together her conception of the
teacher she wanted to be.

Stanza 8

K: *aw* . . . [sigh] . . .
K: um . . . [sigh] . . . a *robot* . . .
K: and one who sort of . . .
K: who doesn't use . . .
K: any *imagination*
K: and a pure *deliverer* of information
K: . . . within a framework
K: that attracts *funding.*

Stanza 9

K: honest . . . ah . . . trust your own decisions
K: you know . . .
K: adapt . . . I suppose . . . your teaching
K: to *different* learning styles.

In a follow-up question, I asked: "How do you reconcile these two positions?"

Kat's response was sure and certain, given with no hesitation: "I just do my own thing, *especially* now I'm a casual." It appears that Kat's new position at TAFE has somehow allowed her to relinquish the tensions that had built up among herself, the curriculum, and the organization.

How is a Critical Spirit Discourse Positioned in Relation to Its Value to Kat?

Because much of Kat's interview was imbued with a sense of endurance within an acrimonious relationship, I wondered if critical spirit might play a part in moderating this experience. Kat described herself as a "survivor" several times and in Stanza 10, I used this to segue into an exploration of critical spirit.

Stanza 10

I: Is an *understanding* of critical spirit
I: part of that *survival* . . . do you think?
K: . . . well, I think it is . . . and
K: you know . . . having it *identified*
K: or um . . . given some sort of name
K: creates a whole new life of its *own*.
K: Because . . . you're able to *think* . . .
K: "*That's* what that is . . .
K: and *that's* why I behave the way I *did* . . ."
K: so . . . I'd like it to build on my *strengths*.

Kat talked of her personal connection to this project and her embracing the attention paid to her by being asked to be included. She contrasted this with a lack of attention paid to her by the TAFE organization. At first she wondered if she had any spirit left at all "after going through the system." In Stanza 11 Kat's sense of self received a boost through the receipt of my interpretation of her case narrative in the form of a credibility check.

Stanza 11

K: I felt good about it
K: because . . . that . . .

K: it *demonstrated* that
K: I really *was* quite passionate about . . .
K: what I was *doing* . . .

The above appeared as a validation of herself as a good teacher. This was opposite to how she thought that she was perceived by the TAFE organization. In Stanza 12 Kat tells of her being in a valueless position.

Stanza 12

K: where . . . you *weren't* sort of . . . valued
K: your professional *credentials* weren't . . .
K: you know . . . just *go get a* Certificate IV . . . and . . .
K: anyone can do it.

Stanza 12 also implicates TAFE in ascribing a lack of value to Kat as a teacher and to the act of teaching. Kat closed this section of the interview by disclosing that being included in the project "was redeeming for my self-esteem."

When asked if the concept of critical spirit was cumbersome, Kat offered different insights. Kat acknowledged its usefulness in terms of its offering a structure upon which to "reflect on my professionalism," yet posited a secondary consideration. In Stanzas 13 and 14, Kat suggested a possible double-edged sword.

Stanza 13

K: if you want to reflect . . .
K: you try not to . . . because . . . sometimes . . .
K: I suppose . . . it's *nice* to be in denial.

Stanza 14

K: also . . . also is um . . .
K: you've *got* to be *careful* . . .
K: you can't be too *spirited*.

In Stanza 13 Kat highlighted that it requires work (the expenditure of intellectual and emotional energy) to reflect upon self, and that being in a state of denial, or a state of not knowing, allows one time just to rest, or possibly to avoid. Possibly, by reflecting using a critical spirit discourse, "one may find out something about oneself that needs changing." This may not be easy for an exhausted teacher. Yet in Stanza 15 Kat articulated an alliance.

Stanza 15

K: I fully support *it* and *it* should be
K: out there a bit *more*
K: . . . it should be nurtured and *recognized*.

Kat's support was sobered by what was akin to a warning. This warning is about being too spirited. Kat had previously identified herself as acting in concert with critical spirit, yet in Stanza 13 she warns us to be careful. In the interview Kat and I laughed about the "eye of Mordor," from the celebrated *Lord of the Rings* trilogy by J. R. R. Tolkien, as an example of oppressive surveillance. Kat's connection with this metaphor implied that, by drawing attention to herself by being spirited, she had produced a surveillance response from management in her TAFE institute, a position that can be juxtaposed to that in Stanza 2, where Kat reported that she had received little attention by way of support for the curriculum development task that she had been asked to manage. This suggests that for Kat one should be spirited in TAFE but not too spirited.

A synthesis of Kat's position, as built by her interview, is evident in Table 7.1. Kat's position was a picture of a tempestuous relationship with TAFE where she was under pressure. Her relationship with a teacher in her team was also one of tension. Kat positioned her subjectivity as not being comfortable with notions of rigidity and hierarchy, stating that TAFE wanted "robot[s]" as teachers. This I believe put Kat in a position of antipathy with regard to the new vocational discourse. Kat reconciled her want to be creative, adaptive, and keeping up with contemporary nursing issues with being "a pure deliverer of information . . . within a framework that attracts funding" by "doing [her] own thing," and stated that her new position as a casual teacher allowed her the opportunity to do this. She demonstrated a preference for being left alone to exercise her professional judgment as a nurse educator/TAFE teacher. The value of critical spirit as either a holistic or a deconstructed concept was left blank, as Kat offered no discussion of the individual elements; all reference to critical spirit was in general terms. For example, it answered some of the questions that she had about herself and her interactions, as when she stated: "[*T*]*hat's* what that is . . . and *that's* why I behave the way I did."

CONCLUSION

The binary produced by Kat's personal notions of what it is to be a good teacher and new vocationalism's notion of what it is to be a good teacher are clearly demonstrated through the above. In particular, part of Kat's position resonates with several of the central sentiments behind lifelong learning: the individual progressive—education for enlightenment, transformation, and a reduction of dependence; democratic informing—education that informs and is evaluative of social action; and adaptive progressive—education that liberates from deprivation through adaptive learning (Bagnal, 2000). Kat puts her students at the center of this position. New vocationalism, on the other hand, attempts to hijack the lifelong sentiments to mean education for skills to service a market economy, education for vocationalism where powerful market players pressure social action toward consumerism and

Table 7.1   A Synthesis of Kat's Position as Obtained From the Analysis of Her Interview

	Degree of perceived tension		Produced by	The place of others
Significance to relationship with TAFE	High	√	• The undertaking of a curriculum project with "no real terms of reference" and an application of "rules" and/ or managerialist surveillance after project implementation left "you feeling . . . really incompetent" • TAFE bureaucracy • Inadequacy of Certificate Level 4 training to prepare for teaching	• Professionals outside TAFE were valuable. These links facilitated for a change in employment • Teaching colleague considered to be out of touch with contemporary nursing
	Medium			
	Low			
Built subjectivities	*Teaching for economic imperatives*		*Teaching for citizenship3*	*Example(s)*
			√	• Uncomfortable with prescribed curriculum; saw it as rigid, out of date, and unimaginative • Taught outside prescribed curriculum. As a casual teacher, "I do my own thing" • "[N]ot good at rigidity and hierarchy" • Preference for professional choice in deploying the dynamic adaptations required for teaching
The value position of critical spirit	How is it valuable? • As a means of gaining greater self-understanding • As validation of self as a good teacher			How is it less valuable? • As another burden on the already exhausted teacher • Making one more visible to managerialist surveillance

where critical perspectives are not valued, and education for individualization and commodification of basic skills to meet the imperative of human capital that focuses on essential, adaptive, flexible; specific skills to meet economic imperatives in the here and now. New vocationalism puts the dollar at the center of its position. The metaphor of the tango, used to convey the push and pull of Kat's positioning between the nominated binary on the surface, looked like a choice between the two positions, but what is clear is that the choices Kat made were more than likely somewhere between the two. For instance, she indicated that there were times when deploying her critical spirit might not be a pertinent choice. The possible corollary of this is that she actively chooses the times and circumstances, when to enact (or not) her critical spirit. This resonates with the strong connection between notions of one's subjectivity and the exercising of agency. Kat did indicate instances when she would exercise her agency by choosing to limit her critical spirit to those contexts and circumstances of her choosing. This illuminates an interesting space for future exploration, the space where Kat is neither the compliant TAFE teacher nor the critical spirit.

When considering the implications that Kat's case study has for other teachers' future practice, several possibilities are illuminated in relation to how critical spirit can be positioned and utilized by teachers; critical spirit—a discourse on an optional subjectivity, a way of exploring actions of contestation, a way of engagement that enables a pathway around or through binaries, and a means of attracting surveillance so as to openly challenge the status quo. Kat's participation in this project enabled her hidden critical spirit to be illuminated and brought into sharper focus. Kat appeared to walk with this image as she grew into its embodiment and recognized its value to her in contesting her status quo, but at the same time she acknowledged that the "sword" had two sides. Contesting for the lead in Kat's tango with VET produced a fracture in their relationship, yet, as suggested by Kat, she will continue to contest and question in other contexts, possibly by deploying her critical spirit. In analyzing this binary between Kat's personal discourse on teacher identities and new vocationalism's, it might possibly be claimed that this had served to reinforce the binary. This may well be so, and others will judge this to be either positive or negative. But what it has done is to highlight a worthwhile target for the deployment of critical spirit. For Kat, it appears that a critical spirit had served her well as a discourse for moving her teaching identity beyond the binary and into new terrain where possibilities await.

NOTES

1. The following identifies the source of discourse chunks: cn—case narrative and cc—credibility check.
2. In order to teach any VET curriculum, individuals are required by the Australian Quality Training Framework (AQTF) (Department of Employment,

and Training, 2007) to have completed a Level 4 VET certification in training. Specifically these are the Certificate IV in Assessment and Workplace Training (BSZ) or its successor, the Certificate IV in Training and Assessment (TAA). This is a requirement for TAFE teachers. Dissatisfaction with the BSZ certificate (see, e.g., Smith & Keating, 2003) led to the development and introduction of the TAA certificate. Criticism of the TAA certificate is also evident—for example, its inability to prepare VET practitioners for increasingly complex educational judgments (McKenna & Mitchell, 2006; Palmieri, 2003).

3. The term *citizenship* was conceptualized as aligning with notions of progressive education, where notions of teachers as liberal educators, with a focus on lifelong learning, personal transformation, collaborative relationships, and social responsibility are prominent. This cell is indicative of Kat's preference for a discourse of liberal education.

REFERENCES

Bagnal, R. (2000). Lifelong learning and the limitations of economic determinism. *International Journal of Lifelong Education, 19*(1), 20–35.

Billett, S., Kavanagh, C., Beven, F., Hayes, S., Angus, L., Seddon, T., et al. (1998). *The CBT decade: Teaching for flexibility and adaptability.* Adelaide, Australia: National Centre for Vocational Education Research.

Brady, L. (2003). *Teacher voices.* Frenchs Forest, Australia: Pearson Education Australia.

Brookfield, S. (1987). *Developing critical thinkers: Challenging adults to explore alternative ways of thinking and acting.* San Francisco, CA: Jossey-Bass.

Butler, E. (1997). *Beyond political housework: Gender equity in the post-school environment.* Sydney, Australia: Premier's Council for Women, Department for Women.

Chappell, C. (1998). *Teachers' identities in new times.* Retrieved from http://www.aare.edu.au/98pap/cha98382.htm

Chappell, C. (1999). Issues of teacher identity in a restructuring VET system. *RCVET Working Paper 99.31.* Retrieved from http://www.uts.edu.au/frac/edu/rcvet

Childs, M. (2000). *The seductive hope of education work.* Paper presented at the Australian Vocational Education and Training Research Association conference, Canberra, Australia.

Darwin, S. (2004). *Vocational teacher education: Bridging the teaching divide toward lifelong education.* Paper presented at the Lifelong Learning conference. Retrieved from http://lifelonglearning.cqu.edu.au/2004/papers/darwin-35-paper.pdf

Department of Education, Employment, and Workplace Relations. (2008). *Reframing the future.* Retrieved from http://www.dest.gov.au/sectors/training_skills/policy_issues_reviews/key_issues

Department of Employment and Training. (2007). Australian Quality Training Framework (AQTF) [Electronic Version]. Retrieved from http://www.dest.gov.au/sectors/training_skills/policy_issues_reviews/key_issues

Elliott, R., Fischer, C., & Rennie, D. (1999). Evolving guidelines for publication of qualitative research studies in psychology and related fields. *British Journal of Clinical Psychology, 38*(3), 215–229.

Gee, J. P. (2005). *An introduction to discourse analysis: Theory and method.* New York: Routledge.

Gouthro, P. (2002). Education for sale: At what cost? Lifelong learning and the marketplace. *International Journal of Lifelong Education, 21*(4), 334–346.

Grabau, K. (1999). Life as a sessional teacher. *The Australian Education News*, *13*, 4.

Harris, R., Simons, M., & Clayton, B. (2005). *Shifting mindsets: The changing work roles of vocational education and training practitioners*. Adelaide, Australia: National Centre for Vocational Education Research.

Hawke, G. (1998). *'Workplaces as components of a formal VET system' in vocational knowledge and institutions: Changing relationships*. Paper presented at the 6th annual international conference on post-compulsory education and training, Brisbane, Australia.

Kronemann, M. (2001a). *TAFE teachers: Facing the challenge*. Retrieved from http://www.avetra.org.au/abstracts_and_papers_2001/

Kronemann, M. (2001b). TAFE teachers speak out. *The Australian TAFE Teacher*, *35*(1), 23–25.

Marginson, S. (1994). *Markets in education: The dynamics of positional goods and knowledge goods*. Paper presented at the (Re)Forming Post-Compulsory Education and Training Reconciliation and Reconstruction conferences, Brisbane, Australia.

McCallum, R. (1999). *Ideologies of identity in adolescent fiction: The dialogic construction of subjectivity*. New York: Garland.

McKenna, S., & Mitchell, J. (2006). *Professional judgment in vocational education and training: A set of resources*. Elizabeth, Australia: Department of Education, Science, and Training.

Oxman-Michelli, W. (1992). Critical thinking as "critical spirit." *Institute for Critical Thinking Resource Publication, Series 4*(7), 1–13.

Palmer, P. J. (1998). *The courage to teach*. San Francisco, CA: Jossey-Bass.

Palmieri, P. (2003). *The agile organisation: Case studies of the impact of flexible delivery on human resource practices in TAFE*. Adelaide, Australia: National Centre for Vocational Education Research.

Seddon, T., & Marginson, S. (2001). The crisis trifector: Education. In C. Sheil (Ed.), *Globalisation: Australian impacts* (pp. 202–218). Sydney, Australia: University of New South Wales Press.

Smith, E., & Keating, J. (2003). *From training reform to training packages*. Tuggerah, Australia: Social Sciences Press.

Tyler, M. A. (2008). Mapping the inner landscape of Australian TAFE teachers' work: Navigating contours by explicating critical spirit. In R. Henderson & P. A. Danaher (Eds.), *Troubling terrains: Tactics for traversing and transforming contemporary educational research* (pp. 119–136). Teneriffe, Australia: Post Pressed.

Tyler, M. A. (2009a). *Torquing up TAFE teacher traction through a critical spirit discourse*. Paper presented at the Australian Vocational Education and Training Research Association 12th annual conference. Retrieved from http://www.avetra.org.au/annual_conference/presentations-2009.shtml

Tyler, M. A. (2009b). *Critical spirit manifestations in TAFE teachers and their work* (unpublished doctoral dissertation). University of Southern Queensland, Australia.

Yates, L. (2004). *Creating identities in the new vocationalism*. Paper presented at the British Education Research Association conference. Retrieved from http://www.education.uts.edu.au/ostaff/staff/publications/BERAvocpap.pdf

8 Beyond the Binaries That Keep Us From Writing With and Like Children

Shelley Kinash and Kirsten Kinash

ABSTRACT

This chapter was written through a mother/daughter partnership. The mother is a university academic with a PhD in educational technology. The daughter is a digital native (which means that she is of the generation of children who have grown up never experiencing a life without computers and the Internet) in primary school. The initial question compelling this collaboration was, "Why aren't children encouraged and acknowledged as authentic authors of scholarly publications." The question was initially framed as a social justice issue about children's rights and epistemological deprivation. However, what became evident is that the assumed victims might not be interested in our advocacy. Children are not protesting exclusion from authorship of static texts because they have moved on to a different medium entirely. In other words, this chapter was conceived to address the binary of adult/child rights and grew to address the binary of adult/child construction and use of text.

INTRODUCTION

> Whether, as Bran Ferrin seriously suggests, reading and writing will eventually disappear after having been a 300- to 400-year "fad" is not clear. What is clear is that reading and writing have already been seriously supplemented—and in some cases almost completely supplanted—in a number of areas of our lives. (Prensky, 2001, p. 91)

The adult version of knowing (epistemology) has moved from orality to literacy (Ong, 2002). In other *words*, whereas our ancestors once relied upon spoken stories to convey truths and instill order through the generations, we now rely upon the written word. The advent of the Internet has altered some presentations of written communication (Wenglinsky, 2005), but our books remain consistently and fixedly formatted in atoms as opposed to bits (Kinash, 2006; Negroponte, 1995). The implication is that, beyond a little variation in size, color and binding materials, a Western *book is a book* in that it is a collection of fastened pages read left to right and top to bottom. Unless new editions are released, the form and content remains the same throughout multiple prints. The author and publisher have full control and the reader cannot respond or contribute. The book continues to be privileged as the highest-esteemed communication medium of adult scholars (Brown, 2006; Ward, 2009).

The knowledge journey of children differs from that of adults. Historically, children were to be seen and not heard (Head, 1998), thereby silencing them from orality. Now that we as adults are doggedly committed to literacy (Horrigan, 2007), we allow children to read and insist that they *learn how* at increasingly younger ages (Iaquinta, 2006). On the other hand, children are still not permitted to read digital sources like the Internet to their full potential (Levin & Arafeh, 2002) nor, as shall be explored throughout this chapter, to write authentically. The children, however, are not protesting, for their epistemological journey has bypassed the adult controls, traditions, and inflexibility (Lenhart, Arafeh, Smith, & Rankin Macgill, 2008). As the Net or N-Generation (Tapscott, 1998), the children are bored and baffled by the school's epistemological fixation on the linear text (Prensky, 2001), where new media are occasionally tacked on as a conflated enrichment (Jardine, Clifford, & Friesen, 2003). When freed from adult constraints, children think, play, and work differently from their parents' and teachers' designs, models, and habits (Lenhart & Madden, 2005). Flew (2008) presented and discussed a model of new media participation ranging from low to high engagement. The children's new media actions are "read, favorite, tag, comment, subscribe, share, network, write, refactor, collaborate, moderate, lead" (p. 32). In other words, when online, children *do, make, create, try,* and *share.* They *skim, jump, leap,* and *link,* and as adults we haven't thought to watch and learn. It is beyond our belief that the children are now the generators and the innovators. We made the shift from orality to literacy and then froze, failing to notice that the children have left us behind.

Publishing conventions and formats are not the only barriers to child voice. Contemporary authors are articulate about the attitudes that keep children from expressing themselves and/or adults from listening. In fact, the issue of suppression of child voice has become such a prominent contemporary issue that Wyness (2006) opened his article with the statement "Children and young people in recent years have become a highly visible social minority group" (p. 209). The media focus on children's rights is a recent phenomenon, but the issue has been debated for centuries. Singer (2005) reminds us that children's voice has been a prominent theme amongst "enlightened pedagogues and progressive psychologists" (p. 618) since the 17th century and that we still have not successfully achieved authentic child voice. Cockburn (2007) wrote about the low power position of children. He explained that, "when children and young people communicate their ideas and viewpoints in public, their voices are often met with patronization or simply not listened to" (p. 447). Cockburn concurs with authors such as Griffiths, Berry, Holt, Naylor, and Weekes (2006), Lundy (2007) and Wyness that where children's rights matter most and make an authentic difference in their day-to-day lives is in the school. These authors advocate ameliorating the school environment so that children are encouraged to contribute their perspectives. Concomitantly, adults must genuinely listen to and act upon the children's ideas. In being coauthored by a child, this chapter actively confronts the barriers to voice.

This is the third in a series that the adult author has coauthored with a child. Whereas the first two adult–child coauthored publications addressed children as school-based researchers, this chapter explicitly and specifically focuses on child as author. There is a binary at play that excludes children from being acknowledged as legitimate scholars capable of published contributions to knowledge. This binary primarily functions at the social level of adult/child. Adults are acknowledged as academic authors, whereas children are not (Kinash & Hoffman, 2008; Kinash & Kinash, 2008). Throughout scholarly literature, children are presented as research objects, subjects, or informants (see, e.g., Burnett, Dickinson, & Myers, 2006; Meehan, Holmes, & Tangney, 2001; Ruttle, 2004; Vasconcelos, 2006), but they are denied the right to claim and identify their own intellectual property. They are not named as authors. In addition, the contemporary writing of children, when the children themselves have control of the form, content, and process, is fundamentally different from that of adults (Lenhart, Arafeh, Smith, & Rankin Macgill, 2008). It is the theses of this chapter that challenging the adult/child writing binary mandates both generations to confront the attitudes and barriers that are blocking the contribution of children's epistemology and the acceptance that is silencing children's complaints (hegemony), and that adults would be well served by updating our publishing form and processes in accordance with what and how children are choosing to write.

This chapter builds upon the foundation that was laid by the two previous publications coauthored with children. The first project was a book chapter by Kinash and Kinash (2008) describing the child author's primary school experience in a small rural Australian school, compared to her prior years spent in a large urban Canadian school. This situated experience was used as the backdrop to explore the process of adult–child coauthorship. The second project was a journal article by Kinash and Hoffman (2008), coauthored with a 12-year-old child, set at the same Australian school as the first project and describing research within and beyond the classroom. Despite multiple searches and enquiries to field experts, to the authors' knowledge these two are the only other published scholarly documents coauthored by a child.

Whereas advocacy to include the child's name as coauthor of the Kinash and Kinash chapter was unproblematic, the inclusion of Hoffman's name as author was a greater challenge. Four differences between the two publications were likely impacting factors. First, like this chapter, we wrote Kinash and Kinash as a mother–daughter partnership, whereas I have no family ties to Madison Hoffman. The editors could assume a level of parental consent for the chapter that they could not for the journal article. Second, the editors of the book are my colleagues and had personally met Kirsten, whereas the journal editors had never made Madison's acquaintance. Third, the explicit topic of the book was *troubling the terrain of educational research*, whereas the journal is within the traditional field of teacher education. The fourth factor (albeit speculative) is that there may be a perception of greater security in releasing a child's name in the print medium of a book, rather than a contemporary journal which is widely available online.

The editors' and peer reviewers' concerns regarding the inclusion of Hoffman's name as author were resolved by: (1) inserting a footnote including Madison's recent exceptional test scores to validate the authenticity of her voice; (2) including a dated and signed letter from Madison's parents indicating informed consent along with the submission; and; (3) through in-text narrative primarily authored by Hoffman, explicitly addressing the topic of risk and security of children identified as author. In response to the question "Do you feel vulnerable with your real name identified through this article once it is published?" Madison wrote,

> The subject of exposure and vulnerability is relevant although I feel that taking the next step to stop my name from being published has gone too far. My name is already published as being in this project from day one along with my other 31 counter-parts [on the school website]. . . . I don't feel vulnerable physically or mentally through being named as author, and both of my parents agreed to it, so I don't feel vulnerable on levels of exposure either. I do understand what your university colleagues are trying to say but personally, it should be mine and your decision to add or remove my name as author on these papers. I don't see how I'm any more vulnerable than you are for having your name identified as author. Someone can Google your name and find out all kinds of information about you too. I have the added advantage of having parents to protect me. (Kinash & Hoffman, 2008, p. 86)

Madison's words describe an adult/child binary. Whereas she sees risk in name authorship for both adults and children and thereby potential vulnerability, she is affronted by the social constraints in that adults have the power to take that risk, whereas children do not. She invites the discussion and problem solving regarding safeguards, but she believes that denying her claim on her own intellectual property is "going too far."

In this chapter, we explore this binary in three parts. First, we subjugate ourselves to our assigned social categories. Independent of each other, we explore the binary positions from the respective social roles of child and adult. Independent narratives provide the opportunity to explore disparate and common views, and the socialized understandings of a child and an adult author.

Second, we engage in dialogic analysis. We coauthor a section wherein we trouble our independent analyses. This second section may also be called a *metalogue*, defined by Bateson and Ryan (2001) as "a conversation about some problematic subject" wherein "not only do the participants discuss the problem, but the structure of the conversation as a whole is also relevant to the same subject" (p. 1). In other words, the term *metalogue* is a play on the notion of dialogue. It is a to-and-fro conversation with the added dimension that the interlocutors invite reflection and open discussion about the communication itself. Our presentation of section two resembles conversation transcripts. This is consistent with Haudrup Christensen's (2004) inquiry into how to research with children. She wrote,

> Over the years I have strongly advocated the importance of re-searchers seeing children primarily as fellow human beings. In my view this entails not treating children as in principle different from adults. This approach does not assume that particular methods are needed for research with children just because they are children, that a different set of ethical standards is required or that the problems faced during the research process are unique to working with children. (p. 165)

The approach that Haudrup Christensen developed over time through her own research with children interweaves three elements. First, the research is deeply and richly based in dialogue. Second, the adult and child researchers are reflective, open, and revealing about the negotiated and evolving relationship between them throughout the research process. Third, power is acknowledged and negotiated as dynamic and embedded in the actions of the child and adult. Haudrup Christensen's depiction of power is consistent with a Foucauldian stance (Foucault, 1972–1977). Writing about writing together was a metare-search activity that required rich dialogue between Kirsten and me not only about our topic but also about our relationship and its power implications.

In the third section of the chapter we present and analyze case studies of adult and child writing to elaborate the exploration of the disparate nature of these two forms. I provide a single example of my writing as an adult academic. Kirsten describes a typical example of her school-based writing. Together we describe examples of writing that are within Kirsten's control. Finally, I present a table depicting the key characteristics of these three conditions.

SECTION 1: THE QUESTIONS—TROUBLING AUTHORSHIP

The three questions framing this section of the chapter are:

1. What does it mean to be an author?
2. Why should children be authors?
3. Why are children not named as scholarly authors?

Kirsten's Responses

What Does It Mean to be An Author?

To be an author it is either sad or happy or amazing or scary. That's the beauty of being an author—you can share your opinion and your emotions the way you want to, and make others feel the way you want them to feel. That's exactly what we are trying to do here in this chapter—share the beauty of our story. It is our way to influence others. For those adults who don't believe that children should write, I'm not saying that you aren't allowed to have an opinion. I am speaking in the voice of a kid and expressing *my* opinion. What we are writing about here is that the adult opinion is published, but the child's opinion is missing. You don't have the chance to read it with the feelings that would help you understand.

To be an author is also a privilege. For example, to be an author with the way things are now, some of the things a kid must do in order to have work published are:

- Wait until you are old enough to write or privileged enough (as some people think) for people to believe that your writing is worth reading.
- Research about what you are writing about.
- Get permission from whom you mentioned in your book.
- Read it and edit over and over again.

And there is a lot more to the whole writing process, so, after you have done everything, only the very committed people "stick to it." It is even harder for kids to *stick to it* long enough and hard enough to get writing published because adults tell us things like, *You must wait until you are older to write this.* Sometimes adults do things that push kids down and don't let them believe they can have power. To be an author is to feel however you want to and help others experience these same feelings.

Why Should Children Be Authors?

Let me explain by giving some specific examples. I could write a children's book and it might even be better than what an adult would write because I *am* a child and I can put my mind into whatever children think.

Have you ever heard the expression that you can't understand what I'm going through until you *walk a mile in my shoes*? As a child, I'm already IN my shoes, so I can just think about what *I* like and how to get the message out to other children. I don't have to imagine it. I *know* it because I'm in my shoes, which are pretty close in size to the ones other children are wearing.

Here's another example. When new girls join synchronized swimming, I know how they feel because I used to be the new and younger one when I first started. If I were to write a book that would teach them about my experiences, and how to do a figure, or how to swim a length, I could write about it in a way that even the coach couldn't. I not only know how to do the skills, but I remember how I *felt*. The feelings are important to the learning, and you can't make them up. You need to experience them in order to understand how to teach them to others.

Here's one more example. This one is about my brother. My brother Josh has a very creative mind. He comes up with excellent ideas for computer games that he wishes were already invented so that he could play them. He writes them all down in a big book that he calls his *Invention Book*. I bet if all of his games were published he would make millions of dollars because he puts his mind into how he thinks a cool game would be like. By the time adults study all of the programming and have to be serious about owning a house and paying bills they seem to lose touch with what is fun to kids and they lose their creative inspiration. When Josh is old enough to create the games, the technology will have changed. For example, Pac Man and Galaga aren't exciting any more to kids. If adults took Josh seriously *now* as a published author and an expert on games creation, then they could be very successful.

I'm going to ask one more BIG question. Why not get children to write adult books? Isn't there anything that adults think that kids might be able to tell them?

Why are Children Not Named as Scholarly Authors?

Why aren't children named as scholarly authors? I've thought about this question for a long, long time and I came up with a very simple answer. There is absolutely no reason at all that children shouldn't be authors.

Shelley's Responses

What Does It Mean to be An Author?

I have been an academic for 15 years. In the 5 years that I have been post-PhD I have produced over 60 research outputs including 3 books, 5 chapters, and 8 scholarly journal articles. I feel like an author. The books are bound with attractive covers and have ISBN numbers. I can find them on

Google Books. To count as an author, the identity construction and the form and destination of the document matter.

I believe that teachers and schools are only halfway there when they facilitate writers' workshops for primary-school children, and tell them that they are "authors" because their works are "published." There is a great sense of pride and accomplishment in authentically being an author. One puts a great deal more effort into production when the words are actually going to be read, and perhaps even make a difference. The problem is that these school initiatives are seldom authentic. When asked to give feedback on these writers' workshops, some of the children comment that they feel "lied to." The child lovingly hands over his masterpiece to the teacher, who tells him that she will return it to him "published." The child looks skeptical when the teacher returns with a stapled, laminated version. He wants to know which bookstores will be selling it, and is crestfallen when told that his "book" is not actually in the bookstore.

The question which logically follows is—Why are adults' books deemed worthy of real publication, whereas children's are not?

Why Should Children Be Authors?

I believe that there are 10 reasons, subdivided into who is to gain—the child, the coauthor, the reader, and society.

1. Overall Reason—I cannot see any defensible reason for children *not* to be included, supported, and acknowledged as authors of scholarly publications.
2. The Child—To express oneself is a basic human right that should not be denied.
3. The Child—Pedagogically, authoring authentic publications is a motivating task, fostering literacy and transferable skills such as persistence and focus.
4. The Coauthor—Writing with children is fun. I found the process exhilarating, reflexive, and void of any angst or threat of judgment. As a mother, the opportunity to engage with my daughter on this level is a spiritual gift. Singer (2005) wrote, "Every . . . parent should be obligated to answer the question of how the child's voice is heard in daily practice, and how the child's voice is evaluated in decision making" (p. 618). Collaborative writing gave Kirsten and me the opportunity to build our relationship and negotiate the power that mediates our lives together.
5. The Reader—Having read Kirsten's narrative just prior to mine, I would venture that you have made comparisons that likely came out in Kirsten's favor. I find children's writing to be compelling, approachable, real, and experiential. I like reading children's writing.

6. Society—It is difficult to find an article that is about a novel topic. When reading journal articles, I am continually faced with the dissatisfied reflection that I have read it before. Children are as yet academically unpublished. They offer a fresh perspective that we have not yet experienced. Arguing that children are indeed capable of philosophizing about their lives, Kennedy (1999) described children as "privileged strangers to the tradition," meaning that, once children are allowed to write, readers will discover a unique and informed tome of knowledge.

7. Society—Children are the experts on their own lives. It is only right that they should be the ones writing about the phenomena that they experience. They know it best. Perhaps we might discover some solutions to children's concerns that adults have not been able to conceive.

8. Society—Authorship makes people reflective citizens. In order to write, authors must think broadly and deeply. This exercise fosters commendable habits of mind that help people to become stronger problem solvers and leaders in their everyday lives.

9. Society—We live in the knowledge era. Children are an untapped resource base to build new knowledge. Researchers such as Farrell, Tayler, Tennent, and Gahan (2002) demonstrated children's capacity to contribute to "social capital" (p. 36).

10. Society—Children are often spoken about and spoken for. Putting their ideas into print provides an undistorted, unrepresented, unfiltered avenue to child voice.

Why are Children Not Named as Scholarly Authors?

I have spent a great deal of time conversing about and contemplating this question in the process of deciding to write about this topic and of getting the two previous works written with children published. I have compiled a list of eight interactive reasons. I can empathize with each of these reasons, but only insofar as using them as measures to ensure that protective measures are put into place so that the safety and well-being of children are not compromised.

1. Distrust—Because adults are not used to reading the published writings of children, some find it difficult to believe the authenticity of the intellectual property. For example, you may question whether Kirsten wrote her own portion of this chapter. You may suspect me of shadow writing. Let me assure you that Kirsten authored her sections, and I authored mine.

2. Perceived Incompetence—Until adults have directly experienced the power of children's writing, many believe that children are incapable of writing anything that adults would want to read. Egan (2002) wrote that our low expectations of children derive at least in part from

"Piaget's low opinion of children's intelligence" (p. 106). This opinion will be challenged as more children's writing becomes available.

3. Intimidation—At home as part of the armchair television audience, have you ever failed *Are You Smarter Than a Fifth Grader?* I have—every time I watch the television show. Reading the writing of children can be intimidating and as we compare ourselves we often have the uncomfortable realization that we come out lacking.

4. Danger—The Internet has brought an era of fears and realities of identity theft, stalking, virtual gender switching, and other predatory behaviors. Legally, parents must sign informed consent to allow public dissemination of the child's name. The article should avoid identifying information that would increase children's vulnerability to predators. While parents should not be falsely assured, predators are likely to choose easier sources of child location than scholarly literature.

5. Pandora's Box—Skeptics have queried whether publishing with children unduly removes boundaries and limits. Some adults believe that published authorship oversteps the appropriate roles and privileges of children. Madison Hoffman's mother, for example, shared that her daughter had difficulty accepting her parents' authority and accumulated knowledge immediately after her successful publication.

6. Stigma and Impression—Research and publication are the lifeblood of many academics. Academics may perceive that coauthoring with children would compromise their perceived scholarship.

7. Prestige—Related to Reason 6 above, editors may feel that including children as authors compromises the perceived value of their journal or book. Publishers might believe that publishing children raises questions as to the legitimacy and value of the whole industry.

8. Elitism—If children are to be published, which ones? There is a concern that only children with the highest grades, or in this case with an academic parent, are going to be the ones to experience this privilege.

SECTION 2: METALOGUE—KIRSTEN AND SHELLEY KINASH

Shelley: Kirsten, when I read your responses to the questions, I was particularly impressed with your use of specific examples. I especially liked the examples you gave to explain why children should be authors. As a university teacher I know that people are more likely to learn and remember if they have feelings about the topics they are studying. Your writing reminded me how important feelings are in writing as well. When you read my responses to the questions, were you struck by anything that you hadn't thought of?

Kirsten: The point that stood out for me is that you have to be lucky to have parents that will help you publish. I hadn't really thought about that, but it's so true. For example, most of my friends don't have parents who work at a university and have never written a book. They wouldn't know how to go about it, so their kids will never have a chance. Some of them don't even think about taking the kids to a library, teaching them how to use the Internet, and how to learn to research. They won't ever have a chance to write and publish like me, at least until they're adults and do it on their own. By that time they might lose inspiration to read and to write because they might not have been encouraged as a child. Lots of parents want their kids to write or to be academic and they might say, You should write more, but are they really supporting them to do so? Also, the parents need to give a more positive attitude about reading and writing by showing that they do it themselves and that they enjoy doing it.

Shelley: How does it make you feel that you have this opportunity when your friends don't?

Kirsten: I feel two opposite emotions. One, that I'm very lucky and privileged to have this chance and a wonderful mum that will do this with me. But, I also feel almost guilty that my friends would probably love to write things like this and would be really good at it, but don't get the chance.

Shelley: Do you have ideas about how we might fix this problem? What can be done to open up more opportunities for children to become published authors?

Kirsten: We've already taken the first step by writing this chapter together. Hopefully people will read this chapter and talk about it with their friends and their own children. Maybe people will write more about it themselves and, even better, invite a child to write with them. I don't think we can do a lot about changing what happens in the home. If parents don't know how to write, then how will they teach their kids the skills? However, schoolteachers have been to university, learnt to write, and enjoy writing. They also enjoy working with children. Teachers are the perfect people to teach kids how to write, help them generate ideas, and encourage them to publish. Wait a minute; why do children need all that help? Why can't they just publish?

Shelley: That's a good question. Remember when we wrote our last chapter together I found the editors and the book that might consider our writing. I talked to them about publishing your work—as a child author. I navigated our way through the process, like the structure, writing drafts, and making the required changes.

This makes me think of another question. Is all of that important? Does it matter to you that our chapter came out in a bound book with a shiny cover and that it is sold in bookstores? Would it be just as meaningful to you to *publish* by putting your writing on a blog or on a webpage that wouldn't require all of the formalities like publishing a chapter in a book?

Kirsten: It would matter! No, I wouldn't like it if it was just on a blog or up on the whiteboard at school. If it's on a blog or up on the whiteboard at school it's read but only by people who go on that blog or go into that classroom. As the author of that kind of schoolwork, I don't usually get to choose what I'm writing about, and the readers don't usually get to choose what to read about. It's all assigned. On the other hand, people who buy a book or take a book out of the library chose it because they wanted to know more about that topic. We chose to write that chapter because we were interested in the topic of schools and we had something to say about it.

I'm proud of our book. Writing a chapter and then seeing and reading the published book is an amazing feeling. When I finish a school assignment it eventually ends up being a bunch of wrinkled papers shoved to the back of my desk. No one reads it. At the end of the year most of it is thrown out. It's a good feeling to see your name published on this book that people want to see and read. Books are important because they could make a real difference.

SECTION 3: CASE EXAMPLES OF ADULT AND CHILD WRITING

Inspiration and innovation can be found in the natural inclinations of children. Observing the way in which children choose to work forecasts the future of authorship when today's children assume the power position of adulthood (Tapscott, 1998). In the tradition of [the positive components of] Piagetian methodology, I have informed my position through in-depth and emotion-infused observation of my own daughter, and in keeping with emergent trends toward reflexive research (Alvesson & Sköldberg, 2000; Etherington, 2004; Kincheloe & Berry, 2004) our positions are deeply influenced through autoethnography. Through writing this chapter, we have developed clarity about ourselves and our own and each other's authorship that we would not have attained without engaging in the process.

In this section of the chapter, Kirsten and I present case descriptions in three categories. The first is adult authorship. I describe and identify the characteristics of a current writing project. The second category is child authorship when controlled by adults. Kirsten elaborates through description of a recent school project. Third, we describe examples of empowered child authorship, operationally defined as those writing pursuits that are not infiltrated by adult intervention. I conclude this section through presenting and interpreting a table of the inherent principles of adult/child authorship.

My chosen writing task is almost definitional to academics—a peer-reviewed journal article. This particular article describes research I conducted as part of a team in a primary school. I submitted the manuscript to a journal chosen for its fit with the article's topic. After a few months, it was returned with a summary of the peer reviewers' suggestions and a note from the editor about which minor edits must be made and submitted prior to publication. I submitted the changes and in a few more months the article will appear in the online journal. The article will be catalogued according to its key terms, and included in multiple electronic databases. A handful of other academics researching in this area will find my article through their database searches. Some of these academics will read the article and perhaps use it in the literature review that forms the rationale for their own research. Perhaps through these researchers the article may even find its way into the hands of a teacher or two who may apply the recommendations to enhance their teaching. In order to increase the chances that the article will be read and thus contribute to the university's public image, library personnel request copyright clearance from the publisher to include a link or a PDF file of the article on an e-publications site linked to my name. This means that searchers will be able to find the article using keyword searches using a standard search engine such as Google. The university will register the article among the annual submission to the higher education body that tabulates Australian university research output. This results in increased funds to the university based on a points-based system. I will insert a record of the publication into my CV and include the full-text document in the portfolio that I will use for evidence when I submit my promotion application.

In summary, I chose what I was going to write about based on my interest in education. I included the required components into the article to ensure that it would be accepted by a peer-reviewed journal. I was motivated to write the article because: the research had positive outcomes for the children at the school site, compelling me to make recommendations for other schools; I enjoy writing; and experience has led me to believe that there is truth in the university maxim of publish or perish. The article will be read, but perhaps not by many, and particularly not by many practitioners who might apply the recommendations.

My writing project varies widely from children's writing projects that are controlled by adults. While employment is the work of adults, school determines and defines the primary work of children. The adults who determine the writing work of children are the school administrators who design and develop the curriculum and the teachers whose lesson plans determine how that curriculum is taught and assessed. Kirsten's description of a school project follows.

Authored by Kirsten

Right now in writing we're doing a project on explanations. It is compulsory that we write our explanations about a natural disaster. I chose bushfires. The teacher went to the school library and brought back books about natural disasters. The books were divided between the three classes, which meant that there weren't a lot of books and choices. We also got to research on the Internet. There are four computers for over 20 kids. It was first come first served. I got around 20 minutes on the computer total. We were given a worksheet that gave spaces for a definition, middle, and conclusion. We did a rough draft and a good draft. Now on a new sheet I'm writing out my final copy. We'll hand it in to the teacher and she'll assess us. I think that this one piece of writing is our whole assessment mark. Our report-card mark will be based on this one cookie-cutter writing process. One of my friends said, "The more boring this is, the higher mark we get." I think she's right.

Authored by Shelley

The writing projects that are inspired, created, and authentically managed by children themselves are radically different from the traditional assignments of school. While one project each sufficed to depict the nature of adult academic work and children's school-based writing, the novelty, complexity, and variety of children's creative empowered writing necessitates the presentation of multiple case examples. Kirsten will write about the first one; the nature of the described case gives me no rights to apply words to it. It is strictly the intellectual property of the children who created it. It is important that I describe the next examples because what I observe is so germane to Kirsten's experience that she cannot step beyond and see what an interruption these activities provide to the essence of authorship for a person of my generation and social positioning.

Authored by Kirsten

The project I have chosen to describe about is opti-minds. Opti-minds is all about thinking outside the box and using creativity. Five of the girls, including me, in our Years 6/7 split class were chosen to be an opti-minds team. One of the great rules in opti-minds is you're allowed no teacher support, which means it's all up to us, the kids. To make sure the teachers didn't give us ideas or help we were sent in to the other side of a divided room so that the teacher could hear enough to make sure we weren't getting in trouble, but not enough to interfere. We are given challenges called spontaneous challenges and one main challenge. Our main challenge was to build a model of an environmentally friendly house and present it through a play. Our main energy idea was getting overweight animals from the Animal Welfare League to run on a treadmill and that gave us power. In the spontaneous challenges we are given a question where we must think outside the box. For example: *look before you leap—Batman leapt. Who is Batman?*

What did he see when he leapt? And why did he say, "Look before you leap"? We had four minutes to talk about our solution and two minutes to present it. Our answer was—Batman was actually a batman or in other words a baseball player. He wasn't even a man—he was a frog because he was leaping. He leapt up because he wanted to get a fly, but then he said, "Look before you leap" because the ball hit him. It was very exciting because our team won the regional competition and now we go on to state finals. It just goes to show that kids can do it without adult help.

Authored by Shelley

The next examples of contemporary authorship are through digital games systems. Kirsten is a member of multiple virtual worlds through Internet sites such as *Club Penguin* and *Webkinz*. These worlds are interactive and creative. The children do not simply participate in others' designs. They construct portions of the environment, choosing locations, colors, and furnishings. Kirsten gives her younger brother ideas within Play Station's *Little Big Planet*, which allows children to create 3D animation, building *worlds* which are played and rated by others online. We recently purchased Play Station's *Buzz*, which is a home armchair version of a television trivia quiz show with interactive buzzers that light up, play customized sound, and activate each player's turn. The evening I brought it home, the children played the game with us for approximately half an hour. They left my husband and me playing the game as is while they went online and created their own trivia quiz, which other people will play and rate. Children demonstrate an expectation that what they do is creative, rewarding, and connected, and allows them to generate content for others. Our proposition is that we can learn from the natural epistemological enactments of children to inform our design and use of the writings of children and, for that matter, of adults. The following table presented summarizes the characteristics of adult authorship and children's authorship when controlled by adults and when in the control of the children themselves.

Table 8.1   The Characteristics of Adult, Controlled, and Empowered Child Authorship

	Adult Authorship	*Child Authorship (Adult Controlled)*	*Empowered Child Authorship*
Content	Determined by disciplinary interest	Determined by curriculum	Determined by sense of fun
Process	Standardized	Repetitive	Creative
Motivation	Mixed	Punishment	Reward
Network	Limited	Largely solitary	Connected
Outcomes	Generative	Solipsistic	Generative

Academics decide what to write based on the conventions of our disciplines. If we want our writing to appear in print, we conform to the publication standards. We are motivated by the stick and the carrot. If we don't publish, we perish. If we do publish, then we might get tenure and/or a promotion. Our collaborative network is limited. We allow others to read our work, but seldom to contribute to it. In so doing, we generate information.

There are similarities and differences between the work of adults and the work of children when it is controlled by adults. There is a curriculum for primary school and curriculums of higher education determined by the disciplines. The academics' writing is largely standardized and, similarly, the children's schoolwork is repetitive. They write the same types of reports year after year, changing only by degrees of vocabulary, grammar, and neatness of handwriting. Whereas the academic is motivated through the carrot and the stick, the child feels as if the only consequence of not satisfying the teacher's expectations is a low grade and resulting punishment doled out by parents. Even though some school rows have given way to grouping, most school assignments are still written independently and teachers mark repeated versions of the same work. The children are not contributing to social capital. Their work is generated for the sole audience of one—the teacher and a few choice pieces selected to show to the parents.

Children's out-of-school writing is fun. The process is creative and intrinsically rewarding. One must only observe the rising statistics regarding children's mobile-phone use to realize how important connectivity is to children. The outcomes of their work are not insular and solipsistic. They are generating content for others to enjoy, benefit from and contribute to.

These characteristics of children's empowered writing are described by Flew (2008) as five characteristics of new media (p. 3). First, they are *manipulable*, or in other words can be changed. Second, they are *networkable*, meaning that they can be shared. Third, they are *dense* in the sense of microchips being able to hold vast amounts of information. Fourth, they are *compressible*, which means that information can be condensed to small units. Fifth, they are *impartial* or apolitical, meaning that anyone can contribute to social capital. Children inherently understand and appreciate these characteristics of new media. In fact, they expect these conditions of the medium and of themselves. What the children produce when they are empowered to do so on their own terms is germane to the characteristics of new media. As adults, on the other hand, we often have to be reminded or enticed to put our paper away and use our computers to their full capacity, to work collaboratively and iteratively, and to share our work and our thinking. We need only watch what and how children write to forecast our own futures—that is, unless we choose to be left behind.

CONCLUSION

In order to inform our conclusion, Kirsten and I read through our entire chapter again, pausing to chat after each paragraph. The paragraphs that inspired the most conversation were the first sections of the introduction about the changing presentation of the written word. Kirsten said that she did not want to leave readers with the impression that children think there should no longer be books. We were working on this section in Kirsten's room. She asked me to look around and I noted the three shelves of chapter books, mostly fiction but also some nonfiction. She said, "I love books!" I concur with her. She said, "I feel proud when I finish reading a thick book." She explained that the authors of books were deliberate about what they included and the order of the contents. She said that this sometimes gives her more of a sense of security than skimming and following links through the Internet. In addition, when she is reading facts, she can trust the truth of a book, whereas she must always remember to question what is written on the Internet. Kirsten said that she hoped that there would always be books. She also hopes that children will be supported to author some of the books.

Whereas we concur that books are an important source of education and enjoyment, we believe that schooling overuses the written text and does not use the computer to its full potential. Kirsten said that her computer experience is repetitive and she attributes this to lack of teacher training. She said that she has been taught PhotoStory software three times in sequential years and she believes that this software was chosen because it is one of the few that teachers feel confident in using. Neither is school a stimulus and catalyst for student voice. As Kirsten described above, with their interest in children and their university training in communications, teachers are the ideal trainers and advocates for student voice. Cockburn (2007) presents schools as a potential living laboratory for children to learn about and practice being democratic citizens in a public arena. However, his research indicates that "children are rarely consulted about the education they receive," leading him to conclude that "children do not really learn democracy in terms of the practices of democracy and decision-making—schools are not mini-democracies" (p. 452). Children continue to be silenced in school.

In summary, a significant interpretation that emerged through the collaborative writing experience between a university academic and a child is that adults must relinquish the epistemological and publication controls that are depriving us of the compelling knowledge produced by children. Children can and should be acknowledged as academic authors as long as the welfare of the child authors is appropriately assured, and reasonable academic rigor and the format requirements for publication in the chosen genre are maintained. The other emergent interpretation is that adults must follow the lead of children to produce and disseminate 21st-century knowledge that is generative, imaginative, multidirectional, and connected.

REFERENCES

Alvesson, M., & Sköldberg, K. (2000). *Reflexive methodology: New vistas for qualitative research.* London: Sage.

Bateson, G., & Ryan, P. (2001). *Metalogue: Gregory Bateson, Paul Ryan.* New York: Paul Ryan.

Brown, A. (2006). Where manuscript development meets faculty development. *Journal of Scholarly Publishing, 37*(2), 131–135.

Burnett, C., Dickinson, P., & Myers, J. (2006). Digital connections: Transforming literacy in the primary school. *Cambridge Journal of Education, 36*(1), 11–29.

Cockburn, T. (2007). Partners in power: A radically pluralistic form of participative democracy for children and young people. *Children & Society, 21*, 446–457.

Egan, K. (2002). *Getting it wrong from the beginning: Our progressivist inheritance from Herbert Spencer, John Dewey, and Jean Piaget.* New Haven, CT: Yale University Press.

Etherington, K. (2004). *Becoming a reflexive researcher: Using our selves in research.* London: Jessica Kingsley.

Farrell, A., Tayler, C., Tennent, L., & Gahan, D. (2002). Listening to children: A study of child and family services. *Early Years, 22*(1), 27–38.

Flew, T. (2008). *New media: An introduction* (3rd ed.). New York: Oxford University Press.

Foucault, M. (1972–1977). *Power/knowledge: Selected interviews & other writings.* (C. Gordon, Ed.). New York: Pantheon.

Griffiths, M., Berry, J., Holt, A., Naylor, J., & Weekes, P. (2006). Learning to be in public spaces: In from the margins with dancers, sculptors, painters and musicians. *British Journal of Educational Studies, 54*(3), 352–371.

Haudrup Christensen, P. (2004). Children's participation in ethnographic research: Issues of power and representation. *Children & Society, 18*, 165–176.

Head, A. (1998). The child's voice in child and family social work decision making: The perspective of a guardian *ad litem*. *Child and Family Social Work, 3*, 189–196.

Horrigan, J. B. (2007). *A typology of information and communication technology users.* Washington, DC: PEW Internet & American Life Project.

Iaquinta, A. (2006). Guided reading: A research-based response to the challenges of early reading instruction. *Early Childhood Education Journal, 33*(6), 413–418.

Jardine, D. W., Clifford, P., & Friesen, S. (2003). *Back to the basics of teaching and learning: Thinking the world together.* Mahwah, NJ: Lawrence Erlbaum Associates.

Kennedy, D. (1999). Philosophy for children and the reconstruction of philosophy. *Metaphilosophy, 30*(4), 338–359.

Kinash, S. (2006). *Seeing beyond blindness.* Greenwich, CT: Information Age.

Kinash, S., & Hoffman, M. (2008). Child and university teacher collaborative research within and beyond the classroom. *Australian Journal of Teacher Education, 33*(6), 76–93.

Kinash, K., & Kinash, S. (2008). Storied by children: Authored by adults. In R. Henderson & P. A. Danaher (Eds.), *Troubling terrains: Tactics for traversing and transforming contemporary educational research* (pp. 29–48). Teneriffe, Australia: Post Pressed.

Kincheloe, J. L., & Berry, K. S. (2004). *Rigour and complexity in educational research: Conceptualizing the bricolage.* Maidenhead, UK: Open University Press.

Lenhart, A., Arafeh, S., Smith, A., & Rankin Macgill, A. (2008). *Writing, technology and teens.* Washington, DC: PEW Internet & American Life Project.

Lenhart, A., & Madden, M. (2005). *Teen content creators and consumers.* Washington, DC: PEW Internet & American Life Project.

Levin, D., & Arafeh, S. (2002). *The digital disconnect: The widening gap between Internet savvy students and their schools.* Washington, DC: PEW Internet & American Life Project.

Lundy, L. (2007). 'Voice' is not enough: Conceptualising Article 12 of the United Nations Convention on the Rights of the Child. *British Educational Research Journal, 33*(6), 927–942.

Meehan, S., Holmes, B., & Tangney, B. (2001). Who wants to be a teacher? An exploration of the theory of communal constructivism at the chalk face. *Teacher Development, 5*(2), 177–190.

Negroponte, N. (1995). *Being digital.* New York: Vintage.

Ong, W. J. (2002). *Orality and literacy: The technologizing of the word* (2nd ed.). New York: Routledge.

Prensky, M. (2001). *Digital game-based learning.* New York: McGraw-Hill.

Ruttle, K. (2004). What goes on inside my head when I'm writing? A case study of 8–9-year-old boys. *Literacy, 38*(2), 71–77.

Singer, E. (2005). The liberation of the child: A recurrent theme in the history of education in Western societies. *Early Child Development and Care, 175*(6), 611–620.

Tapscott, D. (1998). *Growing up digital: The rise of the net generation.* New York: McGraw-Hill.

Vasconcelos, T. (2006). Children's spaces as sites for ethical practices: A 'School-as-a-Tree' in an economically impoverished neighbourhood. *International Journal of Early Years Education, 14*(2), 169–182.

Ward, K. (2009). The future of research monographs: An international set of perspectives. *Progress in Human Geography, 33*(1), 101–126.

Wenglinsky, H. (2005). *Using technology wisely: The keys to success in schools.* New York: Teachers College Press.

Wyness, M. (2006). Children, young people and civic participation: Regulation and local diversity. *Educational Review, 58*(2), 209–218.

9 Burying the Binaries

Getting Discourses to Converge in a Program for First-Year University Students

Robyn Henderson and Karen Noble

ABSTRACT

For many students, especially those who come from groups that often seem disconnected from tertiary study, including those from low socioeconomic, rural, and remote backgrounds, beginning university can be a difficult experience. Traditionally, universities have offered generic study skills programs to assist *new* students to make the transition into the tertiary context. However, recent work about the first-year experience of university suggests that the process of becoming a university student requires more than *top-up* academic programs that are based on a successful/unsuccessful binary about students' capacities to cope with university study.

In a regional Australian university, a program for first-year education students is based on Gee's (1996) theorization of Discourse (with a capital D)—the ways of being, doing, saying, believing, reading, and writing that are shared by a particular social group. In seeing transition into university as a process of learning a new Discourse, the program focuses on the social aspects of transition and embeds the academic within the social. Drawing on data collected during the first two years of the program, this chapter describes the program and how it has worked to dispel the binaries that are so often used to describe new university students, and demonstrates the effects of helping students see the convergences of their different Discourses.

INTRODUCTION

With the massification of university study in Australia in recent years, there has been a dramatic change in the nature of student populations. Whilst tertiary students once tended to represent particular groups within society, today's students are drawn from a diverse range of backgrounds, including ones that traditionally were disconnected from university study. In the university where we work, for example, a large number of students come from low socioeconomic, rural, and remote backgrounds. Additionally, many students are mature-age, second-chance, or 'interrupted' learners, having decided to become university students after choosing a nonacademic career path when leaving school or "missing educational opportunities in their youth" (University of Southern Queensland, 2007, p. 5).

In attempting to cater for student diversity, many universities offer generic study skills programs as a way of helping students make the transition into university study. As an analysis of the webpages of several Australian university sites reveals, library and orientation programs incorporate opportunities for students to top up their academic skills by learning the particular skills and knowledges that are deemed essential for success at university. Library skills, learning skills, academic writing, computing skills, motivation, and time management appear to be favorite topics in many universities, including our own (see, e.g., Griffith University, 2009; James Cook University, 2009; University of Queensland, 2009; University of Southern Queensland, 2009).

While such programs are important and enable students to hone particular skills that are relevant to university study, we question the way that *beginning* university students are framed in terms of a binary—those who have particular skills and those who do not. Such thinking posits that students will be either successful or unsuccessful in their transition into university and that the way of helping students to overcome any difficulties that they experience is to top up their academic skills. Approaches that draw on this logic tend to construct some students as deficient in particular skills, and therefore identify possible solutions to these deficits in programs that offer learning, study, and computer skills (Green, Hammer, & Stephens, 2005; Henderson & Hirst, 2007). Although such thinking might appear to be commonsensical, we argue that binary logic makes top-up programs seem like a panacea for surviving university and thus narrows the options that are on offer to students.

In this chapter, we argue that learning to become a university student is much more complex than learning sets of generic skills. More importantly, we suggest that a shift from binary logic is essential if universities are serious about ensuring that diverse student cohorts are successful in their bid for academic success and university qualifications. To explain our position, we draw on data from a research project that has been examining a support program for first-year university students since the program was established three years ago. The program makes a deliberate attempt to avoid binary thinking and to help first-year students see their arrival at university as requiring the learning of a new Discourse. Drawing on Gee's (1996) theory of Discourses as "ways of behaving, interacting, valuing, thinking, believing, speaking, and often reading and writing" (p. viii), we demonstrate that the avoidance of binaries can provide productive ways of assisting students to become successful learners in the university context.

THE PROGRAM

This chapter draws on data from the first two years of a research project that was conducted in a regional Australian university. It reports on a support program called FYI that caters for first-year students by providing opportunities for social support with embedded academic support. The acronym FYI encapsulates the multiple purposes of the program, including access to relevant information—For Your Information—and the way it operates in the spaces between first-year courses—First Year Infusion. By exploring a selection of students' stories about significant events in their journey to becoming university students, the chapter uses Gee's (1996) theory to show how the program's approach, which deliberately set out to move beyond binaries, assisted students to understand the multiple discourses of their lives and to make the transition into tertiary study.

The program operates as a weekly Learning Circle meeting (Aksim, 1998; Noble, Macfarlane, & Cartmel, 2005; Riel, 2006; Wadick, 2006). A group of academics and faculty support staff, including a librarian and staff from the university's learning and teaching support unit, make a two-hour time slot available to students during each week of the semester. Students are invited to *drop in* to the meeting place, which is a teaching room within the building occupied by the faculty. The Learning Circle operates with no fixed agenda and provides an opportunity for students and staff to engage in discussions about aspects of university study. This student-centered approach allows the meeting to address whatever issues the students identify as important to them at that time. Despite the unstructured approach, however, regular topics of discussion have been academic literacies, information literacies, subject-specific knowledges, and questions about time management and assignments.

The program is underpinned by a belief that successful university study involves social integration and support accompanied by academic preparedness (Noble & Henderson, 2008). It is for that reason that the program uses the Learning Circle approach, offering a social community within which students are able to develop a sense of belonging and connectedness, to focus on interactions and relationships, and to develop a sense of agency and control over their experiences as tertiary students. In particular, the academic and support staff who attend FYI encourage students to use critical reflection as a tool for recognizing that they have skills and knowledges from their lives outside university and that these are generally adaptable to the university context. Furthermore, students are encouraged to take control of their own learning, to be proactive, to ask questions, to seek support when they need it, and to engage in collaborative problem solving.

Also underpinning the program is Gee's (1996) theorization of *capital D* Discourse. Drawing on his notion of Discourses as "ways of behaving, interacting, valuing, thinking, believing, speaking, and often reading and writing" (p. viii), the program takes the perspective that *new* university students are learning to take on a new Discourse—the Discourse of *university student*. As Gee explains, Discourses involve a "usually taken for granted and tacit 'theory' of what counts as a 'normal' person and the 'right' ways to think, feel, and behave" (p. ix). The FYI Program's use of the Learning Circle approach provides opportunities for students to reflect critically on their experiences and on their ways of doing, being, and knowing within the university context.

The academic and support staff encourage students to see themselves as lifelong learners who bring strengths to their university study as well as the ability to learn and problem-solve in new contexts. Learning how to use a new Discourse is regarded as a necessary process for achieving success. By taking this perspective, the program actively discourages deficit discourses and associated binary logic. These two ideas are closely associated. Any approach that sees some students as being successful and others as deficit has nowhere to go but to offer remediation or intervention for those who do not have the perceived requisite skills and knowledges for success in the university context. Such measures can narrow the options on offer and tend to be unproductive in the long term. The worst-case scenario—and we know from experience in other educational contexts that this does happen—is that the gap widens between successful and unsuccessful students (Henderson, 2005; Stanovich, 1986).

What the FYI Program attempts to do is to assist students in their uptake of the new Discourse of university student. Rather than focusing narrowly on academic skills, the wider context, including the social aspects of the students' lives and the wide experiences that they bring to university, is taken into account. While not denying that cognitive, technical, or behavioral skills are involved in learning at university, this approach emphasizes the importance of viewing learning with a "wide lens" (Hill, Comber, Louden, Rivalland, & Reid, 1998, p. 13) rather than focusing exclusively on the individual student. By taking account of the way that being a university student is socially constructed and institutionally located (Hill et al., 1998, p. 13), the place of the social cannot be ignored.

RESEARCHING THE PROGRAM

Because the program began initially for self-identified *at-risk* first-year students, the number of participating students was small. In the first year of the program, only five first-year students attended on a regular basis and participated in almost every meeting. However, other students dropped in when they had specific questions to ask. In the second year, 20 first-year students attended most meetings throughout the year, with other students participating on an ad hoc basis.

Since the beginning of the FYI Program, we have interviewed students and staff toward the end of each semester and kept a log of anecdotal records. In Stake's (2005) terms, we have conducted an intrinsic case study by collecting rich and detailed data about the program and the students who have participated in it. Because of our interest in the program, data collection has been focused on the students, their experiences and perceptions of university, and their reasons for accessing the program.

As part of data collection, semistructured interviews, both individual and focus group, were video-recorded and the audio components were transcribed. Excerpts from those transcriptions are used in this chapter. In the interviews, we asked students about their perceptions of the program and how they thought their study was going. Students reflected on their experiences in their first year of university study, their successful and less than successful experiences, and the place of the FYI Program in those experiences. Many of the students recalled particular times when they realized that they could be successful in the university context. The data used in the chapter draw on the students' descriptions of the times or incidents that they regarded as significant. These critical learning incidents (Byrne, 2001) provide insights about the program from the students' perspectives.

We were quite aware that the interviews were going to yield mostly positive stories, as the program was voluntary and the students were not likely to continue attending the weekly meetings unless they perceived that the program was helpful or beneficial in some way. What we were specifically interested in finding out was whether the interview data would show evidence of the underlying philosophy of the program. In basing the program on a philosophy of not using deficit thinking and not seeing students as deficient, we wanted to know what the students said about becoming university students. In examining the data that were collected, we found that many students described particular incidents that they believed played a critical role in their experience as students.

We begin our discussion of the students' talk by providing a brief overview of the types of issues that emerged from a thematic analysis. We then focus specifically on four of the critical incidents that students described, in order to provide a more detailed discussion of the way that the FYI Program tried to operate. By including contextual information about the students, we locate their stories within the broader context of their university experiences and consider the discourses that might have been on offer.

THE STUDENTS' EXPERIENCES OF UNIVERSITY

In their descriptions of becoming university students, many of the students articulated the difficulties they experienced. Whilst the students varied in age, many identified that a break from formal study—whether that was 5, 10, 20, or even 30 years—had meant that there was a lot to learn about how to study. Time management, learning how to use technology, and finding ways of not being overwhelmed by the tasks they had to do were identified by most of the students as requiring considerable effort.

Many of the students identified the importance of getting to know other students and university staff as part of learning to become university students. In their discussion of this, they highlighted the importance of making friends and identifying study partners, learning how to go about accessing lecturers and the types of interactions that were acceptable, and feeling comfortable in the university context. Even though many of the issues they identified could be described as relevant to the social aspects of university, they linked these to their academic development.

As will be seen in the discussion that follows, the students sometimes used deficit notions to consider their abilities. Nevertheless, there was always an acceptance that they were not bound by these perceived deficiencies. The students were always positive about finding ways of overcoming the problems that they experienced. In focusing on four examples where students identified learning that was significant to their transition into university, the next section of this chapter illustrates how students had moved beyond the binaries that are so often heard. Rather than identifying themselves as on one side of a binary—such as successful/unsuccessful student, able to achieve/not able to achieve, or able to problem-solve/not able to problem-solve—the students seemed to regard the process as one of learning to manage the multiple Discourses of their busy lives.

CRITICAL INCIDENT 1: SPENDING
"THREE WHOLE HOURS!"

The first example involves two students: Margaret and Erin (pseudonyms). Margaret had left school 35 years previously and found that tertiary study had brought many challenges, especially in relation to learning to use information and communication technologies. Additionally, her home was in a small country town over four hours' drive from the university. As a result, tertiary study had brought numerous changes to her usual way of life, including the weekly drive to and from the university. By contrast, Erin had just completed high school and was a high achieving student who often claimed to be "stressed out" by her study and the high expectations she placed on herself.

For the two students, a critical learning incident occurred as they persevered with trying to solve a particular study problem. They had spent several hours working on the problem in the university library. They then sought assistance from one of the academics working in the FYI Program. This move in itself was illustrative of the proactive approach that the program was using—that is, working out *what to do when you don't know what to do*. In an interview, Margaret and Erin described the incident:

Table 9.1 Margaret and Erin's Interview

Margaret:	That's like the day that Erin and I spent 3 hours in the library.
Erin:	Three whole hours!
Margaret:	We tried everything, didn't we? We tried to find out that simple problem, and we eventually thought, "I wonder if—"
Erin:	We have to get help. We went to [the academic]'s office. And she said, "Yes, this is what you need to do." And in 15 minutes—
Academic:	Well, in actual fact, let's go back to that day. I don't actually think I actually said, "This is what you need to do." I think I asked a series of questions and who had the answers.
Margaret:	Well, we both did and we didn't know it, and we'd been up [at] the library for three hours trying to figure it out. But see, that's what . . . you . . . do. I mean, you can see that we know the answers. We know the answers, but you know how to direct the question to use to draw the answer out. And without both [of] you . . . giving us that in the sessions, we would have still had the answers locked inside.

Whilst Margaret and Erin were reluctant to take credit for solving their problem, they recognized that they had the personal resources to work out what to do. For these two students, this incident was a significant point in their understanding about how to achieve in the university context. They had used the processes that the FYI Program had highlighted. In particular, they had worked out what to do when you don't know what to do, by going and talking to one of the academics who worked in the program. From our perspective, Margaret and Erin were developing ways of drawing on what they already knew to solve new problems. In finding a work-around, they were beginning to connect their unsuccessful experiences with successful ones.

CRITICAL INCIDENT 2: BEING IN "A CONSTANT STATE OF PANIC"

Craig (a pseudonym) was a mature-age student who was supporting himself by working as a landscape gardener. He explained that "I needed to get as much help as I could." However, although he attended the FYI Program regularly, he said that it took him a while to get the idea of what the program was about:

> Actually it took me a while before I fully realized what you guys wanted to do. Like I was probably a bit more reserved in the questions I was going to ask. I didn't realize that you were just here available. I thought I'd just sit here and listen to what you guys had to say rather than the other way around.

Initially, Craig thought that he would learn by listening to the academic and support staff working in the FYI Program. It was as if he expected to find an expert/novice binary in play. However, he came to understand that the program was student-centered and focused on *just in time* and *just for me* learnings, with the staff *just here available.*

Another important learning for Craig was about the importance of social relationships and "knowing you've got someone here who's telling you all the time that you can do it." This thinking helped him stay positive and not engage in deficit thinking about himself. Instead, he explained:

> At one time . . . I was in a constant state of panic. That's how I felt at the initial part of it. . . . I just didn't see how I was going to be able to get through all this work, but now I've just—yeah, I've got a lot of confidence now that I can do what's asked and that things are a lot easier than they appear to be.

CRITICAL INCIDENT 3: LEARNING TO TAKE RESPONSIBILITY

Sandra (a pseudonym) was a mature-age student who began part-time study to see if she could fit in being an education student whilst running a household with five sons, four of whom were still at school. For Sandra, learning to trust her family to take on more responsibility was significant in her move toward becoming a successful university student. Empowerment and responsibility became specific considerations:

> I learnt that my children are much more resilient than I give them credit for. And my husband can do a lot more than what he can often say he can do. And also I had to empower myself with the knowledge of where do I go. I didn't have to ask the boys to log me on the computer, or to find out this for me, or Google me that. I could do it myself. So I had to actually take control of my turn on the computer and then I could come out to the library and actually do it as well. A bit empowering, and a bit of taking responsibility and accountability for my own learning.

Sandra noted the changing of roles within her family that had developed during her first year of university study. She began to learn new skills in areas where she had been a novice relying on her more expert sons. This worked both ways, with her husband and sons taking on some of the responsibilities that had originally been hers. Sandra identified the changing roles of all members of her family as significant changes as she learnt to be a university student. Rather than being positioned by the binaries that had operated previously, Sandra's family had learnt to do things in different ways.

CRITICAL INCIDENT 4: MANAGING TIME AND SELF

The final example focuses on Susan (a pseudonym). She had attempted university study as a school leaver but, in her words, had "bombed out big time." In deciding to go back to university over 20 years later, she had a very clear view of what she wanted to achieve. As she explained, "I know where I want to go and I know what I need to do to get there."

In Susan's opinion, time management was a major issue that she needed to address:

I know that's something I'll need as a professional when I am working, but also need to know how to structure my time. And it's really interesting. Like we're all panicking about second semester already and the amount of work. But I'm going, "No, I'm not going to." We've been advizing a friend of ours—breathe—because we've got through first semester and we didn't have any of the skills we've got now. And I'm a lot savvier on the computer and like I said I'm not afraid to ask for help now, not worried about if I need an extension. If I've got reasonable cause, I know that everybody's pretty approachable.

When talking about her experiences, Susan highlighted the need to stay calm and to remember that, as students, they had survived the first semester and were capable of surviving any future semester. Despite the difficulties and the panic she and her friends sometimes experienced, she identified the positive changes that had occurred since her experiences in the first semester. As she explained:

Yes, you get to a point—I think it was in the fourth or fifth week—I just all of a sudden went, "stop, I'm just so overwhelmed; I cannot fit another thing in my head." I honestly couldn't put another bit of information in there if you'd tried. I think that the only way you could have done it was to let some out and put new stuff in.

Rather than see the situation as being too difficult, Susan highlighted the need to reflect on the accomplishments that she and her fellow students had achieved. This focus helped her to see that they had learnt a lot during their first semester and that they would continue to learn how to deal with future difficulties. Additionally, she argued that it was important to give herself "credit when credit's due." She explained that "I have to keep patting myself on the back" and to "ease off myself sometimes." For Susan, this was important as a way of dealing with the pressure that she placed on herself.

CONCLUSION

This chapter used four examples to demonstrate a range of perspectives on coping with the first year of university study. Drawing on short excerpts from interviews with students—Margaret and Erin, Craig, Sandra, and Susan—we hope to have highlighted the variety of strategies that this small group of students used as they learnt to take on the Discourse of university student (Gee, 1996). Through talking about events and understandings that they considered critical and significant to their survival at university, the students showed that they had moved beyond disabling binaries toward enabling ways of thinking about being a student.

Although we cannot say with certainty that the students set out to resist deficit discourses, it certainly appeared that they found ways of working around what might have been potentially disabling binaries. Our plan was that the FYI Program would assist students to see that they could make connections between the social aspects of their lives outside and within the university context, and that they could transfer their problem-solving capacities across contexts and from one Discourse to another (Gee, 1996). In this way, we hoped that the program would avoid binaries that polarize success and failure and often underpin educational interventions or remedial programs.

The use of Gee's (1996) theory of Discourses helped to frame the transition into university as the learning of a new Discourse. Not only was this notion used by the staff who worked in the FYI Program, but it was also taken up by the students in their talk about university study. Rather than setting up the binary of success and failure, the students discussed ways of making changes to their often stressful lives as students. For Margaret and Erin, knowing what to do when you don't know what to do was helpful, whilst for Craig it was important to avoid deficit thinking and to build confidence. For Sandra, seeing changes in herself and her family demonstrated how all of them were learning to do new things, whilst for Susan the need to reflect on successes was highlighted as a way of staying on track. Although all of the students identified difficulties that they were experiencing, they also indicated that they were learning how to deal with the challenges and they were finding ways to move forward. It appeared that the process of learning to be effective students was seen as part of the normative practices of university.

In our opinion, the FYI Program helps to set students up for success by conceptualizing transition into university as requiring the learning of a new Discourse (Gee, 1996). In having a meeting place and space for students to problem-solve whatever issues they think are important, regardless of whether they are social or academic issues, the focus of the program has always been on ways of learning new things to set students up for future successes. Students are encouraged to draw on their existing strengths to solve new problems and to see that they can converge Discourses by bringing particular ways of doing from one Discourse to another.

By avoiding deficit discourses about students, this strengths-based approach not only avoids the success/failure binary but it also stays well away from top-up approaches that focus on academic skill development. Instead, the FYI Program works to develop proactive problem solvers who understand that learning to be a university student is a process of learning to deal with a range of solvable challenges. By moving beyond binaries, the program appears to have helped students see the convergences of their different Discourses, thus enabling success in the university context.

REFERENCES

Aksim, R. E. (1998). *Learning Circle basics*. Retrieved from http://www.magma. ca/~raksim/learning_circle.htm

Byrne, M. (2001). Critical incident technique as a qualitative research method. *AORN Journal, 74*(4), 536–539.

Gee, J. P. (1996). *Social linguistics and literacies: Ideology in discourses* (2nd ed.). London: Falmer Press.

Green, W., Hammer, S., & Stephens, R. (2005, November 22–25). *Locating learning advisers in the new university? What should be our role?* Paper presented at the Language and Academic Skills conference, Canberra, Australia.

Griffith University. (2009). *Self-help resources*. Retrieved from http://www.griffith. edu.au/library/workshops-training/self-help-resources

Henderson, R. (2005). *The social and discursive construction of itinerant farm workers' children as literacy learners* (unpublished doctoral dissertation). James Cook University, Australia.

Henderson, R., & Hirst, E. (2007). Reframing academic literacy: Re-examining a short-course for "disadvantaged" tertiary students. *English Teaching: Practice and Critique, 6*(2), 25–38.

Hill, S., Comber, B., Louden, W., Rivalland, J., & Reid, J. (1998). *100 children go to school: Connections and disconnections in literacy development in the year prior to school and the first year of school* (vol. 1). Canberra, Australia: Commonwealth Department of Employment, Education, Training & Youth Affairs.

James Cook University. (2009). *Learning skills*. Retrieved from http://www.jcu. edu.au/learningskills/

Noble, K., & Henderson, R. (2008). Engaging with images and stories: Using a Learning Circle approach to develop agency of beginning "at-risk" pre-service teachers. *Australian Journal of Teacher Education, 33*(1), 1–16.

Noble, K., Macfarlane, K., & Cartmel, J. (2005). *Circles of change: Challenging orthodoxy in a practitioner supervision*. Melbourne, Australia: Pearson.

Riel, M. (2006). *Learning circles: Teachers' guide*. Retrieved from http://www. iearn.org/circles/lcguide/

Stake, R. E. (2005). Qualitative case studies. In N. K. Denzin & Y. S. Lincoln (Eds.), *The Sage handbook of research* (3rd ed., pp. 443–466). Thousand Oaks, CA: Sage.

Stanovich, K. (1986). Matthew effects in reading: Some consequences of individual differences in the acquisition of literacy. *Reading Research Quarterly, 21*(4), 360–407.

University of Queensland. (2009). *Orientation event planner*. Retrieved from http://uq.edu.au/orientation/st-lucia/index.html

University of Southern Queensland. (2007). *Equity update.* [Report]. Toowoomba, Australia: Author.
University of Southern Queensland. (2009). *Orientation.* Retrieved from http://www.usq.edu.au/orientation/
Wadick, P. (2006). Learning safety: What next? The case for a learning circle approach. Retrieved from http://www.avetra.org.au

10 Not Education Research Binaries
Just Parts of a Whole

Lindy Abawi

ABSTRACT

Reflecting on my lived experience of making the transition from teacher to researcher brought the realization that a number of constructs that I had once taken for granted as being fundamental binaries were in fact just parts of a whole rather than positions on either end of a continuum. For example, I had once considered the constructs of teacher and researcher, silence and speech, making a choice and being chosen, as being obvious examples of the binaries that exist in the world of research. This chapter explores how these binaries were found to be woven into a metaphorical maze of perceptions closely tied to the language used within a specific context. Ultimately language use revealed the lack of substance upon which past perceptions had been built. These revelations emerged from my involvement in three significant pedagogical exploration events: involvement in a school revitalization project called Innovative Designs for Enhancing Achievement in Schools (IDEAS); a Multiliteracies Action Research Project; and an ongoing learning journey which has led to further study and to my becoming a teacher–researcher working on a doctor of philosophy thesis. Hermeneutic phenomenology plays an integral part within this exploration of pedagogy as it forms the methodological stance that helped reveal the insubstantial nature of the binaries and is a key player in the *making a choice and being chosen* scenario.

INTRODUCTION

Drawing on my own lived experience as both a teacher in a primary-school context and a researcher in the throes of a doctor of philosophy (PhD) research project, I aim to capture the essence of my understandings in relation to the constructs of *teacher and researcher, silence and speech,* and *making a choice and being chosen*. I had once seen the relationships between the halves of each pair as being fundamental binaries; however, my lived experience with each in the journey of pedagogical exploration that I have undertaken over the last six years has brought me to the realization that in fact each construct is but half of a whole rather than positions on either end of a continuum.

In searching for the essence of my lived experience of pedagogical exploration, I encountered Max van Manen' s (1997) work and the hermeneutic phenomenological approach to research. The intense searching for the right method with which to undertake research that is entailed in a PhD student's restless quest for what to investigate and how to investigate it came to an abrupt halt when hermeneutic phenomenology found me. From that point on I seemed to have had little choice but to come to grips with the many difficult-to-define aspects of this research method.

Hermeneutic phenomenology explores the depth of understandings gained through listening to multivoiced perspectives combined into an *essence* that reflects the true lived experience of educators and their pedagogic relationship to their world (van Manen, 1997). Hermeneutic phenomenology does not seek to theorize, or prove a theory; instead, the act of writing is seen as a powerful means of disclosing the essence of an experience (Heidegger, 1971; Merleau-Ponty, 1968; van Manen, 1997) and it is through writing that knowledge creation can become transferable on a wide scale. "Only if a practice of teaching is itself teachable, imitable, or somehow conveyable can we meaningfully talk of teacher education or teacher professional development" (van Manen, 2003, p. 2).

By exploring through writing my lived experiences as a teacher I was led to reflect on the many voices and the moments of meaningful silence heard around me and how they impacted on the way new knowledge came into being. Many of the most prominent voices were those of specialists from outside my own school context. It was my application of their external knowledge to my school's internal context that proved most significant in developing my understanding of what ensued. In her research into teacher practice within schools that have undertaken the Innovative Designs for Enhancing Achievement in Schools (IDEAS) revitalization process, Lewis (2003) found this to be of notable significance for many teachers in IDEAS schools. "The creation of contextualized knowledge by teachers overcomes the dichotomous relationship identified by Connelly and Clandinin (1995), between teacher practical knowledge and knowledge received from outside the school" (p. 260).

CREATING CONTEXT

To enable the reader's contextualization of this journey to some degree it is necessary that I briefly explain the two key pedagogical exploration activities that were the starting point for my desire to surge ahead with my own learning journey. These two catalysts were the whole school professional engagement activities called IDEAS, and a Multiliteracies Action

Research Project. Both sets of external facilitators for these projects were researchers who worked in schools both to improve teacher practice and to research teacher practice in order to improve their facilitation. Consequently, the terms *researcher* and *researcher–facilitator* are interchangeable and yet indicate a slight difference of emphasis in their roles at that point in my reflections.

IDEAS is a two-year school revitalization project that has been undertaken by many schools within Australia and has extended beyond Australian shores to schools in India, Singapore, and Sicily. It was developed by a team of researchers, led by Frank Crowther and Dorothy Andrews, at the University of Southern Queensland (USQ). It consists of five key stages: the *i*nitiating stage, the *d*iscovery stage, the *e*nvisioning stage, the *a*ctioning stage and the *s*ustaining stage. There are a number of key IDEAS principles that schools adhere to when undertaking the project. These are that *Teachers are the key*; *Professional learning is the key to professional revitalization*; *Success breeds success*; *No blame*; and *Alignment of school processes is a collective responsibility* (Andrews et al., 2004). Adherence to these principles establishes a climate of collegial trust and together teachers and their communities develop a vision, values, and a set of school-wide pedagogical practices that target improved learning outcomes for all students. Desired outcomes are holistic in nature and focus on developing the *whole child*. Recent research in the Australian state of Victoria highlights the success of the IDEAS process in meeting the needs of diverse school communities (Andrews, 2009). The IDEAS National Learning Forum in 2010 saw the launch of *IDEAS 2 Project* and the establishment of an expert IDEAS network of school personnel who together explore pedagogy and 21st-century learning needs across Australia.

The Multiliteracies Action Research Project was a six-month project developed by Bull and Anstey which emerged from Luke and Freebody's findings within the Literate Futures Report (Luke and Freebody, 2000). Teachers are asked to examine their literacy pedagogy in light of a matrix of quality multiliteracy teaching practices that take into account the vast array of multimodal text types and literacy experiences that students in the 21st century need to access. Each teacher identifies an area in which she or he feels her or his current pedagogical practices are not sufficiently robust, and then puts into place strategies for improvement. Progress made and personal pedagogical understandings developed are then shared in a celebration day. At the school in which I taught, this project was undertaken as a means of exploring and improving personal pedagogical practices. The significance of the Multiliteracies Project was in its contribution to staff professional conversations. These conversations articulated shared understandings of quality pedagogical practices and formed the basis for the school-wide pedagogical framework, the creation of which is an integral part of the IDEAS envisioning stage as it forms the starting point on the way to real school revitalization and improvement.

DRAWING ON LIVED EXPERIENCE

Committing myself to changing my practice in light of the new knowledge that I possessed owing to involvement in these projects caused a subtle and irreversible change in mind-set and the way I viewed both the practice of teaching and the practice of researching. Up until this point in time researchers were seen as entities in universities who, although a part of my learning past, had little to do with the real world of teaching as I now experienced it. Pedagogy was viewed by colleagues, including me, as one of those fancy academic-type words that teachers rarely, if ever, used. However, this language use changed dramatically and pedagogical exploration soon became the catch cry. Teachers excitedly shared their actions and movements forward with academics who were also researchers and facilitators of the projects, and a stimulating new journey of pedagogical discovery had begun. It was at this point that the binary of researcher and teacher became indistinct and as we all worked toward improving practice and improving process the two became parts of a whole educational partnership of learning. Reflections on this dissolving of boundaries are explored later in the chapter.

The desire to capture the essence of the journey meant that, as the researcher I became, I had to reflect on the past in order to understand the significance of my lived experience. The difficulty lay in trying to see the import of words, actions, dialogue, imagery, use of metaphor, and shared understandings in what over the years had become *just the way we do things around here* at my school. At times this proved problematic as there is a fundamental layer of knowledge which is difficult to extrapolate because it lies within the *taken-for-granted* (van Manen, 1997) and thus can easily remain hidden from view. It is therefore necessary that the knowledge seeker listen to the silences within, the moments that make the learner pause and seek the spark of understanding—the essence—of a truth that is reluctant to be revealed.

> Reflection does not withdraw from the world. . . . [I]t steps back to watch the forms of transcendence fly up like sparks from a fire; it slackens the intentional threads which attach us to the world and thus brings them to our notice. (Merleau-Ponty, 1962, p. xiii)

My efforts to capture the elusive nature of these sparks and to convey these clearly are, I feel, inadequate; however, it is this feeling of inadequacy that drives the phenomenologist deeper into self to find the right word, phrase, or metaphoric image to switch on the light of meaning making with *the other* and that ultimately becomes Merleau-Ponty's essence (1962, p. vii) of a lived experience.

The phenomenological other is an intriguing concept. Husserl's relationship with the other, fundamental to transcendental phenomenology, sees each being as having an equal relationship with the other "as cobearer of the world . . . the very same world that is for me real and objective" (1929, as cited in Welton, 2000, p. 149). He sees this relationship with the other as being fundamental to the reduction of description into essence. However, my understanding of the other is more in tune with that of Merleau-Ponty (1962) and in particular with van Manen (1997), who constantly explores pedagogic relationships with the other or others, as cocreators of the world, in a deep search for essence. The other in my sense is therefore the other that is sought out in order to share experience, to ask what an experience is like, and to ascertain the import of lived experiences, while essence is understood as:

> a linguistic construction, a description of a phenomenon . . . not unlike an artistic endeavor, a creative attempt to somehow capture a certain phenomenon of life. . . . [It] is both holistic and analytical, evocative and precise, unique and universal, powerful and sensitive. (van Manen, 1997, p. 39)

These halves of the whole that van Manen (1997) seeks to capture as black marks on a blank canvas are the painters of essence, with essence being both ontic and ontological. Researching lived experience is by name and nature researching the past. By reflecting on the past in light of a current need to know, we interpret an experience within the world in light of certain questions that we seek to answer. Living in the world also entails living in relationships with others. Therefore to some extent this is my story and a concrete description of specific events or moments in time that on reflection seem to hold specific significance, but it also draws on the stories of others to create the essential nature of the lived experience of pedagogical exploration within the context in which it took place.

REFLECTIONS FROM THE PAST—THE STORY BEGINS

Once upon a time I trained as a secondary art and English teacher and went on to teach in the Australian states of Western Australia and Queensland. At various junctures I taught in a remote country town, a thriving metropolis, and a regional inland city. As situational contexts varied, so did my teaching roles. I taught senior art and English, primary-school music, community art and craft, and English as a second language. Within each of these teaching contexts, when professional development opportunities arose that were led by academics coming into the school, the general buzz by teachers at the beginning and end of the learning episode revolved around comments such as *"That's all very well in theory but I bet he/she hasn't been in front of a class in years! What would they know about what it is really like these days?"* In my time I echoed, and no doubt instigated, such comments.

However, in 2003 another page in my story was turned. The school at which I was then Music Specialist commenced IDEAS and the Multiliteracies Action Research Project in the hope of bringing renewed energy and commitment to our staff after a prolonged period of low morale owing to uncertain and disconnected leadership. Both projects targeted teacher understandings of pedagogy. Each was led by external facilitators and each contributed to an irrevocable change in my mind-set with regard to the value of combining teacher practice and academic research under the one mental heading. The Multiliteracies Project empowered teachers to share and compare classroom-based research centered on self-analysis of one's own practice and pedagogy. This action research became a subset of the wider range of pedagogical exploration activities that were to be undertaken as part of the IDEAS project. IDEAS was aimed at promoting the unique culture of a school: celebrating its strengths; assisting staff, students, and parents to detect areas of concern; and formulating a set of school-wide pedagogical principles and accompanying strategies to enable school improvement to occur.

After the Multiliteracies Project ended, facilitation of the IDEAS process by USQ's IDEAS staff continued. Teachers became a part of the IDEAS materials development team and were asked to reflect on and provide insights into elements of the process. Research was continually part of the equation because reflection—the silent pulse of research—was necessary in order to understand the context and move the process forward. Here was research that celebrated the worth of teacher professionalism! Here was research that was authentic! The IDEAS principles of teachers are the key and professional learning is the key to professional revitalization and valuing and empowering teachers to make a difference (Crowther, Kaagan, Ferguson, & Hann, 2009). The IDEAS concept of parallel leadership meant that traditional hierarchical power structures became flattened and more visible. The USQ research team modeled shared leadership and shared understanding in their delivery of the workshop materials.

MY UNDERSTANDINGS AS A TEACHER
IN AN IDEAS SCHOOL

Recently at a school professional development session, exasperated exclamations, similar to those that had once buzzed contentedly around in my head, could still be found reflected in the voices around me. There were still lingering traces of grumblings that floated in the air with the smells of coffee and reminiscences about weekends past.

What a waste of time! *(Did you see that Brad Pitt movie. . . . ?)*

What do they know about classrooms these days? (*Heck, it's been a long day! If I fall asleep—nudge me!*)

Hey! They don't know our kids—how can they possibly understand! *(Okay, everyone—quieten down—let's get started! Groan—Do we have to?)*

Unless what we are about to hear is practical, we don't want to know about it! *(Yeah! I reckon . . . Marg—Where's my coffee?)*

Finally, silence or semisilence descended as manners (or was it guilt, tiredness, or boredom?) took over. On the other hand, for some there was a silence within the silence. This was a special silence—a silence of anticipation—perhaps connecting thoughts to positive past experiences or to the desire to learn so as more effectively to meet the needs of students and therefore fulfill their own need for self-efficacy, professional enhancement, and sense of worth.

The silence within the silence that shimmered in the staffroom at my school that day was a mirror image of the silence that settled in my mind about six months after commencing my involvement with the IDEAS process and the professionals leading us to learning. At this stage the silence in my mind was a little unnerving. The sense of familiarity associated with falling back on easily defamed stereotypes (such as *Academics? Researchers?— What would they know about our real world?*) had been taken away and instead my mind entered a land of mirages—a quicksand land where there were glimmerings of truth but nothing firm to hold on to. There was no solid ground on which to stand because certainties that had become uncertainties had not yet been replaced with other certainties. This is where the valuing and recognition inherent in the IDEAS principle of teachers as the key started to work its magic.

These researchers asked for our opinions; they valued what teachers said. They did not pretend to be the founts of all wisdom and refused to tell us what to do (even when we begged them to!) These researcher–facilitators led from behind. They gently nudged us to ask the questions that only we, as professionals within our specific context, knew needed asking. Inquiry, reflection, informed application of new knowledge, and celebration of progression were part of an ongoing teaching–learning–researching cycle. The more I learned the more I needed to learn!

The direction we, as a school community, set ourselves was a collective choice—it was not insisted on by the researcher–facilitator with whom we worked. It was developed as a team, excitedly and confidently, by using the inquiry and deduction skills that we had developed throughout the process. This level of confidence to explore and research our own context, to define the needs and formulate ways to move forward, crept up on us slowly and subtly. As it became more concrete we started asking our academic–researcher partners questions that they found difficult to answer. Our perspectives and perceptions opened new channels for thinking. At times teachers were the experts and in other scenarios the researchers were the ones to shed light on meaning.

It was the helixical entwinement of researcher and researched perspectives and the narrowing of the initial distance between the two that gave credence to what evolved. The evolution of the process itself ensured that the symbiotic relationship between both halves of the possible binary was to be valued and value added to by all those involved. Teacher culture insisted that practicality and application to classroom practice be an essential value that must be reflected in new understandings and workshop materials. Academic culture insisted that sound research practice and theoretical validity would underpin progress made so that there was a solid foundation upon which new knowledge could be built. Together the synergy of thought and expertise that abounded solidified into ground on which I was happy to stand and became my launching pad into further learning.

Initial differences diminished. Teachers more frequently used theoretical language and researchers more frequently used context-specific, practical, teacher terminology. As the conversations developed, a richness of understanding through shared interaction became apparent (Conway, 2008). With this sense of communicative ease, well-established teachers moved from research shy, to research novice, to research partners, eager to understand more, often inquiring into and raising questions that were

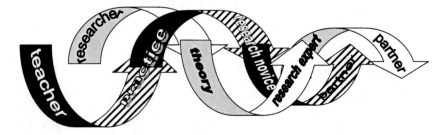

Figure 10.1   The 'helixical' relationship built a closely entwined thread of understanding.

not a part of the original quest. Researchers became teachers leading the learning process and were viewed as the research experts who at the same time were learning themselves, asking their own questions, the other half of the learning/researching partnership.

My interpretation of the transformation of perceptions that occurred within this lived experience is captured in Tables 10.1 and 10.2.

I had become caught up in a world that combined both teaching and researching in an entwined manner. Once I was hooked, a master's and full-time PhD scholarship ensued. At times I felt lost in the whirlwind that had overtaken me but these moments of disbelief were tempered by a sense of overpowering excitement at the possibilities that now arose. I became a researcher in IDEAS schools and developed research partnerships in settings similar to the one in which I had once been a participant.

Table 10.1 The Researcher/Teacher Binary From My Perspective in 2003

Stereotypical Researcher	Stereotypical Teacher
• Head in the clouds • Got their own agenda • Too theoretical/not practical • Watcher rather than participator • Needs grounding in the real world • Puts own twist on data • Out of touch with Gen X, so of what relevance is past research?	• Student-focused practice essential • Skeptical of so-called experts untested in current classroom contexts • Grassroots teaching experts • Self-conscious of sharing practice • Threatened by change if purpose not clearly explained • Know Gen X well

Table 10.2 The Researcher/Teacher Binary From My Perspective in 2007

Researcher partner	Teacher partner
• Focused on the needs and aptitudes of Gen X according to data from current research • Teacher focused to improve student outcomes • Raise the profile of teachers: "Teachers are the key" • Theory backed by practical application and supported by research • Grounded in the real world—big Picture • Learns from teachers • Ask the hard questions	• Focused on the needs and aptitudes of Gen X according to experience • Practice focused to improve student outcomes • Confidence and pride in own teacher professionalism • Practice backed by theoretical application and research • Grounded in the real world—context specific • Learn from researchers • Ask the hard questions

MY UNDERSTANDINGS AS A
RESEARCHER IN IDEAS SCHOOLS

As I moved from teacher to researcher I had the excitement of seeing my understandings of the blurring and blending of the researcher/teacher dichotomy in IDEAS schools being echoed by the teachers in the schools with whom I now conducted my own research. The following excerpts from data collected as a part of my PhD study indicate this.

> Excerpt 1: Guess what—I have started studying again. After our discussions and reflections on what we do here I just have to know more! I have been looking back into what we have done well and where we could improve. I have been asking my staff for their opinions and insights and have decided to re-administer the DI [a research questionnaire] that we did years ago so we can update our data. We have so many new students and families now that we need to understand their current perspectives. It's all very exciting! *(Teaching principal)*

> Excerpt 2: It's been great having you here! I was really nervous having you in my classroom at first. I thought you would be judging me and that made me self-conscious. You just seem to adapt to whatever is happening and extract little insights and bits of information that I am not aware that I am conscious of! You listen to what I say and don't mind it when I ask questions too! It's made me reflect on my practice again and how far I have come as a teacher over the last few years. *(Teacher)*

> Excerpt 3: At only my second visit I realized that at this school the staff (principal, teachers, and teacher-aides) had so much knowledge that needed to be captured for others to benefit from. I had of course suspected that or I would not have approached them to become part of my research, but the supporting evidence to confirm this far exceeds what I had anticipated. The staff are so humble and yet confident about the *why* of their quality teaching practice and are forever reflecting on ways to improve. The principal made me conscious of a perspective on functional grammar use in relation to a technology unit evaluation task that I would never have thought of. What a great approach to reflection on 'best fit'! I am going to link this insight into my own practice. It is very obvious that the learning journey here involves everyone—including me. *(Researcher)*

SEEKING THE ESSENCE

In IDEAS, the trend since its conception has been for researchers and teachers to work closely together collecting and interpreting data. Teachers are seen as vital to the process because they are the leaders of knowledge creation and change in their schools (Crowther, Kaagan, Ferguson, & Hann, 2009). The data sets that emerge from IDEAS schools are a visual and verbal representation of the synergy of combined consciousness (Conway, 2008) that exists. The professionalism of both researchers and participants (generally teachers) is celebrated and worth is attributed to both the teachers' contextual practical understandings and the researchers' *Big Picture* interpretation and analysis underpinned by theoretical understandings.

The reciprocity evident within the snippets of conversations and reflections highlighted here are part of a larger database that links to the essence found within the researcher–teacher relationship. There was acceptance of each other's professionalism; acknowledgment that each individual had much to learn; realization that the questions and the answers were not set in stone; confidence that opinions and insights were valued; trust that the research–teacher relationship would not be abused; and confidence in the capability of each individual to contribute to the whole. As such it became obvious that in this context a teacher/researcher binary did not exist and the hint of the binary mirage "I thought you would be judging me" (Excerpt 2) was quickly dismissed by the teacher as a fallacy, just as I had dismissed it myself many years before.

MOVING BEYOND THE BINARY MIND-SET

Hartle et al. (this volume) identify that the stereotypical views often held by professionals are based on a cultural predilection within each profession toward one extreme rather than another and are in fact rarely believed or manifested in their entirety. In particular, the stereotypical characteristics of the *culture of research* and the *culture of teacher* that I had once accepted as part of each profile were shown to be unreal. In an attempt to find out why the initial binary construct existed, and why it had so emphatically dissolved, I once again explored my inner silence for answers.

Part of this inner seeking led me to reflect on the binary of silence and speech. Initially researcher language had rendered me uncomfortable because it was not the language of teacher talk used in schools. In order not to appear ignorant, I remained silent. In silence is reflection. Reflection is inner speech. At this point the repartee inside my head highlighted the practical nature of what was being said. I was having this silent conversation with myself where I could translate meaning into teacher talk. Familiarity with meaning gave voice to my practical knowledge and this rose to the surface and was finally expressed out loud—often inadvertently. Researcher acknowledgment of the value of teacher knowledge was reflected in their silence. They would listen silently while we spoke, bouncing ideas from one to another and allowing us to explore our inner landscapes as teachers (Palmer, 2007)—quicksands, mirages, and all. At times the teachers would lapse into silence and yet the researchers did not fill this silence straight away because the silence was respected and examined for its import. Over time the language of these professional conversations, whether held in silence or held out loud, became an amalgamation of academic and teacher talk, a hybrid language that was vibrant and alive in its continued evolution.

I realize now that, when academics speak in terminology foreign to teachers and their practice, this knowledge is dismissed without further thought or, even worse, becomes labeled as useless theoretical rhetoric.

> It is well established that people's estimates of what others know, believe, or value tends to be biased in the direction of their own beliefs—what they themselves know. As a result, comprehending the true intention of an utterance may require knowledge far beyond what one possesses, and this may be particularly prevalent when the cultural situations of the parties are markedly different (Krauss & Morsella, 1997, p. 8).

The thought of becoming a researcher myself—if it had ever twinkled for a moment in the corner of my mind with other fanciful maybes—had always been quickly dismissed. This dismissal had been happily fortified by internal reflections based on the cultural stance which many a teacher resorts to when feeling out of their depth and is brought into focus as the words *"I'm only a teacher!"*

These few words once uttered seem to have a life and meaning all of their own and are in complete contrast to my findings and the work of Stenhouse (1983) and Hollingsworth (1995), who believe that teachers should be valued as researchers, who question the logic or even the possibility of separating the performance from the performer, and who insist that professional and curriculum development should be part of the same exploration. Within the IDEAS and Multiliteracies Project, the provision of a process and framework for reflection and school improvement enabled the bringing together of not only professional development and the construction of more effective teaching strategies but also the theoretical understandings that underpin good practice (Andrews & Crowther, 2002; Anstey & Bull, 1996). Therefore, teachers could simultaneously seek understandings and improve practice, thereby embodying the essence of both researcher and teacher.

What became apparent in the pedagogical exploration projects was that the questions that must be asked from both researcher and teacher perspectives also needed to be answered from both perspectives and that neither perspective was to be more valued than the other. In fact it was only when they were combined that a whole picture was created which was deeper, richer, and more meaningful. Creating this whole picture required time, professional conversations, and moments of reflective silence. Another binary had dissolved with the realization that silence was in many cases actually internal speech and that the moments of silence were integral to the meaning to be created. It also became obvious that the words being utilized in these moments of silence and moments of speech were not static.

A moment of enlightenment then occurred—an essence had been identified—the most significant difference between the researcher and the teacher at the outset of these two innovative pedagogical exploration processes was not in the quantity of knowledge possessed, or the levels of confidence and depths of reflection undertaken by both parties, but in the difference of the language used between each of the parties (Marland, 1996) and that both parties used their internal language-in-use to adjust to the other's culture of practice and to ask the questions that needed answering. Some questions seemed to have no clear origin. They emerged out of an ongoing thought from a discussion or an urge for clarity, or perhaps from an echo of an echo that resonated from a silence or from one mind to another. It was the eagerness to question and seek answers that characterized the interactions among all participants in the research process. With this personal understanding now clearly in place, I realized that I too could seek the answers to questions that as yet had no answers and so my decision to become a researcher came to fruition.

CHOOSING A RESEARCH PARADIGM OR BEING CHOSEN?

In my own research, the quest to find the questions that demanded to be answered, and the framework to use that would ensure that such questions would be answered as they should be, required a great deal of reading and delving into the literature and theory related to an endless array of research paradigms. From a teacher's perspective, I had experienced the value, sense of fulfillment, and personal power that I had gained by working within the IDEAS collaborative research paradigm. It was therefore an imperative to locate a research methodology that supported my belief in this type of lived experience research practice.

Today the dimensions of research paradigms have changed to embrace the need for a fundamental understanding of the values underlying each paradigm so that a researchers can choose with more focused clarity the one that suits their need. "If we had to do it all over again, we would make values or, more correctly, axiology (the branch of philosophy dealing with ethics, aesthetics, and religion) a part of the basic foundational philosophical dimensions of paradigm proposal" (Guba & Lincoln, 2005, p. 200). The essence of this statement echoed with the IDEAS focus on establishing clear vision and values as a way to move forward. This was the first hint of the next binary that would sink into the quicksand and emerge as a whole.

As the search for a research method continued, I became moved by the beauty and power captured by Freire (1992, p. 2), fascinated by the transcendental phenomenology of Husserl (1983), and confused by the work of Foucault (1977). Is his the method I should be adopting? It seemed too analytical and semiotic-based for my purposes! Elliott (1991) emphasized the interpretive-hermeneutic nature of inquiry and action research as a pedagogical paradigm—this was closer to where I wanted to be.

Venturing still deeper, it became apparent that phenomenological researchers sought to capture the lived experience of self and others. Further exploration led to the writings of Max van Manen and his work within a hermeneutic phenomenological paradigm.

> Herein lies the irony of a profound contradiction: the language by way of which teachers are encouraged to interpret themselves and reflect on their living with children is thoroughly imbued by hope, and yet it is almost exclusively a language of doing—it lacks being. (van Manen, 1997, p. 122)

Within many IDEAS schools I had a sense that hope was becoming *being* in ways that were new, contextualized, and yet transferable. The need to interpret this sense of being from a variety of perspectives spoke volumes in my inner silence. Phenomenology embodies the essence of qualitative research as

> a situated activity that locates the observer in the world. It (qualitative research) consists of a set of interpretive, material practices that make the world visible. These practices transform the world . . . qualitative researchers study things in their natural settings, attempting to make sense of, or interpret, phenomena in terms of the meanings people give to them. (Denzin & Lincoln, 2005, p. 3)

In the hermeneutic phenomenological research paradigm

> both the interviewer and the interviewee attempt to interpret the significance of the preliminary themes in the light of the original phenomenological question. Both the researcher and the interviewee weigh the appropriateness of theme by asking: "Is this what the experience is really like?" And thus the interview turns indeed into an interpretive conversation wherein both partners self-reflectively orient themselves to the interpersonal or collective ground that brings the significance of the phenomenological question into view. (van Manen, 1997, p. 99)

After waking to moon glow on my wall one night I realized that my inner silence had again been engaged in its own conversation and had accepted that hermeneutic phenomenology had found me. Even though I could barely say it, I could spell it. This was an eerie sensation at the time as I realized that I had to search no longer as the choosing had been done. The concept of phenomenological research met the needs of my research focus and, colored by my own lived experience, reflected the values in which I believed—I decided at that point to go along with being chosen as it was obvious that my inner silence, with total disregard of the choosing or being chosen binary, had agreed that hermeneutic phenomenology was to be the next path taken in my learning journey.

CONCLUSION

Conceptually, binaries in educational research are not clear-cut entities that have boundaries of carefully constructed meaning. So many under-standings and half-understandings, experiences and suppositions, are tied up in educational binaries. Each half of a binary can have differ-ent connotations for different people depending on the learning journeys undertaken and the cultural backgrounds from where they originate. As both a researcher and a teacher, my lived experience has colored my understandings of a number of binaries that I had once taken for granted. When first I turned to the research page of my never-ending story, I discovered thoughts, feelings, experiences, preconceptions, and fallacies about which I had been previously unaware.

The feeling of *best fit* associated with moving beyond preconceived beliefs and into a synergistic interpretive research paradigm, such as hermeneutic phenomenology, heralds a clear direction for future research that I plan to undertake on completion of my thesis. IDEAS as a process lends itself to this interpretive form of research, as teachers develop the skills to carry out "sophisticated research skill development and mutualistic relationships with external researchers" (Austin & Crowther, 2000, as cited in Erwee & Conway, 2006, p. 182). The very nature of hermeneutic phenomenological research means that the many interpretations still to be made assure that this story will remain in the realms of the *to be continued* for a long time to come. As a consequence, I wonder how many more educational binaries will sink into the quicksand only to reemerge as essences of a whole.

REFERENCES

Andrews, D. (2009). *The Victorian IDEAS Project: Research report.* Toowoomba, Australia: University of Southern Queensland.

Andrews, D., Conway, J. M., Dawson, M., Lewis, M., McMaster, J., Morgan, A., & Starr, H. (2004). *School revitalisation the IDEAS way* (monograph). Melbourne, Australia: ACEL.

Andrews, D., & Crowther, F. (2002). Parallel leadership: A clue to the contents of the "black box" of school reform. *International Journal of Educational Management, 16*(4), 152–159.

Anstey, M., & Bull, G. (1996). *The literacy labyrinth.* Sydney, Australia: Prentice Hall.

Connelly, F. M., & Clandinin, D. J. (1995). *Teacher's professional knowledge landscapes.* New York: Teachers College Press.

Conway, J. (2008). *Collective intelligence in schools: An exploration of teacher engagement in the making of significant new meaning* (unpublished doctoral dissertation). University of Southern Queensland, Australia.

Crowther, F., Andrews, D., Dawson, M., & Lewis, M. (2002). *Innovative designs for enhancing achievement in schools: Facilitation folder.* Toowoomba, Australia: University of Southern Queensland.

Crowther, F., Kaagan, S., Ferguson, M., & Hann, L. (2009). *Developing teacher leaders: How teacher leadership enhances school success.* Thousand Oaks, CA: Corwin Press.

Denzin, N. K., & Lincoln, Y. S. (Eds.). (2005). *The Sage handbook of qualitative research* (3rd ed.). Thousand Oaks, CA: Sage.

Elliott, J. (1991). *Action research for educational change.* Buckingham, UK: Open University Press.

Erwee, R., & Conway, J. (2006). Cocreation of knowledge: Roles of coresearchers in research teams. *The Educational Forum, 70*(2), 171–184.

Freire, P. (1992). *Pedagogy of hope.* London: Continuum.

Foucault, M. (1977). History of systems of thought. In D. F. Bouchard (Ed.), *Language, counter-memory, practice: Selected essays and interviews by Michel Foucault* (pp. 119–204). Ithaca, NY: Cornell University Press.

Guba, E., & Lincoln, Y. (2005). Paradigmatic controversies, contradictions and emerging confluences. In N. Denzin & Y. Lincoln (Eds.), *The Sage handbook of qualitative research* (3rd ed., pp.191–215). London: Sage.

Heidegger, M. (1971). *Poetry, language, thought* (A. Hofstadter Trans. & intro). New York: Harper & Row.

Hollingsworth, S. (1995). Teachers as researchers. In L. Anderson (Ed.), *International encyclopedia of teaching and teacher education* (2nd ed., pp. 16–19). Cambridge, UK: Cambridge University Press.

Husserl, E. (1983). *Ideas pertaining to a pure phenomenology and to phenomenological philosophy: First book: Gneral introduction to a pure phenomenology* (F. Kersten. Trans.). Dordrecht, The Netherlands: Kluwer Academic Publishers.

Krauss, R. M., & Morsella, E. (1997). *Communication and conflict.* Retrieved from http://www.columbia.edu/~rmk7/PDF/Confl.pdf

Lewis, M. (2003). *The dynamics, implications and effects of knowledge creation in professional learning communities* (unpublished doctoral dissertation). University of Southern Queensland, Australia.

Luke, A., & Freebody, P. (2000). *Literate futures: Report of the literacy review for Queensland State Schools.* Queensland, Australia: Department of Education.

Marland, P. (1996). *Teaching literacy: Teachers' practical theories.* In G. Bull & M. Anstey (Eds.), *The literacy lexicon.* Sydney, Australia: Prentice Hall.

Merleau-Ponty, M. (1962). *The phenomenology of perception.* London: Routledge and Kegan Paul.

Palmer, P. J. (2007). *The courage to teach: Exploring the inner landscape of a teacher's life* (2nd ed.). San Francisco, CA: Jossey-Bass.

Stenhouse, L. A. (1983). *Authority, education and emancipation.* London: Heinemann Educational.

van Manen, M. (1997). *Researching lived experience: Human science for an action sensitive pedagogy* (2nd ed.). London: Althouse Press.

van Manen, M. (2003). *Writing in the dark: Phenomenological studies in interpretive inquiry.* London: Althouse Press.

Welton, D. (2000). *The other Husserl: The horizons of transcendental phenomenology* (Studies in continental thought). Indianapolis, IN: Indiana University Press.

11 Beyond the Binary of Researcher/Researched

The Complexities of Participatory Action Research

Karen Hawkins

ABSTRACT

This chapter explores the binaries of researcher/researched and, to a certain extent, objectivity/subjectivity by outlining a participatory action research (PAR) project situated in early childhood contexts. To do this it delves deeply into the project's methodological concepts and therefore may be considered a conceptual chapter. The background and justification as to why PAR was the design of choice for this project are offered.

It is argued that action research, while overlapping significantly with the qualitative paradigm, has distinct differences in the way in which action researchers work with others and that the distinction between researcher and participants becomes blurred during the collaborative relationship. The chapter highlights that this study was carried out *with* and *by*, as opposed to *on*, participants and so it bypassed the traditional division between researcher and researched. Although PAR is considered a socially just mode of inquiry, it is not without its tensions, complexities, and challenges, which the chapter explains.

However, it also puts forward strategies that the study adopted to address these tensions, complexities, and challenges. It offers strategies to assist the facilitator of a PAR project; strategies to assist coresearchers form a coherent PAR team; and strategies to assist the PAR team forge ahead and address the complex web of power and privilege. These strategies go a long way in confronting and addressing the binary of researcher/researched.

INTRODUCTION

PAR is not an easy undertaking for any participant. Indeed, it is often referred to as messy and complex owing to the blurring of the roles of researcher and researched (Herr & Anderson, 2005; Maguire 2006; McIntyre, 2008). To explain this messiness and complexity, this chapter highlights the difficulties and intricacies of PAR by examining one particular study. This study was set in two preschool classrooms (Preschools A and B, with preschool defined here as providing noncompulsory, before formal school years care with an educational purpose). The study examined the specific pedagogical strategy of utilizing children's literature during classroom storytime sessions as a means to teach for social justice. The research team consisted of a preschool director, a preschool teacher, and a preschool assistant from Preschool A; a preschool director/teacher and a preschool assistant from Preschool B; and myself. All team members embraced the study because we had an interest in teaching for social justice and wished to explore pedagogical strategies that would assist in implementing such a curriculum into early childhood settings that would impact positively on preschoolers' understandings of social justice issues. Indeed, the methodology of action research attracts people of similar interests, dreams, and aspirations (Kemmis & McTaggart, 2005; Skolimowski, 1995; Torres, 2004). Herein lay the first clue to a shift away from the binary of researcher/researched as, in most research endeavors, participants are usually selected and not the other way around as was the case in this research project. This is further explained later in the chapter.

The project incorporated an orientation phase (which this chapter discusses in depth) and an action phase. During the action research phase, the research team met weekly to view and analyze videotaped storytime sessions from each of the preschools. Most of the picture books involved in these storytime sessions were critical books that highlighted social justice issues related to difference, diversity, and human dignity. The research team analyzed the preschool teachers' and the preschoolers' responses during the storytime sessions. From this analysis action plans for the following storytime sessions were proposed.

From the above explanation of the action research project highlighted in this chapter, it may appear to be a relatively straightforward exercise rather than a messy, complex, and daunting task. I propose that, on the contrary, the PAR team faces many tensions, complexities, and challenges and that these issues can be analyzed in terms of the blurring of the boundaries between researcher and researched. This chapter also offers strategies that were adopted by the PAR team that addressed these complex issues. However, before these complexities are examined it is advantageous to explore why and how PAR was adopted for the study as the design itself challenges the binaries of researcher/researched and objectivity/subjectivity.

BACKGROUND

The objective of education research should not stop at deconstructing the obvious and simply unpacking reality, but should produce analyses that possess a certain strategic edge to recognize those elements that have the potential to change or oppose the social reality (Troyna, 1994). Through action research this objective may be realized. The methodology of action research was chosen for this study based on three considerations. Firstly, action research reflects a participatory worldview by which this action research project was framed. The research project outlined in this chapter was founded on a profound belief that the world is shaped by participation and collaboration with one another and it was underpinned by a deep interest in and concern for social justice. Secondly, action research is a collaborative inquiry method that values participant knowledge, skills, and expertise and seeks to empower and give voice to those involved in the study and who will use the findings. Lastly, action research engages an ethical commitment to improving society and making it more just; to improving ourselves so that we may become more conscious of our responsibility as members of a democratic society; and ultimately to improving our lives together as we build community (Jones, 2006).

The research project focused on social justice understandings. Therefore, prior to the commencement of the research project I investigated collaborative methodological practices that would move beyond the binary of researcher/researched and promote a socially just mode of inquiry and would value and uphold the integrity of each participant involved in the study (myself included) and give each a valued voice. The most obvious response to critical concerns regarding representation is empowerment research and PAR has been cited as the most developed genre of this type (Gergen & Gergen, 2003). "While notions of 'voice' or representation are problematic . . . it is the intention of PART (participatory action research teams) to explicitly deal with this to ensure agency, as participants act in the framing and intervention practices of the issue" (Martin, lisahunter, & McLaren, 2006, p. 176).

PAR is a relatively new and collaborative approach to research (Torres, 2004). In the 1980s action researchers from Australia and Europe raised the initiative to develop more overtly critical and emancipatory action research (Carr & Kemmis, 1986). Following this, a new generation of action researchers emerged through social movements in the developing world supported by such notable activists as Paulo Freire (1993) and Orlando Fals Borda (1988). These researchers believed that research should represent "educational transformation and emancipation by working with others to change existing social practices and by using critical reflection and social criticism as key research processes" (Mac Naughton, 2001, p. 210). Such research is necessarily collaborative, orientated to change and visibly political. Denzin and Lincoln (2005) refer to this type of inquiry as "liberation methodology" (p. 1123).

The research project outlined in this chapter easily aligned itself with the above generation of action research as it transformed the pedagogy of the early childhood educators involved in the study from using children's literature during storytime sessions as simply a filler activity between, for example, the end of the day and the collection of children to a catalyst for teaching about social justice issues. However, it also aligned with a new generation of critical PAR that emerged during the 1990s as part of a dialogue aimed at critiquing itself and providing a frame of reference for understanding its own research journey (Kemmis & McTaggart, 2005). This again displays a move away from the binary of objective/subjective whereby the research looks inward and examines its own process. The research team involved in this research project aspired to become part of this international dialogue by critiquing its own process and journey through collaborative discussions, reflection, and reflexivity (more on this later in the chapter).

Action research is a research design that has become particularly attractive to educators because of its practical, problem-solving emphasis, because practitioners carry out the research, and because the research is directed toward greater understanding and improvement of their own practice (Bell, 2000). Action research involves "researching with people to create and study change in and through the research process. In early childhood settings it can produce changed ways of doing things and changed ways of understanding why we do what we do" (Mac Naughton, 2001, p. 208).

Action research became appealing to me as a research design; however, I did not fully understand how I (as a researcher) could fit into this type of research. Was I still caught up in the binary of researcher/researched? I found reassurance in that many action researchers recognized that the coconstruction of knowledge and the material gathered from, with, and by any community—including a preschool—constituted a participatory process (Fine, Torre, Boudin, Bowden, Clark, Hylton, et al., 2004). The term *participatory process* emphasized the fact that research need not be done on participants as objects but can be a collaborative practice. Indeed, "action, participatory, and activist-orientated research is on the horizon" (Denzin & Lincoln, 2003, p. 29) and blurs the lines between researcher/ researched. My philosophy and worldview aligned with this new direction of qualitative research where together stakeholders and researchers cocreate knowledge that is realistic and pragmatically useful and is rooted in local understandings (Greenwood & Levin, 2005).

Because an aim of this research project was to empower and enable all participants, I sought a research design that would in itself become a social practice that encouraged a social process of collaborative learning and transformation, opened communicative space (Habermas, 1996), upheld prior knowledge, and listened to and valued the voice of each participant. This meant that all participants were afforded a valued voice, debate and discussion were encouraged, action agreed upon collaboratively was promoted, and each participant was represented in every stage of the project.

To achieve the above, participatory research requires those involved to form empathetic and compassionate ties that cement the research project together (Bray, Lee, Smith, & Yorks, 2000). The difference between

objective research and participatory research is that the former is underpinned by objective consciousness while the latter is underpinned by
compassionate consciousness (Skolimowski, 1995). Therefore, participatory research:

> is the art of dwelling in the other, is the art of penetrating from within, is
> the art of learning to use the language of the other; in short, is the art of
> empathy. . . . What clinical detachment is to objective methodology, empa-
> thy is to the methodology of participation. (Skolimowski, 1995, p. 182)

To this end, PAR encourages and opens communicative space between
those involved. The process of PAR is one of mutual and collaborative
inquiry aimed at reaching intersubjective agreement, mutual understanding of a situation, unforced consensus about what to do, and a sense that
what people achieve together will be *legitimate* not only for themselves but
also for every reasonable person (a universal claim). Participatory action
research aims to create circumstances in which people can search together
collaboratively for more comprehensible, true, authentic, and morally right
and appropriate ways of understanding and acting in the world (Kemmis &
McTaggart, 2005, p. 578).

Therefore, because of its collaborative strength, the design of PAR was
adopted as the design of this research project. Informed by Skolimowski
(1995) and Kemmis and McTaggart (2005), the project became a compassionate, communal inquiry that attracted like-minded people who wanted
to investigate collaboratively for more understandable, accurate, reliable,
and ethically right and suitable ways of exploring children's literature during storytime sessions to promote their students' awareness of, and sensitiv-
ities to, social justice issues. PAR involves reflection, discussion, decision,
and action as people of like minds participate in research concerning problems that influence and interest them (Torres, 2004).

The application of PAR was appropriate for this study because it was a
means that produced knowledge and improved practice through its collaborative nature: the direct involvement of participants in setting the sched-
ule, data collection and analysis, and use of findings (Greenwood & Levin,
2005; Kemmis & McTaggart, 2005; Mac Naughton, 2001). PAR signifies
a position within qualitative research methods, an epistemology that aligns
well with a participatory worldview and believes knowledge is embedded
in social relationships and most influential when produced collaboratively
through action (Fine et al., 2004). To this end the research team undertook
the cyclical, spiraling action research process. Figure 11.1 depicts how different aspects of the PAR process are fluidly interwoven with one another
in a spiral of reflection, planning, action, observation, and further reflection, further planning, further action, further observation, and still more
reflection (Bell, 2000; Kemmis & McTaggert, 2005; Kemmis & Wilkinson, 1998; Mac Naughton, 2001; McIntyre, 2008; Reason & Bradbury,

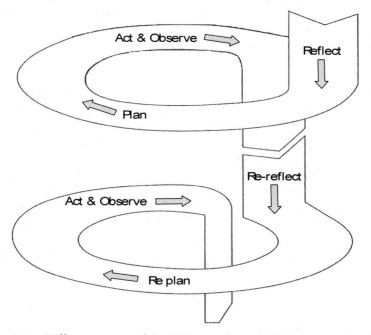

Figure 11.1   Different aspects of the PAR process are fluidly interwoven with one another (adapted from Kemmis & Wilkinson, 1998).

2006; Torres, 2004). This spiral can take many cycles before reaching clear understandings and drawing conclusions.

PAR is influential to the social justice movement (Torres, 2004) and therefore was quite appropriate to this study, because its participative nature and transformative action allowed teachers and children critically to scrutinize their understandings of, and appreciation for, justice, difference, diversity, and human dignity. By actively and collectively shaping and reshaping these understandings through storytime sessions, children became more sensitive to and aware of social justice issues, and teachers developed strategies for teaching for social justice. However, as noted previously the study was not without tensions, complexities, and challenges, which the chapter now examines.

THE TENSIONS

My philosophies and my participatory worldview encouraged me to value participatory collaborative research; however, it was not an easy task and fraught with many challenges for all participants. Indeed, the concern of power and privilege is ever present in collaborative research (Ryan &

Campbell, 2001). How the research team dealt with these concerns is discussed later in this chapter. In this section I wish to raise quandaries regarding my own position in the research project and explain how I worked through the binary of researcher/researched.

I was a PhD university researcher inviting participants into what I initially described as my study. However, as time went on I began to problematize my own position in the research project. I related to Wadsworth (2006) when she commented on the unease that she felt when writing about her own experiences in facilitating PAR (for want of a better term—Kemmis and McTaggart [2005] and McIntyre [2008] have also struggled for an appropriate term for the university researcher involved in PAR). Wadsworth (2006, p. 323) states that "the presumptuous claims of the immodest Royal 'I' (as in 'I did this' and 'I did that') sit uncomfortably with a hard-won 'we.'" I, too, felt this unease. Although I instigated the research project, it was, indeed, the educators and preschoolers who took ownership of the evolving findings. Therefore, this research project was as much theirs as it was mine, which is exactly how collaborative action research is intended. So how could I participate in this project on an equal footing with the coresearchers and not assume a leadership role such as head of the research team? How could I dispense with the binary of researcher/researched?

Addressing Tensions: Standpoints for the PAR Facilitator

According to Heron and Reason (2006), the initiating or facilitating researcher has, from the beginning of the research project, three fundamental and interdependent issues to consider. Firstly, group members should be thoroughly orientated and inducted into the methodology so that they can accept it as their own. Therefore an orientation phase that addressed this understanding was built into the research project. This consideration empowered participants cognitively and methodologically. Secondly, the initiator, or facilitator, should strive for emergent participative decision making and collaboration so that the inquiry becomes cooperative. To this end all research meetings were a participative endeavor where decisions were democratically collaborated upon. This consideration empowered participants politically. Thirdly, a climate of mutual respect, warmth, and trust should be created to allow open and free expression. This consideration was largely addressed during the orientation phase and is discussed later in this chapter. This last consideration empowered participants emotionally and interpersonally. Indeed, getting these issues clear from the outset "makes for good practice" (Heron & Reason, 2006, p. 151).

I also acknowledged Wadsworth's (2006) ideas that assisted my understanding of my position in this research project. The research project was the participants' inquiry and they became coresearchers with me as facilitator. As facilitator I assisted an iterative, emergent inquiry that was continuous and responsive, carried out over time. As facilitator I involved and worked with the coresearchers to choose the methods and questions to be asked, facilitated meetings, and circulated the responses among them; together we interpreted, analyzed, and drew conclusions and decided on new actions, and then experimented with these and monitored them continuously and over time. Disparities of power required me as the facilitator to encourage the research team to devise strategies that empowered all involved to speak and be heard accurately and with respect. The facilitator enters into an engaged, intersubjective process with participants, and together they hold up "mirrors and magnifying glasses" (Wadsworth, 2006, p. 333) to themselves and one another over a sequence of cycles so that more and more desirable changes may be a result of the inquiry. As facilitator I desired the best possible results that revealed new insights were gained by all the relevant players and were applied in practice without the need for executive direction.

Thus, it can be seen that the facilitator of PAR has a responsibility not only to produce rigorous, trustworthy research but also accountability and responsibility to those coresearchers and participants involved in the study. Therefore, when instigating and participating in this research project I endeavored to address Heron and Reason's (2006) three fundamental issues for the facilitator of action research from the beginning of the inquiry. I was also attentive to Wadsworth's (2006) explanation regarding the standpoints of the facilitator of PAR and incorporated them into this research project.

THE COMPLEXITIES

During the orientation phase the research team met fortnightly to discuss storytime, the research design, children's literature, social justice issues, our philosophies that underpinned our personal and professional lives, and a framework that we could refer to when conducting our collaborative research project. The latter involved defining the characteristics of how our research group would function. This collaborative putting together of a "group constitution" (Bray et al., 2000, p. 72) is a very important component of collaborative research and sustains collegiality, solidarity, and support (Bray et al., 2000; Whitmore & McKee, 2006). Therefore, this orientation phase was invaluable in building a strong, collaborative, caring research team that moved beyond the binary of researcher/researched.

Conversations, dialogues, and reflections during this orientation phase of the inquiry encouraged us to delve deeply into our philosophical and epistemological positions. Like most action research, it was not only the research questions that were investigated but also our philosophies and the way partnerships and relationships were supported and maintained (Goldstein, 2000; Ryan & Campbell, 2001). Individually we were very different people with different backgrounds, ages, personalities, and personal commitments. However, collectively we were all driven by the same resolve: to explore pedagogical strategies that would work to teach for social justice in early childhood classrooms. Therefore we set about to *"make this thing work, and work well!"* (Preschool B Director/teacher, meeting minutes, April 26, 2006). So how could we make sure that partnerships and relationships were supported and maintained in an atmosphere of equality and collegiality throughout the research project?

Addressing Complexities: Using Feminist Communitarianism to Build a Research Constitution

As a team we talked about our philosophies and without exception the words *caring, empathy, trust, honesty, solidarity, and open communication* were articulated by every team member. However, our understandings of how to build a research team on these virtues did not happen overnight. We undertook individual and team research over the course of the orientation phase that explored the work of proponents of an ethic of care (e.g., Greene, 1995; Noddings, 2005) and feminist communitarianism (e.g., Christians, 2006; Maguire, 2006). This was a complex task for all coresearchers (including myself); as one coresearcher explained, *"I've never done anything like this. I can see the merits, but it hurts my brain sometimes!"* (Preschool A assistant, meeting minutes, June 20, 2006).

After much research, reflection, and discussion, our research team adopted the feminist communitarian model through which to conduct this inquiry. The feminist communitarian model for conducting research is underpinned by an ethic of care. An entire chapter could be devoted to this model; however, constraints of space preclude further explanation (see Christians, 2006). Briefly it calls for trusting, collaborative, nonoppressive relationships among coresearchers. "Such an ethic presumes that investigators are committed to recognizing personal accountability, the value of individual expressiveness and caring, the capacity for empathy, and the sharing of emotionality" (Denzin & Lincoln, 2003, p. 52).

From our understandings of an ethic of care and feminist communitarianism, we based our research approach on seven principles (similar to Whitmore and McKee's [2006] six principles) that guided our research team through the inevitable ups and downs of this collaborative research endeavor. Our research team's constitution involved:

1. *Noninvasive collaboration.* All ideas, opinions, and verbalizations, however different from one's own, will be respected and collaborative resolutions considerately decided upon. Honesty will be combined with respect and accord. We respectfully and sensitively give constructive feedback.

2. *Solidarity.* All humanity, without exception, is sacred, connected, interdependent, and interrelated in a shared common journey. We are one in support.

3. *Mutual trust.* Everyone has the capability to understand and create her/his own realities. We trust each person to do this and still remain an integral part of a team.

4. *Genuine respect.* This mutual trust can be built among all people irrespective of class, race, age, gender, ability, sexuality, or background. This trust and respect take concerted time, patience, and perseverance, which we are prepared to give.

5. *Equality.* All are considered equal, as the Universal Declaration of Human Rights states. We are equal team members.

6. *Mutuality.* Transparency is important to our collaboration; therefore, we will make our agendas, interests, and goals explicit.

7. *The importance of process.* Collaborative partnerships necessitate emotional as well as intellectual involvement. This involvement goes beyond a detached working relationship to one of personal shared emotionality and connectivity. We are empathetic about the physical, emotional, mental, and spiritual needs of our coresearchers.

Therefore, the philosophical frameworks for the research project were established by the research team before the completion of the orientation phase.

THE CHALLENGES

Pushing boundaries and moving beyond binaries are challenging and, as explained, PAR does both. It is demanding for all involved (Ryan & Campbell, 2001), and this study was no exception. It was quite clear from the outset that anyone who engaged in this research project was a committed and dedicated professional who had an enthusiastic and vested interest in teaching for social justice; someone who was willing to devote a considerable amount of personal time to the research project; and someone who desired not only to reflect upon and analyze her own teaching practices but also to engage with others in this reflection and analysis. These requirements (especially the latter) became issues for many potential participants. It was always very apparent that I was not selecting participants as much as the participants were selecting the research project and me as a coresearcher. It was also understood that each participant coresearcher was interested not only in the research project but also in the others as research partners. Understandably, all this compounded the difficulty of establishing a research team.

However, when the research group *was* formed, further challenges were faced. There did exist identities of perceived power (e.g., the perceived power differentials between a university researcher and teacher researchers; preschool directors and preschool teachers; preschool teachers and teacher assistants), and, even though our research constitution endeavored to address such issues, they needed to be constantly and continually checked. How could we ensure that the research constitution was being upheld and that the research was being conducted in a manner of equality? Was the research of equal significance to each coresearcher? Was the binary of researcher/researched being displaced?

Addressing Challenges: Utilizing Reason and Bradbury's (2006) five issues on the quality and validity of action research

To address the above questions, the research team regularly reflected upon Reason and Bradbury's (2006) five issues on quality and validity of action research and adapted their suggested questions for discussion:

Issues of Emerging and Enduring Consequence

Are ideas emerging that will help us to continue to explore how children's literature impacts on our preschoolers to teach for social justice in the future?

Issues of Outcomes and Practice

Are we developing a critical and self-critical understanding of our situations? Is this research project assisting us to transform ourselves, our teaching practices, and our preschool settings positively? If yes: how and in what way? If no: how can we improve this?

Issues of Significance

Is our analysis of each storytime session of significance to each setting? How, why, and could we improve? Is the research project still important to you? If not, why not and how can we help?

Issues of Relational Practice

Do you feel an equal coresearcher? Do you feel invigorated and empowered? Are we developing critical consciousness that engenders new insights into our situations? If so, what and how? If not, how can we address this deficit?

Issues of Plural Ways of Knowing

Are we discovering what we need to know to use storytime to teach for social justice better? How are we valuing one another's knowledge?

The above reflective questions helped the research team move beyond the binary of researcher/researched and perceived power differentials in an empowering way. By way of example I offer a vignette taken from the penultimate meeting of the action research phase (pseudonyms are used):

Shelley (Preschool B Assistant): Well, I can honestly say that I really feel an equal co-researcher and I wish Pip [Preschool A Assistant] was here because I think she'd say the same. We felt funny at the beginning but, you know, I think, for me, it changed when Kate was away and I took the reading that week. Yeah, at first I felt awful listening to myself on tape. I hate my gravelly voice, but yeah, I felt that I was contributing, [pause] that my teaching practices were being looked at [pause] and because we were all involved in this [pause] I mean, all supportive, I don't know, it just didn't feel scary any more.

Lisa (Preschool A Teacher): Exactly! That's exactly how I felt about three weeks in. I suddenly thought, "Hey, this isn't so frightening [pause], scary. It's okay".

Kate (Preschool B Teacher/Director): Yeah and I think that answers the question of empowerment. It took a while because at first I was so conscious of the videotape and [pause], well, self-conscious. But after a few weeks I began to look past my self-consciousness to see ways that this was helping my practice. I guess instead of being caught up in the superficial thoughts of "Oh, no, I look terrible on TV" I moved through to the deeper issue of how I am going to teach for social justice and how important this was to me.

Lisa (Preschool A Teacher): Yeah, Kate [pause] I guess it's all about new insights into our situations. This has changed the way I look at books and storytime and the importance I place on what children say. It's made me so aware.

Karen (University Facilitator): This is great, but how is this happening [pause]? What is it that we're doing?

Kate (Preschool B Teacher/Director): Well, I think it's through the strong support we give one another, and encouragement.

Lisa (Preschool A Teacher/Director): And it's the nitty gritty stuff [pause] the really critically looking at our practices, the constructive criticisms, the suggested strategies [pause] all of that.

Kate (Preschool B Teacher/Director): Yeah, this has been worthwhile.

CONCLUSION

This chapter has highlighted the methodology of PAR and the tensions, complexities, and challenges involved for all participants. Indeed, it is time consuming; often emotionally, physically, and mentally draining; and confronting. However, it can be empowering, transformative, respectful, and collaborative. It was not the aim of this paper to dissuade researchers from embracing PAR. On the contrary, by making explicit its tensions, complexities, and challenges and offering strategies that may address these issues, it is hoped that the chapter has also highlighted the value and empowering nature of PAR and encouraged those who dare to go beyond the binary of researcher/researched.

REFERENCES

Bell, J. (2000). *Doing your research project*. Buckingham, UK: Open University Press.
Bray, J., Lee, J., Smith, L. L., & Yorks, L. (2000). *Collaborative inquiry in practice*. Thousand Oaks, CA: Sage.
Carr, W., & Kemmis, S. (1986). *Becoming critical*. London: Falmer Press.
Christians, C. G. (2006). Communitarianism: A third way. *Media Ethics*, 17(2), 5–16.
Denzin, N. K., & Lincoln, Y. S. (2003). *The landscape of qualitative research: Theories and issues* (2nd ed.). Thousand Oaks, CA: Sage.
Denzin, N. K. & Lincoln, Y. S. (2005). *The Sage handbook of qualitative research* (3rd ed.). Thousand Oaks, CA: Sage.
Fals Borda, O. (1988). *Knowledge and people's power*. New Delhi, India: Indian Social Institute.
Fine, M., Torre, M. E., Boudin, K., Bowden, I., Clark, J., Hylton, et al. (2004). Participatory Action Research: From within and beyond prison bars. In L. Weis & M. Fine (Eds.), *Working method: Research and social justice* (pp. 95–120). New York: Routledge.
Freire, P. (1993). *Pedagogy of the oppressed*. London: Penguin Books.
Gergen, M. M., & Gergen, K. J. (2003). Qualitative inquiry: Tensions and transformations. In N. K. Denzin & Y. S. Lincoln (Eds.), *The landscape of qualitative research: Theories and issues* (2nd ed., pp. 575–610). Thousand Oaks, CA: Sage.
Goldstein, L. S. (2000). Ethical dilemmas in designing collaborative research: Lessons learned the hard way. *Qualitative Studies in Education*, 13(5), 517–530.
Greene, M. (1995). *Releasing the imagination: Essays on education, the arts and social change*. San Francisco, CA: Jossey-Bass.
Greenwood, D., & Levin, M. (2005). Reconstructing the relationships between universities and society through action research. In K. N. Denzin & Y. S. Lincoln (Eds.), *The landscape of qualitative research* (2nd ed., pp. 131–166). Thousand Oaks, CA: Sage.
Habermas, J. (1996). *Between facts and norms* (W. Rehg, Trans). Cambridge, MA: MIT Press.
Heron, J., & Reason, P. (2006). The practice of co-operative inquiry: Research 'with' rather than 'on' people. In P. Reason & H. Bradbury (Eds.), *The handbook of action research* (pp. 144–154). London: Sage.
Herr, K., & Anderson, G. L. (2005). *The action research dissertation: A guide for students and faculty*. Thousand Oaks, CA: Sage.
Jones, J. K. (2006). Work in progress: The Magic Gardens project. *International Journal of the Arts in Society*, 1(1), 85–96.
Kemmis, S., & McTaggart, R. (2005). Participatory action research: Communicative action and the public sphere. In N. K. Denzin & Y. S. Lincoln (Eds.), *The Sage handbook of qualitative research* (3rd ed., pp. 559–603). Thousand Oaks, CA: Sage.

Kemmis, S., & Wilkinson, M. (1998). PAR and the study of practice. In B. Atweh, S. Kemmis, & P. Weeks (Eds.), *Action research in practice: Partnerships for social justice* (pp. 21–36). New York: Routledge.

Mac Naughton, G. (2001). Action research. In G. Mac Naughton, A. Rolfe, & I. Siraj-Blatchford (Eds.), *Doing early childhood research: International perspectives on theory and practice* (pp. 208–223). Crows Nest, Australia: Allen & Unwin.

Maguire, P. (2006). Uneven ground: Feminisms in action research. In P. Reason & H. Bradbury (Eds.), *The handbook of action research* (pp. 60–70). London: Sage.

Martin, G., lisahunter, & McLaren, P. (2006). Participatory action research (teams)/action research. In K. Tobin & J. Kincheloe (Eds.), *Doing educational research—A handbook* (pp. 157–190). Rotterdam, The Netherlands: Sense.

McIntyre, A. (2008). *Participatory action research.* Thousand Oaks, CA: Sage.

Noddings, N. (2005). What have we learned? In N. Noddings (Ed.), *Educating citizens for global awareness* (pp. 122–135). New York: Teacher's College Press.

Reason, P., & Bradbury, H. (2006). Introduction: Inquiry and participation in search of a world worthy of human aspiration. In P. Reason & H. Bradbury (Eds.), *Handbook of action research* (pp. 1–14). London: Sage.

Ryan, S., & Campbell, S. (2001). Doing research for the first time. In G. Mac Naughton, S. A Rolfe, & I. Siraj-Blatchford (Eds.), *Doing early childhood research: International perspectives on theory and practice* (pp. 56–63). Crows Nest, Australia: Allen & Unwin.

Skolimowski, H. (1995). *The participatory mind: A new theory of knowledge and of the universe (Arkana).* London: Penguin.

Torres, M. (2004). The role of participatory democracy in the critical praxis of social justice. In J. O'Donnell, M. Pruyn, & R. Chavez Chavez (Eds.), *Social justice in these times* (pp. 15–32). Greenwich, CT: Information Age.

Troyna, B. (1994). Blind faith? Empowerment and educational research. *International Studies in Sociology in Education, 4*(1), 3–24.

Wadsworth, Y. (2006). The mirror, the magnifying glass, the compass and the map: Facilitating participatory action research. In P. Reason & H. Bradbury (Eds.), *Handbook of action research* (pp. 322–334). London: Sage.

Whitmore, E., & McKee, C. (2006). Six street youth who could . . . In P. Reason & H. Bradbury (Eds.), *Handbook of action research* (pp. 297–303). London: Sage.

12 Understanding Cultural Differences Between Western and Confucian[1] Teaching and Learning

Peng Zhou and Cec Pedersen

ABSTRACT

Cultures of the West and the East are often seen as a binary with different values and assumptions underlying each. Differences between Western and Confucian cultures can result in frustrations and confusion for cross-cultural learners and therefore impact on their learning performance. This chapter explores differences between Western and Confucian cultures from an international education perspective to draw implications for Western educators involved in transnational or international education. In particular, a conceptual framework is presented to help move beyond the binary. Using the conceptual framework, the authors argue that, while Confucian culture may impose constraints on Confucian-heritage students' study of Australian business courses in terms of teaching and learning styles, it is possible to develop Confucian-heritage students to meet Western education requirements if measures are taken and efforts are made to bridge cultural gaps in two-way understanding and adaptation. The chapter draws from literature on cross-cultural teaching and learning as well as the authors' experiences in teaching Confucian-heritage students under transnational arrangements.

> *"Culture is more often a source of conflict than of synergy.*
> *Cultural differences are a nuisance at best and often a disaster."*
> *—Dr. Geert Hofstede*

INTRODUCTION

The trend toward globalization has brought about many fundamental changes and developments in the international education sector for Australian universities. One such development in the past few decades is the rapid growth of Australian-sourced transnational education programs in neighboring Southeastern Asian markets. This rapid expansion of transnational education programs for Australian universities comes at a time when Asian economies are growing more quickly than their Western counterparts (Sugimoto, 2006). Furthermore, recent developments in information technology and in particular the greater availability of the Internet make Australian higher education services more accessible and affordable for those Asian students who prefer to study toward a Western degree in their home countries (Ziguras, 2001).

According to IDP Education Australia (2008), offshore international students enrolled in Australian transnational education programs in Semester 1, 2007, accounted for 24% of all international students studying with Australian universities. The top five source countries were Singapore, Malaysia, Hong Kong, China, and Vietnam, which in total had 49,709 students studying with Australian universities under transnational partnership arrangements with local educational institutions in those five countries. Of particular note is that China is emerging as Australia's biggest transnational education market with 300 joint education programs in operation with Australian universities and some 30,000 students enrolled in these joint programs in 2007, up 42.4% from the previous financial year (Australian Education International, 2007).

As a result of the continued internationalization of Australian universities, academics are being challenged to teach an increasingly diverse student population from different cultures with different learning styles. In particular, teaching offshore international students in China often exposes Australian academics to "cultural shock" because they may need not only to adjust their personal lifestyles to suit local customs but also to adapt their pedagogical approaches to meet the Confucian-heritage students' needs. On the other hand, cultural differences in terms of learning styles have been identified as a more serious obstacle than language proficiency for international students from a Confucian heritage to study with Australian universities (Egege & Kutieleh, 2004), as they may often find themselves being challenged to cope with demanding academic requirements with which they are not familiar.

Given the above background, this chapter aims to discuss cultural differences between Western and Confucian teaching and learning traditions and their implications for pedagogical adaptation, based on the authors' involvements in teaching an Australian bachelor of business administration program to offshore Confucian-heritage students under a transnational arrangement with two Chinese partners. A conceptual framework elaborating the Western and the Confucian binary is developed from a teaching and learning perspective to reflect both dynamic interchanges between the Western and the Confucian paradigms and static attributes that are perceived to be associated with each of the two paradigms. Based on this conceptual framework, such binary opposites between the Australian and the Confucian-heritage teaching and learning orientations as analytic versus holistic thinking, active versus passive learning, deep versus surface approach, and abstract versus practical reasoning are discussed with implications drawn for Western academics involved in teaching Confucian-heritage students. The discussion then considers how to go beyond the Western—Confucian binary in a globalization era, followed by a brief conclusion to reflect the authors' key standpoints.

THE WESTERN AND CONFUCIAN BINARY

A typical approach to addressing cultural differences between Western and Confucian cultures is to posit them as a binary. For example, Hofstede (1980) developed a framework to understand broad differences in national cultures based on five binary dimensions. In the same spirit, this chapter proposes a conceptual framework (refer to Figure 12.1) that depicts binary differences between the Western and the Confucian traditions of teaching and learning, based on the contrastive *yin-yang* principle of Chinese Taoist philosophy. This conceptual framework will guides further discussion in this chapter.

The yin-yang circle at the heart of Figure 12.1 suggests that relationships between the Western and the Confucian paradigms are so dynamic and complex that each paradigm may influence the other via interchanges

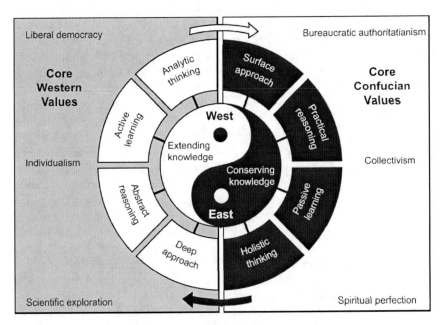

Figure 12.1 A conceptual framework to illustrate cultural differences between the Western and the Confucian traditions of teaching and learning (developed by Peng Zhou).

between the two. As suggested by Rizvi (1997), cultures are dynamic and engage in constant interchanges with each other to survive and develop. In other words, culture is not constant and it changes as the world changes (Crawford, 2009). The eight binary attributes in the outer circle are distinctive features associated with each of the two competing paradigms of the Western and the Confucian, in contrastive colors of white and black. These culturally specific attributes may evolve over time but are relatively static in the short term, thus allowing differences between cultures to be captured and interpreted. The outside layer (illustrated in the split square boxes) reflects broader core cultural values underpinning each of the Western and the Confucian teaching and learning traditions.

Three core value differences between cultures are identified as sources to explain opposite features of those traditions. The first value difference lies in the individualism versus collectivism dimension. While the Western tradition is characterized by individualism, the Confucian is associated with collectivism (Hofstede, 1980; Trompanaars, 1993). The second value difference is reflected in the liberal democracy versus bureaucratic authoritarianism binary. In the egalitarian and rationality dominated West, liberal democracy is upheld as a fundamental guiding principle for education because it is perceived as vital for a nation to operate both dialectically and spatially (see Dewey, 1950). However, in the hierarchical and relationship-oriented Confucian societies, a bureaucratic authoritarian approach that regards knowledge as residing with authorities is widely accepted because it is believed to be beneficial for maintaining harmonious relation between teacher and student (Hu, 2002). The final value difference is identified in the scientific exploration versus spiritual perfection dichotomy. While education in the West has centered on scientific disputation since Socrates (Olsen, 2010), teaching and learning in the Confucian societies have long been viewed as an important avenue for cultivating a student's moral qualities (Scollon, 1999).

From an educational philosophy perspective, the individualistic Western approach to knowledge acquisition is assumed to be value independent with active learning and individual development as a central focus in education (Ryan & Louie, 2007), while in a collectivist, Confucian heritage students are often perceived as passive rote learners because of their tendency to memorize mechanically without real understanding (Wong, 2004). Furthermore, liberal democracy and scientific spirit in the Socratic tradition have underpinned analytic thinking in Western educational philosophy (Olsen, 2010), while a typical bureaucratic authoritarianism and spiritual perfection orientation favor holistic thinking in the Confucian teaching and learning tradition (Graham & Lam, 2003; Lloyd, 1996). Accordingly, Western learners are assumed to take an active, deep approach to learning and are thus able to understand abstract theories and apply them to practice. By contrast, Confucian-heritage students are often criticized for taking a surface approach to learning and can handle only concrete facts (Biggs, 1996).

As shown in Figure 12.1, analytical thinking, active learning, abstract reasoning, and a deep approach to learning have their roots in the Western tradition of liberal democracy, individualism, and scientific exploration (Dewey, 1950; Olsen, 2010). By contrast, holistic thinking, passive learning, practical reasoning, and a surface approach to learning are more in accordance with the Confucian-heritage tradition of bureaucratic authoritarianism, collectivism, and spiritual perfection (Tweed & Lehman, 2002). For example, while capabilities such as critical questioning, independent learning, and analytical reasoning are dominant Western educational values (Egege & Kutieleh, 2004; Mason, 2007), other ideals like a tempered questioning of authority, dependent learning by following clear instructions, and harmony of thought as well as harmony in relationships are more valued in traditional Confucian-heritage cultures (Liu, 2008). These different traditions of thinking and learning are products of their own cultural history and social development, which evolved over a long time in eras of isolation and separation owing to geographic distances and lack of communications.

ANALYTIC VERSUS HOLISTIC THINKING

Many studies have documented cultural differences in traditions of thinking and systems of reasoning (e.g., Nisbett, Peng, Choi, & Norenzayan, 2001; Norenzayan, Smith, Kim, & Nisbett, 2002). An analytic mode of thinking has been found to be more prevalent in low-context Western cultures. This mode focuses on the object and tries to separate the object from its context and then uses rules to explain and predict the object's behavior. By contrast, a holistic mode of thinking has been held to be more prevalent in high-context Confucian-heritage cultures (Graham & Lam, 2003). This mode examines the context or field as a whole with a focus on relationships among objects and on object–field relationships, often involving intuitive and *dialectical* reasoning to seek the *middle way* between conflicting propositions (Norenzayan et al., 2002). Western students are typically regarded as verbal/analytic learners who favor abstract analysis based on formal logic, whereas Confucian-heritage students are often stereotyped as visual/holistic learners who either tend to think illogically or are incapable of critical thinking (Thompson & Ku, 2005).

More particularly, the analytic mode of thinking can be traced to the Socratic rationality tradition that is dominant in Western cultures, while the holistic mode of thinking is more prevalent in relationship-focused Confucian-heritage cultures. The Socratic rationality tradition values the seeking of formal logic knowledge in education through critical inquiry, scientifically sound research, and evidence of good reasoning, and this tradition rests on the assumption that truth exists and should be sought after as the ultimate goal of study in any knowledge discipline. However, this Socratic rationality tradition is in strong contrast to the Confucian-heritage ideal that relies on analogy, intuitive induction, and circular reasoning (Egege & Kutieleh, 2004; Graham & Lam, 2003; Lloyd, 1996). Also, Confucian philosophy advocates the end objective of any study should be that the moral perfection of one's own self (On, 1996) rather than seeking truthful knowledge for its own sake.

The distinction between analytic and holistic thinking has implications for transnational education in a globalized era. For example, many Western academics are often bewildered to find that their Confucian-heritage students tend to prefer indirect, or inductive, reasoning. They normally present the details first in order to establish the context and relationships. This indirect writing approach taken by Confucian-heritage students contrasts with the Western linear thought of putting the main point up front and then supporting it with more specific details (Roberts & Tuleja, 2008). On the other hand, many Confucian-heritage students are uncomfortable when their performances are assessed based on unfamiliar criteria of analytic thinking which has never been explicitly taught to them either in their previous education with Chinese secondary schools or in their current study at Western universities. This raises the issue of critical or analytic thinking needs being incorporated into a well-developed transition program which prepares Confucian-heritage students for their Western education environment (Egege & Kutieleh, 2004).

It was found that Confucian-heritage students could improve their assignment writing in English more easily if this vital difference of thinking between the two cultures were explicitly explained to them by their Australian lecturers. For example, during our teaching visits to our Chinese partnership institutes, we purposefully embedded such fundamental academic writing skills as critical and analytical thinking as well as essay and report writing into our intensive, face-to-face lectures. We normally began our teaching sessions with explicit explanations of cultural differences between Australia and China in terms of university business assignment writing. Once the students had some fundamental understanding of these academic cultural differences, we would then introduce them to the basic structures of academic essays and reports. In this way, we gradually familiarized our Confucian-heritage students with such foreign notions of critical and analytical thinking and taught them how to use these fundamental academic writing skills in their essay and report assignments.

ACTIVE VERSUS PASSIVE LEARNING

Another significant difference between Western and Confucian-heritage learning cultures is that active, independent learning is desired and valued in Western universities, whereas students from a Confucian heritage are often stereotyped as rote learners who passively receive established knowledge and seldom challenge the authority of their teachers (Wang & Moore,

2007). More specifically, the emphasis in Western education systems is on individual development, self-esteem, autonomy in learners, participative learning, and two-way dialogue (Robinson, 1999). By contrast, the Confucian educational philosophy values self-perfection, behavioral reform, compliance with authority, pragmatic learning, and seeking knowledge from authorities (Tweed & Lehman, 2002).

This difference can be explained by cultural differences between the Western and the Confucian teaching and learning traditions in terms of knowledge acquisition and dissemination. In accordance with the liberal democracy and scientific exploration tradition of the West, knowledge is something that exists with the learners (De Man, 2006), which can be discovered or constructed only through critical questioning and probing. Individual intelligence or ability plays a key role in the knowledge acquisition process (Li, 2002). By contrast, Confucian learning philosophy believes knowledge exists with authorities (Chan & Chan, 2005) and students can acquire such knowledge from their teachers only through personal willpower and effort (Tweed & Lehman, 2002). Intelligence is not an inhibitor to a person's educability (On, 1996). Put in another way, it has been argued that the West values creation or extension of knowledge while the Confucian tradition emphasizes accumulation and conservation of knowledge (Ballard & Clanchy, 1991). In other words, the Chinese search for *Virtue* while their Western counterparts search for *the Truth.*

However, recent studies challenge this claim of a static difference of learning style between Western learners and their Chinese peers. For example, Confucian-heritage students were found to memorize with understanding rather than rote learning without understanding (Marton, Alba, & Kun, 1996). Furthermore, their learning style has been found to be flexible and depends on the educational environment they are exposed to (Volet & Kee, 1993). That is, while many Confucian-heritage students get used to the passive learning style as a result of the highly competitive examination system in traditional Confucian-heritage societies, their learning style can be adaptive when they are introduced to the Western way of teaching (Wong, 2004). Indeed, Confucian-heritage students have been found to be very responsive to their teachers' instructions (Liu, 2008). Nevertheless, this adaptation process needs to take a progressive approach to help the Confucian-heritage students gradually transit from their passive memory-oriented and content-based learning style to a more active student-centered and problem-based one (Huang, 2005).

With this understanding of the Confucian-heritage students in mind, we also explained to the students why they would be expected to write essays and reports during their study at Australian universities. In particular, caution was paid to emphasize that the Australian essay and report writing types of assignments encourage students to develop their independent learning capacity through active searching for information and critically evaluating the opinions of others rather than passive memorizing of textbook contents and blindly believing the views of authorities. Of note is that, if the Australian lecturers did not explain such important issues as how to avoid unintentional plagiarism through proper referencing, paraphrasing, and synthesizing clearly to the Confucian-heritage students, then quite likely many of the students would resort to their old style of learning by directly copying and pasting large proportions of their writings from the sources even without using quotation marks.

DEEP VERSUS SURFACE APPROACH

Closely related to the active versus passive learning, a deep versus surface approach has been identified as a distinctive feature between Western learners and Confucian-heritage students. Western learners are portrayed as being more inclined to adopt a deep approach to learning because they are more likely to accept involvement and learning through understanding. On the other hand, Confucian-heritage students are often perceived to take a surface approach to their study because they are assessment-driven and lack engagement in the learning process, and their practice of mechanical memorization does not enhance understanding (Wong, 2004). However, this distinction between the Western learners, and Confucian-heritage students' preferred learning styles fails to explain the fact that many Confucian-heritage students outperform their Western counterparts in terms of academic performance (Biggs, 1996).

Research also indicates that not all Western learners are the assertive and independent deep thinkers they are assumed to be (Kember & Gow, 1991; Ryan & Louie, 2007), and that the Confucian tradition of memorization through repetition can be used to deepen understanding and achieve high levels of academic performance (Cooper, 2004). Indeed, there is a distinction between rote/surface and repetitive learning. While rote/surface learning is commonly described as learning without understanding, repetitive learning has the intention to understand (Biggs, 1996). Confucian-heritage students can be deep learners because they tend to memorize through repetitive learning with a purpose to understand (Marton, Alba, & Kun, 1996).

However, this distinction between a deep versus surface approach has implications for transnational education involving Western academics teaching Confucian-heritage students. On the one hand, Western educators need to tailor their teaching approaches to suit the Confucian-heritage students' learning style to make their teachings effective (De Man, 2006). For example, well-structured teaching notes and detailed explanations of study requirements may need to be prepared by Western academics for their Chinese audiences who might show lack of initiative and be teacher-centered. On the other hand, Confucian-heritage students also need to better understand their Western educators' expectations and their own learning approaches to enable effective learning to happen in the classroom.

More specifically, Western educators need to take an incremental approach to introducing gradually the Confucian-heritage students to the Western way of independent and in-depth thinking, based on better understandings of their learning styles and study environments. For example, while many Confucian-heritage students were found to copy one another's assignments and write superficially on a given topic, it turned out one important reason behind this phenomenon was that they did not know how to search the university's library databases to find the right information required for their assignment writing. Therefore, they had to rely on the same limited information located by a few top performing students. To help the Confucian-heritage students master the fundamental skill of information searching for academic purposes, we had personally to demonstrate to the students how to find the right type of information for their assignment writing purposes. More importantly, we had to show them how to incorporate the information into their own writings and split a broad given topic into logically related smaller parts so as to demonstrate their analytic thinking capability.

ABSTRACT VERSUS PRACTICAL REASONING

A final contrast between the Western and Confucian-heritage learners lies in the dimension of abstract versus practical reasoning, as illustrated in Figure 12.1. Western teaching philosophy highly values abstract reasoning about concrete situations in the forms of principles, laws, and rules, whereas the Confucian way of learning is more sense-based, focused on concrete facts (De Man, 2006), and more likely to emphasize the practical outcomes of education (Tweed & Lehman, 2002). In contrast to the Western belief that only objective knowledge obtained through scientific inquiry is truth and that subjective knowledge based purely on personal experience is mere opinion, consolidation of experience is still the dominant mode of knowledge building and an important means of teaching even in modern Chinese societies (Chan & Chan, 2005).

The practical orientation to learning in the Confucian-heritage culture is similar on the surface to the pragmatic approach to education advocated by Dewey (1950) but lacks his philosophical underpinnings. While Confucian teaching emphasizes history and accumulated experiences, and practical knowledge is implicit in the Confucian doctrine of the unity of knowledge and action, its main focus is on the development of one's own self as a morally functioning person who is flexible and adaptable (Chan & Chan, 2005). However, Dewey did not place the same emphasis on history or culture, although he believed in practical human experiences and regarded them as finalities. Dewey also believed that learning should be its own end and that education loses meaning if focused on an extrinsic goal (Tweed & Lehman, 2002).

The contraction of abstract versus practical reasoning between the Western and the Confucian education philosophies has practical implications for Western academics involved in teaching international students of Confucian heritage. Firstly, Confucian-heritage learners may find learning abstract Western-style business theories and concepts boring or at least less interesting. Western academics may need to adapt their teaching styles to accommodate the practicality preference of the Confucian-heritage students by including more contextualized case studies to make understanding of the abstract theories easier for the students. Secondly, metaphors and personal experience–based stories have been found to be effective in teaching Confucian-heritage students because they cater for their demand for concrete facts. In addition, Western academics should demonstrate with examples rather than simply explain in words how abstract theories could be used to resolve practical problems (De Man, 2006).

By understanding the Confucian-heritage students' underdevelopment of abstract reasoning and developing a central focus on practicality, we had to develop different strategies to help cultivate their potential. For example, when lecturing about leadership course theories, one of the authors tried to relate the Western charismatic leadership theory to such well-known Chinese entrepreneurs as the Lenovo founder Liu Chuanzhi and Haier CEO Zhang Ruimin. Also, once the Confucian-heritage students were familiarized with such Western academic writing skills as critical and analytical thinking, essay and report structure, and referencing, practical examples from past students' assignments were utilized to show how these skills were actually used by different students in the past and what sort of common problems students might have with composing similar types of assignments for their studying at Australian universities. It was found that Confucian-heritage students learnt more quickly through examples that are relevant to their own cultures and contexts.

BEYOND THE WESTERN–CONFUCIAN BINARY

In the globalized era of transnational education, Western educators involved in teaching Confucian learners need to be aware of the distinctive characteristics of their students if they aim to achieve sustainable and effective teaching results. Although many of those binary opposites identified above often tend to be overstated or even misinterpreted in the literature, they provide an important basis for understanding the interface between Confucian-heritage learners and Western modes of education (Gu & Schweisfurth, 2006). Indeed, failure to acknowledge these contrastive differences will put an educator at risk of being inconsiderate of the cultural context in which the teaching and learning take place (Smith & Smith, 1999). As noted by Hofstede (1997), one of the basic skills for surviving in a multicultural world is to understand "the cultural values of the others with whom one has to cooperate" (p. 238).

However, the Western–Confucian binary should not be viewed as a static and unchangeable status quo. As observed by Rizvi (1997), throughout its long history, the Confucian tradition of teaching and learning prospered in China and neighboring Southeastern Asian countries because of its capability to adapt to different local contexts. Even nowadays, while the Confucian tradition of teaching and learning may be incompatible with the Socratic method of Western education (Chan & Chan, 2005), Confucian-heritage students have been found to be eager to learn foreign-sourced knowledge and they are capable of adapting to Western-style educational environments (Gu & Schweisfurth, 2006; Kennedy, 2002). Indeed, they often outperform their Western counterparts once they get over the initial hurdle of cultural adaptation.

To go beyond the Western–Confucian binary, as Western educators, simply knowing the distinctive characteristics of Confucian learners and adjusting pedagogical approaches accordingly are not enough to ensure their teaching effectiveness in the globalized era of education. To fully embrace the changes brought about by internationalization of higher education, Western academics should take one step further to try to expand their own knowledge of teaching and learning by observing and absorbing different pedagogical approaches from other cultures (Kennedy, 2002). By borrowing ideas from different traditions, Western academics can not only better accommodate their international students' different needs and learning styles but also better service their domestic students with more effective methods of instruction (De Man, 2006), in order to educate their students to be globalized citizens who can appreciate cultural diversity and handle intercultural conflicts (OECD and the World Bank, 2007).

One way globalization can really facilitate changes in the internationalization of higher education is to bring along a two-way appreciation of the Western/Confucian paradigms in the form of a hybrid approach, as suggested in the conceptual framework (Figure 12.1) developed for this chapter. Taking a Western value-laden assimilationist or universalist approach by simply changing students' learning styles through remedial education is inadequate because it runs the risk of educational imperialism (Evans, 1995) or cultural imperialism (Chambers, 2003; McBurnie & Ziguras, 2007). It is also unfeasible to implement a Chinese accommodation approach by requiring Western academics to adapt their teaching styles to suit every single Confucian student's needs. This would be unrealistic and improper (Volet, 1999). What really can be done is for Western educators to have a deeper understanding of the cultural contexts of Confucian-heritage students and for the Confucian-heritage students to learn to adapt to Western educational environments (Vardanega, Hatcher, & Crombie, 2003). Arguably, perhaps only the hybrid approach that is becoming a basic characteristic of globalization can provide a practical solution to the problem (Crawford, 2009; Rizvi, 1997; Robinson, 1999).

CONCLUSION

Discourses of the internationalization of higher education often take the binary logic to position Western and Confucian teaching and learning styles as being either incompatible or incommensurable opposites. As identified in the conceptual framework presented in this chapter, such binary opposites as analytic/holistic, active/passive, deep/surface, and abstract/practical are often used to illustrate distinctive differences between the Western and the Confucian teaching and learning traditions. While these static binary opposites should not be taken for granted, they do provide a useful basis to gain a clearer insight into the interface between Confucian learners and Western modes of education. Moreover, the conceptual framework suggests that to go beyond the West and the East binary a hybrid approach brought about by globalization may engage the Western and the Confucian paradigms in intercultural dialogue and therefore provide a solution to the perceived incompatible or incommensurable problems between Western teaching and Confucian learning styles.

As observed by Spizzica (1997), different cultures value different types of knowledge and skills differently. The surface approach is popular with Confucian-heritage students simply because traditional Confucian education philosophy emphasizes learning through memorizing classics and conserving knowledge by accumulating established authorities' wisdom, which is not conducive to the development of analytical thinking and active learning. Furthermore, Confucian-heritage students prefer concrete examples and have a tendency to seek the middle way of resolution so as to maintain harmony in societies. As a result, they are generalized as weak in abstract reasoning and lacking in critical thinking. However, Confucian-heritage students are not passive rote learners as they are perceived to be. Indeed, they are flexible with their approaches and are capable of adapting to the requirements of new educational environments, but Western educators need to understand that there are many implicit academic conventions as well as institutional requirements and disciplinary expectations that have to be explicitly explained to Confucian-heritage students.

More practically, while Western students' learning journeys start with exploration and are then followed by the development of skills, Confucian-heritage learners typically believe that skills should be first developed and performance will follow as a result (Wong, 2004). To help Confucian-heritage students settle into Western education environments more effectively, Australian universities should develop a well-wrapped transition program to help to equip these students with such fundamental academic skills as information searching, critical and analytical thinking, essay and report writing, referencing during an orientation process. Likewise, Australian educators involved in teaching Confucian-heritage students either onshore or offshore may consider incorporating these fundamental academic skills in their own lecturing about disciplinary courses so that they will not be disadvantaged because of not possessing these important skills in their prior study under a Confucian education system.

NOTES

1. Within this chapter, the term *Confucian students* is used as a term that denotes students from mainland China, rather than Chinese students per se. These students have typically been educated in a system that is based on strong Confucian values.

REFERENCES

Australian Education International. (2007). *Market data snapshot: People's Republic of China*, Number 16, May 2007. Retrieved from http://aei.gov. au/Aei/

Ballard, B., & Clanchy, J. (1991). *Teaching students from overseas: A brief guide for lecturers and supervisors*. Melbourne, Australia: Longman Cheshire.

Biggs, J. (1996). Western misperceptions of the Confucian-heritage learning culture. In D. Watkins & J. Biggs (Eds.), *The Chinese learner: Cultural, psychological and contextual influences* (pp. 45–67). Hong Kong: Comparative Education Research Center & Australian Council for Educational Research.

Chambers, E. (2003). Cultural imperialism or pluralism? Cross-cultural electronic teaching in the humanities. *Arts and Humanities in Higher Education, 2*(3), 249–264.

Chan, K. L., & Chan, C. L. W. (2005). Chinese culture, social work education and research. *International Social Work, 48*(4), 381–389.

Cooper, B. J. (2004). The enigma of the Chinese learner. *Accounting Education, 13*(3), 289–310.

Crawford, R. D. (2009). *East of West and West of East*. Retrieved from http://www.authorsonline.co.uk/book/763/East_of_West_and_West_of_East/

De Man, H. (2006). *Teaching management to Chinese students: A few notes from theory and practice*. Paper presented at the "Teaching the Chinese Learner," seminar, Leiden University, The Netherlands.

Dewey, J. (1950). *Democracy and education: An introduction to the philosophy of education*. New York: Macmillan.

Egege, S., & Kutieleh, S. (2004). Critical thinking: Teaching foreign notions to foreign students. *International Education Journal, 4*(4), 75–85.

Evans, T. D. (1995). Globalisation, post-Fordism and open and distance education. *Distance Education, 16*(2), 256–269.

Graham, J. L., & Lam, N. M. (2003, October). The Chinese negotiation. *Harvard Business Review*, 2–11.

Gu, Q., & Schweisfurth, M. (2006). Who adapts? Beyond cultural models of 'the' Chinese learner. *Language, Culture and Curriculum, 19*(1), 74–89.

Hofstede, G. (1980). *Culture's consequences: International differences in work-related values.* Newbury Park, CA: Sage.

Hofstede, G. (1997). *Cultures and organizations: Software of the mind.* New York: McGraw-Hill.

Hu, G. (2002). Potential cultural resistance to pedagogical imports: The case of communicative language teaching in China. *Language, Culture and Curriculum, 15*(2), 93–105.

Huang, R. (2005). Chinese international students' perceptions of the problem-based learning experience. *Journal of Hospitality, Leisure, Sport and Tourism Education, 4*(2), 36–43.

IDP Education Australia. (2008). *Fast facts: Higher education.* Retrieved from http://www.idp.com/research/fast_facts/higher_education.aspx

Kember, D., & Gow, L. (1991). A challenge to the anecdotal stereotype of the Asian student. *Studies in Higher Education, 16*(2), 117–128.

Kennedy, P. (2002). Learning cultures and learning styles: Myth-understanding about adult (Hong Kong) Chinese learners. *International Journal of Lifelong Education, 21*(5), 430–445.

Li, J. (2002). A cultural model of learning: Chinese "heart and mind for wanting to learn." *Journal of Cross-Cultural Psychology, 33*(3), 248–269.

Liu, J. (2008). From learner passive to learner active? The case of Chinese postgraduate students studying marketing in the UK. *International Journal of Management Education, 7*(2), 33–40.

Lloyd, G. E. R. (1996). *Adversaries and authorities: Investigations into ancient Greek and Chinese science.* Cambridge, UK: Cambridge University Press.

Marton, F., Alba, G. D., & Kun, T. L. (1996). Memorizing and understanding: The keys to the paradox? In D. Watkins & J. Biggs (Eds.), *The Chinese learner: Cultural, psychological and contextual influence.* Hong Kong: Comparative Education Research Center & Australian Council for Educational Research.

Mason, M. (2007). Critical thinking and learning. *Educational Philosophy and Theory, 39*(4), 39–49.

McBurnie, G., & Ziguras, C. (2007). *Transnational education: Issues and trends in offshore higher education.* London: Routledge.

Nisbett, R. E., Peng, K., Choi, I., & Norenzayan, A. (2001). Culture and systems of thought: Holistic versus analytic cognition. *Psychological Review, 108*(2), 291–310.

Norenzayan, A., Smith, E. E., Kim, B. J., & Nisbett, R. E. (2002). Cultural preferences for formal versus intuitive reasoning, *Cognitive Science, 26,* 653–684.

OECD and the World Bank (2007). *Cross-border tertiary education: A way towards capacity development.* Paris: OECD.

Olsen, G. W. (2010). Introduction. In C. Dawson (Ed.), *The crisis of Western education* (pp. vi–xx). New York: The Catholic University of America Press.

On, W. (1996). The cultural context for Chinese learners: Conceptions of learning in the Confucian tradition. In D. Watkins & J. Biggs (Eds.), *The Chinese learner: Cultural, psychological and contextual influence* (pp. 25–42). Hong Kong: Comparative Education Research Center & Australian Council for Educational Research.

Rizvi, F. (1997). Beyond the East–West divide: Education and the dynamics of Australian-Asia relations. *Australian Educational Researcher, 24*(1), 13–25.

Roberts, E., & Tuleja, E. A. (2008). When West meets East: Teaching a managerial communication course in Hong Kong. *Journal of Business and Technical Communication, 22*(4), 474–489.

Robinson, B. (1999). Asian learner, Western models: Some discontinuities and issues for distance educators. In R. Carr, O. Jegede, W. Tat-meng, & Y. Kin-sun

(Eds.), *The Asian distance learner* (pp. 33–48). Hong Kong: Open University of Hong Kong.

Ryan, J., & Louie, K. (2007). False dichotomy? 'Western' and 'Confucian' concepts of scholarship and learning. *Educational Philosophy and Theory, 39*(4), 404–417.

Scollon, S. (1999). Not to waste words or students: Confucian and Socratic discourse in the tertiary classroom. In E. Hinkel (Ed.), *Culture in second language teaching and learning* (pp. 13–27). Cambridge, UK: Cambridge University Press.

Smith, P. J., & Smith, S. N. (1999). Differences between Chinese and Australian students: Some implications for distance educations. *Distance Education, 20*(1), 64–80.

Spizzica, M. (1997). Cultural differences within "Western" and "Eastern" education. In Z. Golebiowski & H. Borland (Ed.), *Academic communication across disciplines and cultures* (pp. 248–257). Melbourne, Australia: Victoria University of Technology.

Sugimoto, K. (2006). Australia's transnational higher education in the Asia-Pacific region: Its strategies and quality insurance. In F. Huang (Ed.), *Transnational higher education in Asia and the Pacific region (RIHE international publication series 10)* (pp. 1–19). Hiroshima, Japan: Research Institute for Higher Education, Hiroshima University.

Thompson, L., & Ku, H. Y. (2005). Chinese graduate students' experiences and attitudes toward online learning. *Educational Media International, 42*(1), 33–47.

Trompanaars, F. (1993). *Riding the waves of culture.* London: Nicholas Brealy.

Tweed, R. G., & Lehman, D. R. (2002). Learning considered within a cultural context: Confucian and Socratic approaches. *American Psychologist, 57*(2), 89–99.

Vardanega, L., Hatcher, D., & Crombie, K. (2003). *Maintaining sustainable learning environments in a cross cultural context.* Paper presented at the 16th ODLAA biennial forum conference, Canberra, Australia.

Volet, S. E. (1999). Learning across cultures: Appropriateness of knowledge transfer. *International Journal of Educational Research, 31*, 625–643.

Volet, S. E., & Kee, J. P. P. (1993). *Studying in Singapore—studying in Australia: A student perspective.* Melbourne, Australia: School of Education, Murdoch University.

Wang, T., & Moore, L. (2007). Exploring learning style preferences of Chinese postgraduate students in Australian transnational programs. *International Journal of Pedagogies and Learning, 3*(2), 31–41.

Wong, J. K. (2004). Are the learning styles of Asian international students culturally or contextually based? *International Education Journal, 4*(4), 154–166.

Ziguras, C. (2001). Educational technology in transnational higher education in South East Asia: The cultural politics of flexible learning. *Educational Technology & Society, 4*(4), 8–18.

Part III
Considering Contexts

Part III Introduction

Alison Mander

In this final part of the book, the underlying theme is *Considering Contexts*. Here the authors have engaged with the problematic surrounding the common use of binaries in specific research contexts to explore alternative ways of working within these situations. The foundation of these research chapters is the practical working out of resolutions to commonly framed binaries. The contexts are diverse and original and range from higher education in different countries to specific workplace competencies, and from how the print media represent gender to how disability impacts on the student learning journey. The most common motivation of these contextualized examples is to disrupt entrenched and simplistic attitudes in order to generate more socially just and sustainable perspectives on action.

In Chapter 13, Sara Hammer, Jill Lawrence, and Henk Huijser tackle the deficit discourse commonly perpetuated in international courses at university. The cultural binaries limit the learning experiences of students and teachers, and so they have developed a conceptual framework for cultural sustainability which advocates critical engagement and reflection. Sherilyn Lennon describes in Chapter 14 some of the ways that gender is being discursively constituted and perpetuated in one media form, which impacts on students' perceptions of school and appears to reflect community views.

In Chapter 15, Sara Hammer, Shalene Werth, Peter Dunn, Kym Lawson, and Danielle d'Abadie describe the impact of the ability/disability binary on students in a tertiary institution. Their research advocates support for students by providing more choice of pathways through courses, and enhanced understandings by academics of these issues to assist the development of a range of alternative ways of meeting the same standards.

Keith Cardwell gives in Chapter 16 a very clear account of the world of recreational diver instructor training, demonstrating the gaps between what instructors learn through their courses and what they need to be able to know and do in order to perform the job safely and competently. His description of the differences among formal, informal, and incidental learning shows the complexities involved in certification and how the predefined nature of competencies can tend to limit aspects of the development of the professional judgment necessary to perform the tasks.

In Chapter 17, Sean Mehmet's focus is on the quality of the pedagogical relationship between foreign-language teachers on fixed-term contracts and their Japanese students at a Japanese tertiary institution. He advocates a conceptual framework based on leadership theory to unpack some of the complexities and expectations involved in these teaching and learning interactions.

Finally, R. Todd Hartle, Rosemary J. Smith, Stephen Adkison, DJ Williams, and Paul Beardsley clearly demonstrate in Chapter 18 some of the barriers to learning and the emergence of good professional communication between educators and school practitioners where binaries exist. They have developed a model of professional culture axes as a useful tool to enhance the effectiveness of professional partnerships.

Focusing on research contexts permits powerful lenses to view the complex, interacting elements facing practitioners. These studies highlight the limitations of binary perspectives and allow the creation of a robust middle ground to assist the resolution of issues.

13 From Maintaining to Sustaining

Moving Beyond Binaries Toward a Framework for Cultural Sustainability in Higher Education

Sara Hammer, Jill Lawrence, and Henk Huijser

ABSTRACT

Ever-accelerating globalization has generated a number of global flows in a variety of spheres: for example, the flow of capital, media, and information and, importantly for our purposes here, the flow of people and knowledge. There are many benefits of this increased fluidity of movement beyond existing national borders—it can be perceived as liberating, for example—by widening access to travel, work, and education. However, such flows can at the same time be perceived as profoundly destabilizing and threatening, for example, because of perceived threats to security or a stable sense of identity. Within this broader context, the concept of *cultural sustainability* is concerned with a contemporary conception of being in the world that is not restricted by rigid binary oppositions, and that is open and flexible, whilst also sustaining cultural traditions, languages, and knowledges. This chapter applies the concept of cultural sustainability to the higher education sector.

INTRODUCTION

The concept of cultural sustainability is about finding a sustainable balance between cultural maintenance and cultural evolution, between keeping what is perceived to be good and developing the ability of adapting to new circumstances. In this chapter we mostly use culture in Raymond Williams's (1981) conceptualization of the term, as referring to the meanings and practices of everyday life, rather than a more limited sense of culture as artifacts, unless otherwise indicated. As a logical extension, we define cultural sustainability as the ways in which those practices and meanings can be strengthened into the future.

Overall, this chapter aims to develop a conceptual framework for guiding cultural sustainability within the context of higher education (HE), and thus as a way to allow us to become more precise about what it means to produce *global citizens*. Specifically, the chapter explores the way long-established cultural binaries such as Australian/international, host/visitor, elite/mass, and minority/majority function to impede the development of university students as global citizens. This may be because these cultural binaries frame international students as outsiders who must adapt to and integrate with the host culture, including its educational practices and norms. The host culture is thus firmly positioned in the center in an unproblematic fashion. We therefore begin by critiquing civic concepts such as *tolerance* and *cultural maintenance* because they tend to reinforce cultural binaries. We claim that a global citizenship discourse is also inadequate because it valorizes adaptability and diversity in an unproblematic fashion without necessarily challenging their existence. The framework for *cultural sustainability* we propose is instead based on reflective engagement and critical practices. The strength of this framework is that it moves beyond cultural binaries by placing each student, as well as staff member, regardless of context or culture, on a cross-cultural journey of engagement. The strategies that will result from this conceptual framework, and that will form the next step, will help staff and students to understand what is *cultural* about their own and others' cultures, including that of the university itself, and how to apply this understanding in their engagement with other individuals and cultures. As a result, these strategies help to develop a form of *cultural literacy* that can be integrated into university curricula and into the learning and teaching journey.

WHY WE NEED A NEW FRAMEWORK

The initial identification of a need for a new framework that emphasizes cultural sustainability emerges from discussions about managing diversity in the classroom (Devlin, 2009). Specifically, it is grounded in a desire to shift what is arguably an extension of the deficit discourse about the increasing diversity of the student cohort in HE. In the traditional deficit view, students who are unfamiliar with HE culture are sometimes conceptualized as inferior, or as the *other* in comparison with traditional elite students. These others now make up increasing numbers of the student cohort as a result of the *massification* of HE (Star & Hammer, 2008; Warner & Palfreyman, 2001). It is possible to see the arrival of increasing numbers of international students as an extension of this phenomenon because they join a potential group of domestic students who are also unfamiliar with the cultures of HE in Australia. Yet the impetus to deal with this increasing diversity has never been greater, particularly since Australia's export of education services is now the third biggest income earner in Australia (Birrell, 2009).

The need for a new framework that emphasizes cultural sustainability also emerges from a perception that there are limitations to some of the existing theoretical frameworks that relate to cultural diversity. This is because such frameworks are often implicitly based on maintaining firm cultural binaries (Tambini, 2001; Van de Vijver, Breugelmans & Schalk-Soekar, 2008). Global citizenship is a key concept used in relation to frameworks that address cultural diversity. The concept of global citizenship reflects a historical context where the nation-state is seen as an increasingly irrelevant construct, and where questions are increasingly posed about its viability as a political and social unit. It is a response to the advent of a global era, which has seen growing flows of capital and people across borders, a revolution in telecommunications, and the increasing importance of transnational governing bodies (Castells, 1999). However, the extremity of the global citizenship paradigm projects it into a binary with the movement to preserve national civic identities, or what we have referred to as cultural maintenance: in such movements *culture* and *nation* are often treated as interchangeable.

At the local level, the concept of global citizenship is so broad that it also tends to skate over existing cultural binaries. It ignores the ways in which individuals negotiate global contexts and identities in their everyday lives. Within the context of debates about globalization, locality tends to be conceived in relation to a particular form of cultural sustainability where small local or minority communities maintain and revive themselves through planned community activities and targeted state expenditures. Such a conception is often framed within a binary of local or minority culture versus invading global or minority cultures (Huijser, 2009).

Another conception of culture and citizenship that exists under the umbrella of the nation-state is that of multiculturalism and the related requirement to manage cultural diversity. Multiculturalism can be seen in three ways: firstly, as a demographic concept of social poly-ethnicity; secondly, as a state policy relating to diversity; and thirdly, as an attitude that relates to "acceptance of and support for the culturally heterogeneous composition of one's society" (Van de Vijver et al., 2008, p. 93). Ideas of cultural maintenance and the traditional liberal idea of tolerance both sit within this multicultural framework, as well as the related question of who maintains and who tolerates. However, even if multicultural citizenship stretches tolerance to acceptance of cultural diversity, it remains a model that is predicated on a majority/minority binary, or—at best—an ideal of harmonization between ethnic groups, rather than at the level of interaction between individuals. This is why nation-states often frame multiculturalism within a cultural rights discourse, where individual cultures are seen as discrete entities that fit together as in a mosaic (Ang, 2001).

Moving beyond binaries toward a view of cultural sustainability that operates at the level of the individual is important. This is because, as Tambini (2001) argues, *postnational citizens* need concrete abilities to be culturally flexible: they need to be able to cross cultural boundaries and engage with constantly changing and evolving social and cultural contexts. Important components of the framework for cultural sustainability that we are proposing here are ideas such as adaptability and an active valuing of cultural diversity. More specifically, our conceptual framework emphasizes the capacity of individuals to engage critically with cultural difference, as well as the ability to recognize the shifting complexities of cultures themselves. Such a model is *active*, rather than *reactive*, and is *contextual*, rather than *essentialist*. It focuses on where you're at, rather than where you're from, which means that it allows for context-specific, critical engagement with cultural difference, including critical engagement with one's own culture, however hybrid or contested that may be (Hall, 1996). Nakata (2007) affirms this perspective when he speaks about Indigenous peoples in the Australian context. He speaks of the *Indigenous standpoint* as something that has to be produced, rather than something that preexists:

> It is not a simple reflection of experience and it does not pre-exist in the everyday waiting to be brought to light. It is not any sort of hidden wisdom that Indigenous people possess. It is a distinct form of analysis, and is itself both a discursive construction and an intellectual device to persuade others and elevate what might not have been a focus of attention by others. It is not deterministic of any truth, but it lays open the basis from which to launch a range of possible arguments for a range of possible purposes. (Nakata, 2007, p. 11)

The attraction of the cultural sustainability framework proposed here is that it goes well beyond cultural maintenance and tolerance. Instead, it advocates a type of critical engagement and reflection, which simultaneously recognizes and values the importance of a particular cultural perspective, without privileging such a perspective as unchanging and finalized. The framework requires everyone involved in a cross-cultural context to engage critically with cultural difference in the present. In the framework proposed here, culture is seen in its widest sense, so it includes material artifacts and cultural practices, as well as culturally-based value systems. Moreover, culture is seen as living, forever in flux, and constantly in need of renegotiation. There have been many attempts to define what skills are needed to function effectively in the 21st century, especially in a higher education context (e.g., Bradwell, 2009; Oblinger & Oblinger, 2005). Banks (2004) identifies the needs of contemporary citizens as follows:

> Citizens in the new century need the knowledge, attitudes, and skills required to function in their ethnic and cultural communities and beyond their cultural borders to participate in the construction of a national civic culture that is a moral and just community that embodies democratic ideals and values, such as those embodied in the Universal Declaration of Human Rights. Students also need to acquire the knowledge and skills needed to become effective citizens in the global community. (p. 13)

While Banks' definition of effectiveness is not entirely clear, the main points of this paragraph are useful for our purposes. This is because those points allow us to focus the attention of cultural sustainability on knowledge, skills, and attitudes, which are traditionally the bread and butter of HE. From this perspective the next question is: What does cultural sustainability look like, in practice, and how can it be taught?

Table 13.1 Preliminary Differences Between Concepts

Frame-work	Maintenance/ Rights	Global Citizenship	Multiculturalism	Sustainability
Setting	Local, regional, national	Global	National	Situational
Key problem	Loss of cultural/ethnic identity, marginalization	Enduring national (civic) identities	Loss of government advocacy, ethnic group conflict, rigid cultural boundaries	Stereotypes/ assumptions, interpersonal skills
Defining logic	To preserve, reclaim, equalize	To transcend	To enrich, to harmonize	To attain transparency, to translate, to choose, to practice critical analysis and reflection; to understand the cultural stand-point of self and others.

Table 13.1 outlines some preliminary differences between the concepts discussed in this section.

DEFINITION OF CULTURAL SUSTAINABILITY

This section develops the conceptual framework for cultural sustainability that will enable practitioners to move beyond the binaries described in the preceding section.

The framework incorporates three intersecting and dynamic practices that act to enhance an individual's capability for cultural sustainability. They contest, for example, the Australian/international, host/visitor, and majority/minority binaries that function to impede the development of university students as global citizens as well as challenging the view of diversity as deficit (Lawrence, 2005a). The framework demonstrates how engagement can be negotiated, enabling host culture staff and students to engage with international students' and each other's cultures, disturbing the binary of the dominant and the deficit and, in the process, enhancing cultural literacy and sustainability.

Our conceptual framework is inspired by that of Treleaven, Freeman, Leask, Ramburuth, Simpson, Sykes, et al. (2007), who argue that cultural sustainability occurs when we actively value "diversity and conceptualize culture as situated, evolving, and potentially transformative" (p. 9). For others (Landis, 2008; Liu & Louw, 2009; Mak, Westwood, Barker, & Ishiyama,

1998; Ting-Toomey, Kimberilie, Yee-Jung, Shapiro, Garcia, Wright, et al., 2000), a framework for cultural sustainability must necessarily emphasize cultural competencies and skills rather than knowledge (even if one doesn't preclude the other) because it enables practitioners to treat culture as changing, situated, and heterogeneous. Such a framework would also value effective, interpersonal engagement, uphold cultural transparency (rather than acculturation), and highlight both a respect for diversity and individual choice.

A FRAMEWORK FOR CULTURAL SUSTAINABILITY

The framework (see Figure 13.1) presents three practical, intersecting, and dynamic practices—reflective, engagement, and critical practices—which can be used to operationalize the view of cultural sustainability developed in this chapter.

REFLECTIVE PRACTICES

The notion of reflective practice emerges from both sociological (Bourdieu, 1999; Giddens, 1996) and educational (Boud & Walker, 1990;

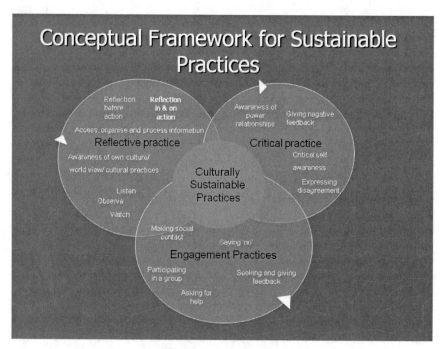

Figure 13.1   Operationalizing cultural sustainability.

Nakata, 2007; Schön, 1987) literature. Reflective practice facilitates individuals' capabilities to challenge their own assumptions, become familiar with different cultural practices, and prepare for communication with other cultures. In the classroom, reflective practice involves the learner's[1] awareness of and knowledge about the culture and cultural understandings, belief systems, worldviews, and cultural practices. Without this kind of critical self-reflection, learners may not comprehend the differences that can exist between the culture they bring with them and the university culture in terms of the different forms of capital (sociocultural, linguistic, and academic as well as economic) (Bourdieu, 1999). Reflective practice also emphasizes our capacity to observe, to watch, and to listen to the cultural practices occurring at a particular site. Reflective practice thus involves the concepts of *reflection in action* and *reflection on action* (Schön, 1987) as well as *reflection before action* (Boud & Walker, 1990). An associated feature of reflective practice is for students to access, organize, and process information.

Through these processes of reflection, learners continually reshape their approaches to cultural engagement and develop wisdom or artistry in their cross-cultural negotiations. If such processes of critical engagement and reflection are developed progressively through university curricula, as our framework suggests they should, they will in turn allow students from a wide variety of cultural backgrounds to negotiate cultural diversity in different contexts productively in a way that is both flexible and sustainable, for example, by being able to focus on what is most beneficial in the particular cultural context they find themselves in, and therefore to be able to negotiate sustainable solutions to localized problems, rather than make decisions that come from a centralized cultural space.

ENGAGEMENT PRACTICES

Engagement practices lie at the heart of the framework as they constitute practical strategies we all use. Broadly speaking, engagement practices in HE that address the issue of culture are informed by a combination of constructivist learning approaches and cross-cultural communication theory. Constructivists emphasize the role of the environment, including interactions with others, in engaging learners (Plourde & Alawiye, 2003). Research in this field places a particular emphasis on the benefits of peer learning, where learners learn from, or through, others (Azzarito & Ennis, 2003; Duncan, Gallacher, Mayes, Smith, & Watson, 2004). Engagement practices in cross-cultural communication theory also place a strong emphasis on context and the educational value of interacting with others. Although it is generally applied to international students only, cross-cultural communication theory is important for our model of cultural sustainability, which applies to all students.

Cross-cultural communication theorists contend that learners need to establish interpersonal relationships and communicate effectively in order to reap maximum benefits from an unfamiliar context. Integral to these learning processes is the development of each individual's sense of self-efficacy: the belief that he or she can successfully perform social behaviors in academic and everyday situations (Bandura, 1986). Bandura's (1986) social learning model is utilized as the basis of a cross-cultural communication program, *ExcelL: Excellence in Cultural Experiential Learning and Leadership Program* (Mak et al., 1998). ExcelL enables learners who have recently arrived to become competent and effective in dealing with specific aspects of the host context rather than adapting to the host culture. ExcelL not only emphasizes the role of sociocultural competencies in helping new learners to interact successfully with others in an unfamiliar culture; it also prioritizes specific practices. These are seeking help and information, participating in a group, making social contact, seeking and offering feedback, expressing disagreement, and refusing requests. There are versions of each of these skills that are relevant to the HE context: for example, seeking help and information correlates to a key HE competency of accessing sources of help and information (Lawrence, 2005b).

Such skills are especially pertinent in an individualist culture like Australian HE, where help is available but only if it is asked for, and there is often a concern about spoon-feeding students. Literature in HE also acknowledges group participation and effective social contact as a successful means of helping people from both diverse and mainstream cultures become more familiar with other cultures (Tinto, 2009). Competencies learned as a result of group participation and social interaction can also lead to the development of mentors, networks, learning communities, communities of practice, friendship groups, and increased access to helpful information and sources of help.

An essential feature of sustainable cultural practice is that it is socially and culturally appropriate or fine-tuned to a particular context, literacy, or discourse that is being engaged with. The specific verbal and nonverbal means of asking for help or participating in a group can differ in different contexts, cultures, disciplines, and workplaces. For example, in terms of verbal communication, learners need to consider appropriate language and conventions: whether to ask directly or indirectly for something, and whether or not to provide an explanation for the request. When making social contact, some topics are taboo in some contexts or cultures but acceptable in others. For example, in many contexts it would be considered rude to discuss personal information on first acquaintance. In terms of nonverbal communication, learners need to think about body language—whether their nonverbal behaviors like posture, eye contact, tone of voice, pace, volume and pitch, how close they stand, and so on, are appropriate to the situation and to the task.

The use of practices is also more complex than it first appears. This is because it is dependent on the prior experience, belief systems, and understanding that each learner embodies and brings to every new context. Seeking help, for instance, may not be culturally valued in individualist, self-reliant cultures, because it is seen as an indication of weakness or a lack of confidence in others. Some learners may feel they have no right to ask for help or they equate it with remediation or inferiority. Others may equate it with being *uncool* or *sucking up*. Many of these reactions are unreflective, culturally conditioned responses. For this reason, critical practice is an essential component of cultural sustainability, since it helps students and staff to understand such assumptions and expectations as artifacts of culture.

CRITICAL PRACTICES

Critical practice encompasses twin capacities: critical self-awareness and critical self-reflection—or the capacity of individuals to understand and acknowledge their own belief systems and cultural practices, and their critical awareness as learners of power configurations, including discourses that may impact on their transition to and progression within HE. Overall, this awareness provides students with the capacity to analyze reflexively the education process itself (Fairclough, 1995).

Kelly (2003) suggests that critical self-awareness requires a "continued attention to the place from which we speak" (p. 3), which aligns closely with Nakata's (2007) aforementioned outline of cultural standpoint. Gee (1999) describes it as the need to make visible to ourselves who we are and what we are doing. It incorporates learners' capacity to unpack reflectively their own cultural perspectives and belief systems, as well as their readiness to challenge these and to transform them if the need arises.

Critical discourse awareness differs from critical self-awareness in that it concentrates on the linguistic representation of power configurations operating within a specific context or setting (Fairclough, 1995). As such, critical discourse awareness offers the possibility of social and/ or cultural critique within a specific educational context. Within the suggested framework of cultural sustainability, learners might engage in reflective assessment tasks that require them to evaluate critically their own cultural assumptions, and explore those of their host HE institution. Critical practice is also relevant to the more overtly interpersonal engagement practices that include providing feedback (both positive and negative), expressing disagreement, and responding to requests because these are all practices that require some level of negotiation between different cultures. Such practices can be risky in that there is a potential for offence; however, their use is essential if learners are to master and demonstrate some level of capacity for intercultural communication or literacy. For example, Lawrence (2005b) documents the particular difficulties that people from some cultural backgrounds experience in giving (negative) feedback to a high-status lecturer in an HE context.

Overall, critical practices are important as they assist us to manage ongoing change within our own cultures, to understand implicitly that all cultures evolve (and are therefore not static, complete, protected), and that there are both local and global factors that impact on such change. Critical practices also enhance our capacities to test our awareness of our own actions, to understand the behavior of others, and potentially to transform our own individual practices: all are essential characteristics of cultural sustainability.

DYNAMIC PRACTICES

The three practices outlined above are dynamic and interdependent. The successful use of one of these practices often depends on the use of another and, if implemented together, they can be more effective in effecting cross-cultural engagement. For example, observation and reflection are prerequisites for fine-tuning engagement practices to a particular context that is being engaged. Likewise, the sociocultural properties of these practices rely, in HE for example, on learners' capacities to reflect on and provide (appropriate) feedback about the mainstream practices. All three practices also depend on learners' capacities to appraise not only their own cultural assumptions and expectations but also the external, and often hidden, assumptions and power configurations that have an impact within the new learning context. The capacities of learners to challenge and, where possible, to transform the unhelpful policies and practices operating in particular contexts also rely on learners' use of practices such as offering feedback, expressing disagreement, and responding to requests.

POTENTIAL APPLICATIONS OF CULTURAL SUSTAINABILITY IN THE CURRICULUM

Teaching staff can actively facilitate students' use of the three practices outlined in Figure 13.1. They can do so, firstly, by creating safe, supportive learning environments where students can practice and receive constructive feedback from lecturers, tutors, and peers on their developing interpersonal, intercultural, and other necessary skills and competencies. Examiners and tutors can also facilitate intercultural communication and interaction in tutorials, foster dialogue between different cultural groups, and encourage students' utilization of group work and discussion groups, study groups, study partners, learning circles, and peer mentors. The feedback and facilitation processes can take place either face-to-face in the classroom or online in discussion fora or other modes of communication. Examiners can also facilitate students' use of the three practices by consistently embedding them in authentic assessment tasks.

Curriculum design can be used specifically to develop students' critical, reflective capabilities. Students can understand how they learn by completing learning-style questionnaires. They can reflect about how they learn by engaging in reflective journaling. Other core aspects of assessment design can assist students in navigating their way through their own, and university, culture. Criteria sheets and marking rubrics can assist staff to make expectations about student performance clear, and students can plan what and how much they wish to learn by completing learning contracts.

Ultimately, explicit learning and teaching of interpersonal and intercultural literacies can help students develop the cultural competencies they will require to succeed in their future professional practice. In this way, higher education practitioners can contribute positively to cultural sustainability.

CONCLUSION

For the common HE graduate attribute of global citizenship, and the increasingly ubiquitous notion of internationalization, to be enriching and meaningful, each must move beyond the binaries of host/visitor, majority/minority, and Australian/international in a practical sense. This chapter has argued that in the HE context such binaries serve to marginalize international students and place the responsibility to adapt on their shoulders. This disadvantages both international and Australian students—with the latter missing valuable opportunities to develop intercultural competencies that would allow them to be truly global citizens. In response to such disadvantages, the chapter has outlined a conceptual framework for cultural sustainability that assists students in HE to move beyond the binaries explored here. Within it, culture is treated as situated, negotiated, evolving, and potentially transformative. The framework also moves beyond the binaries that are either reinforced or left unacknowledged by concepts such as global citizenship, cultural maintenance, and multiculturalism. This is because it does not privilege any particular culture but is instead based on reflective engagement and critical practices. Each of these practices can be supported by learning and teaching strategies to help all students and staff members, to engage critically with their own culture, and to better engage with individuals from cultures other than their own.

NOTES

1. In this chapter the framework is applied to the HE context and thus uses learners as its "subjects." The examples provided are from a number of research studies conducted by one of the authors (see Lawrence, 2004, 2005a, 2005b, and 2009).

REFERENCES

Ang, I. (2001). *On not speaking Chinese: Living between Asia and the West.* London: Routledge.
Azzarito, L., & Ennis, C. D. (2003). A sense of connection: Toward social constructivist physical education. *Sport, Education & Society, 8,* 179–198.
Bandura, A. (1986). *Social foundations of thought and action: A social cognitive theory.* Englewood Cliffs, NJ: Prentice Hall.
Banks, J. A. (Ed.). (2004). *Diversity and citizenship education: Global perspectives.* San Francisco, CA: Jossey-Bass.
Birrell, B. (2009). Exports of educational services attributable to the overseas student industry in Australia. *University World News.* Retrieved from http://www.universityworldnews.com
Boud, D., & Walker, D. (1990). Making the most of experience. *Studies in Continuing Education, 1,* 61–80.
Bourdieu, P. (1999). *The weight of the world: Social suffering in contemporary society.* Cambridge, MA: Polity Press.
Bradwell, P. (2009). *The edgeless university: Why higher education must embrace technology.* London: Demos.
Castells, M. (1999). Flows, networks, and identities: A critical theory of the informational society. In M. Castells, R. Flecha, P. Freire, H. A. Giroux, D. Macedo, & P. Willis (Eds.), *Critical education in the new information age* (pp. 37–64). Lanham, MD: Rowman & Littlefield.
Devlin, M. (2009). *Socioeconomic status and Indigenous background: Implications for first year university curriculum.* Paper presented at the First Year Experience Curriculum Design symposium, Brisbane, Australia.
Duncan, B., Gallacher, J., Mayes, T., Smith, L., & Watson, D. (2004). *Understanding learning cultures in community based further education: Working together towards enhancement.* Paper presented at the TLRP annual conference, Cardiff, UK.
Fairclough, N. (1995). *Critical discourse analysis: The critical study of language.* London: Longman.
Gee, J. P. (1999). *An introduction to discourse analysis: Theory and method.* London: Routledge.
Giddens, A. (1996). *In defence of sociology: Essays, interpretations and rejoinders.* Cambridge, MA: Polity Press.
Hall, S. (1996). New ethnicities. In D. Morley & K.-H. Chen (Eds.), *Stuart Hall: Critical dialogues in cultural studies* (pp. 441–449). New York: Routledge.
Huijser, H. (2009). *The multicultural nation in New Zealand cinema: Production-Text-Reception.* Saarbrucken, Germany: VDM Verlag.

Kelly, P. (2003). *Responding to diversity in tertiary teaching and learning.* Presentation to the USQ Academic Staff Development Program, University of Southern Queensland, Toowoomba, Australia.

Landis, D. (2008). Globalization, migration into urban centers, and cross-cultural training. *International Journal of Intercultural Relations, 32,* 337–348.

Lawrence, J. (2004). *University journeys: Alternative entry students and their construction of a means of succeeding in an unfamiliar university culture.* Unpublished doctoral dissertation, University of Southern Queensland, Australia.

Lawrence, J. (2005a). *Addressing diversity in higher education: Two models for facilitating student engagement and mastery.* Paper presented at the HERDSA annual conference, Sydney, Australia.

Lawrence, J. (2005b). Reconceptualising attrition and retention: Integrating theoretical, research and student perspectives. *Studies in Learning, Evaluation, Innovation and Development, 2*(3), 16–33.

Lawrence, J. (2009). *Two conceptual models for facilitating learners' transitions to new post-school learning contexts.* In J. Field, J. Gallacher, & R. Ingram (Eds.), *Researching transitions in lifelong learning* (pp. 106–120). New York: Routledge.

Liu, S., & Louw, E. (2009). Cultural translation and identity performance: A case of Chinese business people in Australia. *China Media Research, 5*(1), 1–9.

Mak, A. S., Westwood, M. J. Barker, M. C., & Ishiyama, F. I. (1998). *The excell program: Excellence in experiential learning and leadership.* Brisbane, Australia: Lyonco.

Nakata, M. (2007). The cultural interface. *The Australian Journal of Indigenous Education, 36,* 7–14.

Oblinger, D., & Oblinger, J. (Eds.). (2005). *Educating the Net generation.* Boulder, CO: Educause.

Plourde, L. A., & Alawiye, O. (2003). Constructivism and elementary preservice science teacher preparation: Knowledge to application. *College Student Journal, 37,* 334–342.

Schön, D. A. (1987). *Educating the reflective practitioner: Toward a new design for teaching and learning in the professions.* San Francisco, CA: Jossey-Bass.

Star, C., & Hammer, S. (2008). Teaching generic skills: Eroding the higher purpose of universities, or an opportunity for renewal? *Oxford Review of Education, 34*(2), 1–15.

Tambini, D. (2001). Post-national citizenship. *Ethnic and Racial Studies, 24*(2), 195–217.

Ting-Toomey, S., Kimberilie, K., Yee-Jung, R., Shapiro, B., Garcia, W., Wright, T., et al. (2000). Ethnic/cultural identity salience and conflict styles in four US ethnic groups. *International Journal of Intercultural Relations, 24,* 47–81.

Tinto, V. (2009). *Taking student retention seriously: Rethinking the first year of university.* Keynote paper presented at First Year Experience Curriculum Design symposium, Brisbane, Australia.

Treleaven, L., Freeman, F., Leask, B., Ramburuth, P., Simpson, L., Sykes, C., et al. (2007, December). Beyond workshops: A conceptual framework for embedding developments of intercultural competence in business education. *HERDSA News,* 9–11.

Van de Vijver, F. J. R, Breugelmans, S. M., & Schalk-Sokar, S. R. G. (2008). Multiculturalism: Construct validity and stability. *International Journal of Intercultural Relations, 32,* 93–104.

Warner, D., & Palfreyman, D. (2001). *The state of UK higher education: Managing change and diversity.* Buckingham, UK: Open University Press.
Williams, R. (1981). *Culture.* London: Fontana.

14 Exposing Bush Binaries
Using the Media to Problematize Gender

Sherilyn Lennon

ABSTRACT

In problematizing some of the ways gender is being discursively constituted and perpetuated by a small rural newspaper in western Queensland, Australia, this chapter models for educators an approach to disrupting gender beliefs and practices that can work to inhibit students' schooling and life performances. It provides both a method and a model for moving beyond the limitations imposed by gender binaries to a more socially just and equitable world. This chapter spills out of a larger research project being conducted in a western Queensland community. That project adopts a case study approach to explore and question local gender discourses, ideologies, and practices.

GENDER REPRESENTATIONS IN MEDIA DISCOURSES: AN INTRODUCTION

Since 2009, mainstream Australian media outlets have been uncompromising in their eagerness to broadcast a *bad boys* discourse that pathologizes male football players and their clubs as misogynist, predatory, and violent. Headlines such as "Change Attitudes to Women or Get Out" ("Change attitudes," 2009), "Sex Scandal: All Players Should Apologize, Says Sharks Chief" (Robinson, 2009), and "Melbourne Storm Star . . . Arrested Over Assault Over Girlfriend" (Butler, 2009) are working to focus public attention on what is being presented as a particularly unsavory element of Australia's footballing culture.

By contrast, since the mid-1990s, orders of media discourse (Fairclough, 1995) across Australia, the United Kingdom, and the United States have set about conceptually homogenizing males as repressed victims of overly feminized social and schooling systems. Poor boys' and failing boys' discourses portray males as needing to work at reclaiming ground lost to women's rights movements and disproportionately high numbers of achieving female students (Charlton, Mills, Martino, & Beckett, 2005; Kenway, 1995, 1997; McLean,

1996, 1997; Mills, 2004; Mills, Martino, & Lingard, 2007). Newspaper headlines such as "Girls Pip Boys in Student Scores" (Chilcott & Johnstone, 2009, p. 15) and "Top Marks Go to the Girls" (Livingstone, 2006, pp. 8–9) are helping to contribute to public perceptions of girls as society's educational winners with boys positioned as its losers. The perpetuation of such binaries can lead to the implementation of one-dimensional solutions aimed at correcting this perceived injustice and enabling "under researched approaches to colonise teacher practices" (Keddie & Mills, 2007, p. 17).

This chapter will argue that some students' poor schooling performances can be attributed to influences beyond teachers and their classroom practices. It will put forward a case for linking some boys' schooling underperformances to the ideological messages they are receiving from community discourses and practices that promote narrow masculine hierarchies and have, over generations, become entrenched. The chapter will further submit that a purposefully conducted critical examination of community discourses with students can work to make visible and disrupt limiting cultural beliefs and practices whilst offering liberatory alternatives. Such a process is capable of inspiring transformative thinking that can, ultimately, lead to improved student outcomes.

The chapter begins with a discussion of the media's role in constituting, reflecting, and perpetuating potentially restrictive gender binaries before narrowing its focus to make transparent some of the discourses and ideological messaging located in the texts of a small rural newspaper in western Queensland, Australia.[1] Specifically, the linguistic and visual features from a selection of this newspaper's texts will be analyzed for how they are discursively constructing relationships between males and females and for the ideological messages which might be resulting from these constructions. Whilst acknowledging that generalizability from such an approach is problematic, the chapter's content should be viewed as a demonstration of the potential usefulness of media texts as resources for disrupting gender binaries which work to limit and oppress.

RESPONSES TO POOR BOYS' AND FAILING BOYS' DISCOURSES

One response to the poor boys' and failing boys' discourses referred to earlier has been a call to remasculinize schools and/or males. An example of the former can be found, dressed up as common sense, in the following extract from an ABC radio interview with then Australian Prime Minister John Howard:

> I mean, there are 250 public or government schools in New South Wales, according to my advice, who have no male teachers. Now we're trying to do something about this. We're not trying to wind back the

Sex Discrimination Act; nobody wants to wind it back. We're just asking that a little bit of common sense be applied. (2004)

Another response has been an exhortation to return to more traditional ways of performing gender. Qualities considered appropriately masculine by such discourses include "physical strength, adventurousness, emotional neutrality, certainty, control, assertiveness, self-reliance, individuality, competitiveness, instrumental skills, public knowledge, discipline, reason, objectivity and rationality" (Kenway & Fitzclarence, 2005, pp. 41–42)— qualities considered unsuitable are often those associated with femininity. A headline on the front page of Australia's *Sun-Herald Magazine* taunts its male readers with "You've Learnt to Cook, Clean and Cry, but Can You Fix the Car?" ("How to be a man," 2003, p. 1) and promptly refers readers to an article extolling the benefits of returning to "The Basics of Being a Bloke" (Hammerschmidt, 2003, p. 10). A similar article in another popular Sydney newspaper demands that we "Bring Back Real Men" (Casamento, 2003, p. 131). Articles such as these seek, ideologically, to associate masculinities—and being male—with concepts of physical strength and power over others whilst relegating practices associated with nurturing, domesticity, or emotion to the feminine.

Keddie and Mills (2007) acknowledge that some boys are performing poorly at school but, in explaining why, offer an alternative view to the poor boys' and failing boys' discourses so often perpetuated by the media. They claim that "gender regimes can work in oppressive ways to police and normalize particular behaviours and constrain achievement" (p. 42). Beckett (2001) concurs with this thinking through her case study of Caleb, who, earlier in his schooling, had been a high achiever, but "became a youth obsessed with manliness, basketball, showmanship and girlfriends, all to the detriment of his school work" (p. 69). Beckett posits that narrow constructions of masculinity can place some boys in the position of resisting schooling and, alongside others (Dillabough, McLeod, & Mills, 2008; Francis & Skelton, 2008; Keddie, 2003, 2004; Keddie & Mills, 2007, 2009; Kenway & Fitzclarence, 2005), argues strongly for schools to make teaching time available to students for the critiquing of gender discourses. I contend that the media provide us with material aplenty to do just that.

According to Fairclough (1989, 1995, 2003), the media's discursive practices can covertly contribute to and significantly influence power imbalances in today's societies. He claims that media platforms are often used by publishers and politicians to perpetuate discourses which work to inform and legitimize spending, initiatives, and actions that advantage some whilst disadvantaging others. The media achieve this by "putting across the voices of the powerful as if they were the voices of 'common sense'" (Fairclough, 1995, p. 63). Utilizing a poststructuralist argument, Jones (1997) adds to Fairclough's theorizing by claiming that the discourses with which individuals come in contact daily help to shape or constitute them. She uses theoretical concepts such as *positioning* and *subjectivity* to convey a doubled sense of the subject as someone who can be discursively produced and discursively producing. In this way she places language at the center of who we are, what we believe and do, and how we are shaped and shape others.

THE ISSUE AND A WAY IN

The focus of this chapter is on making transparent some of the narrow or limiting gender discourses being reflected in, and perpetuated by, the contents of a small media outlet in rural Queensland. Fitzclarence, Hickey, and Matthews (1997) claim that "the forces of hegemonic masculinity, reinforced via the media, provide young males with powerful messages" (p. 25). The texts analyzed in this chapter make transparent those messages associating being male with power over others, a sense of privilege, physical prowess, risk-taking behavior, and the objectification, denigration, or domination of females. Connell (1995) has coined the term *hypermasculine* to describe these discourses and the behaviors they inspire. As an educator, looking through a feminist poststructuralist lens, I find these discourses particularly worrying because of their tendency to essentialize gender and construct masculinity in opposition to femininity. If mainstream media and public discourses continue to associate being female with, amongst other things, academic success and being male as the binary opposite of all things female, then they are establishing some dangerous cultural, social, and educational protocols. By locating and critically analyzing some of the gender discourses appearing in the publications of a small, but highly popular, newspaper in a western Queensland community, this chapter offers educators a method and a model for challenging and disrupting gender binaries which can work to limit and/or oppress schooling performances and, ultimately, lives.

It should be noted that it is not my intention to vilify or denounce the local newspaper for causing community gender inequities or some boys' schooling underperformances. That would be a ludicrous response to a very complex issue. Whilst acknowledging that the media serve to constitute, reflect, and perpetuate wider community discourses, beliefs, and practices, I also embrace its potential as a resource pool for challenging social inequities. Viewing media texts as cultural artifacts turns them into useful classroom tools for making transparent, and questioning, power imbalances. These power imbalances can polarize in communities to manifest as binaries that serve to limit and restrict lives. Not only do media texts provide us with a means of exploring and questioning oppressive binaries; they can also provide us with alternative ways of being that splinter and dislodge such binaries.

The Wheatville Times (a pseudonym) has a circulation of approximately 3,000 within a population of approximately 10,000. In 2006 the newspaper publicly questioned local boys' academic underperformances in an article entitled "Where Are the Boys?" However, the newspaper does not appear to recognize its own contribution to the perpetuation of heteropatriarchal and/or heteronormative discourses and ideologies, which, for some boys, can manifest as a resistance to schooling. Fairclough (1995) defines ideologies as implicit assumptions that work to create "'reality' as an effect" (p. 44). He argues that, when left unchecked, ideologies can become unquestioned norms that manifest as practice. In *catching* (Davies, 2005) the text in the act of constituting and perpetuating hypermasculine discourses, valuable insights can be gained into how social structures and practices evolve and are sustained. The process of doing this also works to disrupt and challenge these structures and practices, ideally creating the conditions for a rethinking of gender practices to occur.

Texts critiqued in this study have been purposefully selected from *The Wheatville Times* over a period of two years. They have been chosen because they offer examples of how media texts can contribute to, and resist, the constitution and perpetuation of gender binaries. The selected texts include articles which report on local events and individuals' achievements, advertisements, gossip-column entries, and community members' opinions. I acknowledge my gender-justice lenses and the deeply ideological, political, and subjective nature of the decision-making processes which have led to text selection, interpretation, and analysis (Kincheloe & Berry, 2004; Kincheloe & McLaren, 2005). Kenway (1995) posits that multiple and often conflicting discourses, including hegemonic discourses associated with masculinity, are able to coexist in social settings. I concede that I could have used more examples than I have of articles from *The Wheatville Times* that demonstrate broader and more inclusive representations of gender. However, the limitations imposed by a single chapter have made that difficult here. Suffice to say that no text is neutral—including this one.

AN APPROACH FOR EXPLORING DOMINANT MEDIA DISCOURSES

In his seminal work *Language and Power* (1989), Fairclough developed an approach for linking social to linguistic analysis, which has become known as Critical Discourse Analysis. This approach describes, interprets, and explains the discourses presenting in texts for their connections among language, power, and ideologies. In doing so it creates transdisciplinary knowledge that elucidates power as being part ideological and part discursive (Fairclough, 1995). Critical Discourse Analysis involves three layers of analysis: a description of the linguistic properties present in the text; an interpretation of the relationship between the discursive practices involved in the production, distribution, and consumption of the text; and an explanation of the relationship between the discursive and social practices evident in the text. Wodak (2004) sums this up in stating that "discourse is the place where language and ideology meet, and discourse analysis is the analysis of ideological dimensions of language use, and of the materialization in language of ideology" (p. 204). Essentially, this study uses Critical Discourse Analysis to answer the following questions: What are the linguistic and visual features of the texts? How are these texts discursively constructing relationships between males and females? What ideological messages might result from these constructions?

Whilst Critical Discourse Analysis provides its users with an approach to help structure and connect the analyses of texts and their discourses, it also acknowledges the subjectivity and provisional nature of this type of research. In this way Critical Discourse Analysis epistemologically aligns itself with both critical and poststructuralist thinking (Henderson, 2005) and, hence, this chapter.

THE LOCATION

The town of Wheatville (a pseudonym) operates as a service center supporting the surrounding industries of dry land cropping, grazing, cotton, and irrigation. Wheatville is made up almost entirely of fourth-, fifth-, or sixth-generation white Australians and has managed to remain a proud and thriving community despite prolonged drought. Here the passing of land from father to son is something which has become naturalized over generations, as has the sending of local landowners' children to elite private boarding schools in the country's capital and regional cities. Within the town of Wheatville there are three well-resourced schools—two primary and one secondary—but tradition and distances of up to and more than an hour's drive preclude many who live on farms from sending their children to them. A number of smaller one- and two-teacher schools exist in the outlying regions of the shire in order to cater for primary students who would otherwise have to travel excessive distances. However, the local secondary school tends to draw its clientele almost exclusively from the town of Wheatville with only a handful of students traveling in from surrounding properties.

In 2006 *The Wheatville Times* challenged its readers to answer the question "So Where Are the Boys?" in an article written to highlight the absence of boys amongst the academic prize winners at the annual secondary school awards night. The previous week this newspaper's editor had lamented that "at last week's Awards' night we couldn't help but notice the dearth of male students who walked on stage to accept a major academic award." Three years later very little appears to have changed, with the newspaper reporting all five of the awards night major academic prizes being won by girls.

The Wheatville Times has also provided a platform for the concerns of community members who feel worried that an excess of female teachers might be impeding the quality delivery of educational programs in the region. One father of school-aged children complained, "[I]t's hard to attract 'quality teachers'. We don't want a girl who's going to get pregnant after six months and go." Another proffered, "I believe teachers should be better paid. A good wage will attract quality teachers and we need to get more male teachers into our schools."[2] Appropriately, there have been criticisms from some academics challenging the oversimplistic and discriminatory nature of attitudes like these for their inability to recognize that the issue of schooling underperformance is a far more complex one than just having more male teachers or, as some would imply, having too many uncommitted female ones (Alloway, Freebody, Gilbert, & Muspratt, 2002; Francis, 2008; Kenway, 1997; Mills, 2004; Pallotta-Chiarolli, 1997; Zyngier, 2009). However, what specifically are these complexities and where indeed are our boys if they are not amongst the academic prize winners at school awards nights?

LOCATING THE BOYS THROUGH THE MEDIA

The Wheatville Times often portrays local males as men/boys of action pursuing sport and drinking—all with equal fervor and success—as demonstrated by the following contribution to the gossip column (a regular feature of this newspaper):

> Two brothers we know . . . one of whom was renowned far and wide for his ability to hit red cricket balls . . . played golf recently. . . . [They were] watching as opposition tipped back beer after beer and struggled to remain vertical. But while they sank the beers, they also sank the shots. . . . Both [brothers] are back in serious 'training', but has nothing to do with golf.

Another article, reporting on a junior tennis tournament, includes an image of three primary school–aged boys who appear to be drinking out of beer stubbies immediately under the declarative headline "Wheatville Tradition Continues." Whilst the caption clarifies that the boys are only drinking ginger beer, a first glance of the image—and the wording of the headline—could invoke a different reponse among readers: a response which associates the Wheatville tradition with male alcohol consumption and implies that another generation of young males is well on its way to understanding this community's expectations of them. As a means of reinforcing this message, and perhaps unintentionally, a liquor advertisement using the slogan "Great Mates" has been placed immediately below the image.

One perspective of texts such as these is to see them as celebrating, and perhaps romanticizing, Wheatville's strong and successful male sporting traditions and camaraderie. However, a visual and linguistic count of the references to alcohol in many of the newspaper's articles quickly identifies another form of interdiscursivity and hence a different interpretation. In this community being male, participating in sport, socializing, and drinking alcohol would appear to be all closely related and considered part of normal male practice.

LOCATING THE GIRLS THROUGH THE MEDIA

In exploring media representations of masculinity it is important to consider representations of femininity, as, through relational ontology, these also work to constitute and police gender norms (Reay, 2001). In an article published in *The Wheatville Times* to help promote a locally written cookery book, a headline using the imperative mood tells its readers to "Try These, They're Great." The remainder of the text details "three generations of cooks" who have contributed to the book. There are two accompanying images. The larger one is of three local middle-aged women described as "top cooks," holding plates of biscuits and cakes towards the camera as though serving. The women are all well groomed and smiling. The smaller inserted image is of the cookbook and more biscuits. The headline, the accompanying photographs, and the ensuing story all work dialectically to represent these women in roles associated with food preparation and servitude. The smiling faces of the women signify that it is, quite possibly, a role they are happy to embrace.

Another article, reporting on a course offered by the local high school, incorporates an image of a group of smiling female students holding battery-operated prosthetic babies on their laps. The headline reads, "Students Get Lowdown on Motherhood." Whilst "students" is a gender-neutral term, motherhood is not—nor is the image accompanying the headline. One inference which can be read into this text is that the nurturing of and caring for babies is something that is considered especially important for girls to learn in this community. Another article in the same edition reports on the annual debutante ball. Its caption describes the debutantes as "enchanting." The story is accompanied by two images: one, a studio photograph of a girl dressed in virginal white, smiling, styled, and posing for the camera, resplendent in long white gloves and diamante earrings; the other, an image of 22 debutantes standing respectfully behind the local bishop and matrons whilst holding their corsages of flowers. The text's semiotic references to the girls as modest and innocent are many. The long white dresses and gloves, fresh flowers, the presence of a church representative, and the absence of any young males all work to construct a particularly pure, Christian, and traditionally Western representation of young white womanhood in this community.

The representations of females in these texts operate in stark contrast to those of the women represented on the front page of an earlier edition of the newspaper. In it the one-word oversized headline "BASHED!" makes use of the declarative mood, capitalization, and an exclamation mark to arrest the reader's attention. This front-page headline is placed above a large color photograph of two unsmiling Indigenous women who are looking squarely at the reader. The one in the foreground has a visibly swollen and bruised right eye. She is wearing a T-shirt and black front-zip sweater. The woman in the image standing supportively behind her is wearing a football jersey. The article's emotivity is increased through its reference to children in the subheading: "Children watch from car while woman bashed." It goes on to detail the injuries received by one of the photographed women as "a black eye, a broken nose and a suspected broken cheek bone" and inform its readers that the incident may have resulted as a retaliatory response to an earlier verbal altercation between the victim and her attackers. The children who watched from the car are later identified as those of the attackers. The racial othering (Walkerdine, 1990) of the women represented in this article is established using visual, semiotic, linguistic, and semantic cues. These cues work to construct those involved in the incident as violent, anti-social, and poor parental models providing a demonstration of how texts can work to disempower within as well as across genders.

LOCATING MALE AND FEMALE RELATIONSHIPS THROUGH THE MEDIA

In exploring media texts representing both males and females I have selected two texts: another entry from the gossip column in *The Wheatville Times* and an advertisement placed by one of the local football codes for a forth-coming Bachelor and Spinsters (B & S) ball.[3] As with the earlier gossip-column entry, the first text has been written using a familiar conversational tone giving it a person-to-person quality.

A buck's party went off recently with boy's (sic) digging deep to buy some scantily clad entertainment. Front-row seats were hard to come by but boys made way to let some elderly mates have a better vantage point. Perhaps they were worried their eye-sight might not have been up to it if they were too far back. No truth however that there'll be a "health inspection" for party-goers at the next family bucks' show.

Fairclough (1995) has noted the use of informal spoken language in media texts as a growing tendency of formal public discourses.

Whilst the modality used in this entry is hesitant ("Perhaps"), even nega-tive ("no truth"), and the identity of the male participants ("boy's" [*sic*], "party-goers," "elderly mates") and female participants ("scantily clad entertainment") are protected, what can be illuminated through one inter-pretation of this text is that it is assumed amusing to be newsworthy, and socially acceptable for adult males of all ages to pay for, and spectate at, "family bucks' show(s)" involving erotic female entertainers. The further implication of male partygoers as needing "health inspections" could be interpreted as implying that some male attendees have contracted a sexually transmittable disease from the females responsible for the entertainment. The reference to females as "scantily clad entertainment" and the implica-tion that they may have been responsible for spreading sexually transmit-table diseases is dehumanizing, objectifying, denigrating, and trivializing. This text prickles with its misogynist undercurrents and is, through gender-justice lenses, a troubling one indeed.

Another advertisement for an annual B & S ball also raises gender-jus-tice eyebrows ("Book Now Online" [classifieds]). Dominated by a cartoon image of a male bird (the emblem of the local football team) holding a can of beer and towering over a prostrate female bird with legs splayed, it invites local youth to book online for the annual B & S ball. The female bird in the cartoon is sporting high heels, long eyelashes, and a bewildered facial expression. Her prostrate position, a reference in the caption beneath the cartoon to a plucked bird, and the surrounding flying feathers imply that a possibly nonconsensual sexual act has just occurred between the two animals. Masked by humor, the implicit messages are clear. The dominat-ing pose and aggressive glare of the male figure leave the reader in no doubt as to which gender holds power and how male and female roles are to be enacted on the evening in question. This text, and the preceding one, use humor to make palatable patriarchal discourses of white male hegemony and broadcast their harmful gender messages.

FINDING ALTERNATIVES

In attempting to disrupt restrictive and limiting orders of gender discourse it is important that educators locate and put forward alternatives which move beyond binary notions of gender. If students continue to associate masculine, or hypermasculine, behavioral practices solely with males, and those behaviors deemed feminine solely with females, sex and gender become conflated, fixing individuals' performance possibilities to that of a choice between either masculine behaviors for boys or feminine behaviors for girls. In failing to critique alternatives with our students, we run the risk of contributing to the perpetuation of essentialist notions of gender (Francis, 2008). Educators need to seek out and provide alternatives that celebrate diversity and work to blur those gender boundaries that limit and confine us.

The final texts to be analyzed from the pages of *The Wheatville Times* offer examples of gender representations which work to broaden gender performance possibilities beyond heteropatriarchal models of white male entitlement. An article reporting on the death of a 55-year-old local Indigenous man who has, allegedly, been "assaulted" in a nearby regional city incorporates a picture of a smiling well-groomed man above a headline referring to him as a "family man" ("This Family Man Died"). The deceased is described as "well respected" and "much loved." His funeral is reported as being "one of the biggest funerals ever seen in Wheatville" and he is remembered by one family member as being liked by all "because he made people laugh." Whilst the article goes on to suggest that the family of the deceased man are seeking justice for what they believe to be discriminatory police practices, it can be inferred from the images and lexicalization in the text that the Indigenous subject central to the story was popular, well liked, embraced by his family, respectable, and respected. Whilst this representation of an assault victim operates in stark contrast to that of the Indigenous subject reported in the article critiqued earlier ("BASHED!"), it also works to depict a nurturing model of masculinity which moves beyond the hypermasculine discourses located in some of the previous texts.

In another article which reports on three Indigenous women's successes in the art world, an Indigenous woman states, "Making artwork makes me feel good about being an Aboriginal person, I am able to create works that express how I feel inside." The article's visual and linguistic references promote the artistic process as a "family affair." The accompanying series of photographs portray smiling indigenous women surrounded by family members and the artwork they produce. The visuals and celebratory tone of the written text combine to represent the women as successful, creative, productive, connected, and valued members of both family and society. The implicit cultural messaging in this text is very different from that located in the earlier article covering the story of an Indigenous woman who had been bashed ("BASHED!").

Whilst media and public discourses in this community often associate the arts and its practitioners with femininity, the final text to be explored works to challenge and disrupt this idea as well. An article celebrating the artistic successes of a former Wheatville male uses visual and semantic cues to capture and broadcast its subject's success ("Anthony Makes His Mark in the Art World"). The article reports on the artist's recent successes at two art events: one the local Wheatville art show and the other a prestigious exhibition held annually in Brisbane. The successful artist is shown in an accompanying photograph dressed casually in jeans and T-shirt, smiling whilst resting against one of his sandstone sculptures. A smaller image of a stick painting is overlaid onto the larger image. It is a photograph of the painting which has given the artist so much success. In the article, the artist credits Wheatville with inspiring much of his landscape work: "I want to capture the mood of the town." This article also provides an alternative version of masculinity to that located in the hypermasculine discourses of some of the previously critiqued texts. It is through an awareness of contradictory positions such as this that possibilities for empowerment and change are created (Fairclough, 1995).

A STARTING POINT FOR MOVING FORWARD

As stated earlier, the discursive representations of gender and the ideological positionings to be found in media texts are multiple and varied. In this chapter I have deliberately selected those texts which offer educators useful starting points for confronting gender binaries and moving forward. Whilst some provide alternative and less restrictive models for performing gender, others are worrying for the way in which they represent and perpetuate restrictive hegemonic orders of discourse founded in white male supremacy. The use of humor in some of these texts simultaneously to deflect and reify "boyo extremism" (Keddie & Mills, 2009, p. 35) and the accompanying denigration, objectifying, and/or trivializing of the feminine work to forge powerful gender binaries which both privilege and oppress. Kenway and Fitzclarence (2005) have discovered links among the denigration of women, violence against women, and "'only joking' motifs" (p. 44). They claim that traditional and patriarchal views can lead to a belief that violence against women is an acceptable method of dealing with conflict. Other discourses reflected in this newspaper would appear to demonstrate a belief that local schools are being disadvantaged because they have become overly feminized places where girls have a greater chance of academic success than boys. Left unchecked, these discourses can create versions of reality which demonize female teachers and reinforce machismo, power over others, and the subjugation or devaluing of the feminine as appropriate behavior for males.

In addressing boys' schooling underachievements, it is vital that educators locate, explore, contest, and offer alternatives to hypermasculine discourses of white male entitlement that denigrate or trivialize the feminine (Keddie & Mills, 2007). Tellingly, a five-year longitudinal case study conducted by Keddie (2007) shows evidence of a link between these discourses and male educational underperformance and disengagement at school. Media platforms provide the vehicles for broadcasting, reflecting, constituting, and perpetuating *poisonous pedagogies* (Kenway & Fitzclarence, 2005) which help to determine who we are, what we believe, and what we do. Ironically, they can also provide us with useful alternatives for challenging these harmful discourses.

So where to from here? Connolly (2004) claims that "the key factor to address in terms of boys' poor educational performance is masculinity itself" (p. 61). I would posit that in identifying and problematizing heteropatriarchal discourses of white male entitlement we might just find a way of doing this. By exposing the media at work pedaling restrictive gender discourses, educators can begin to irritate and transcend socially unjust practices which have become naturalized.

The discourses located in the newspaper articles referred to in this chapter provide rich fodder for critical pedagogues wanting to challenge and disrupt inequitable gender beliefs and practices that work to limit and oppress. Martino and Meyenn (2001) argue that "gender regimes are more shifting and contradictory than theorists supposed in the seventies and eighties" (p. xi). In appreciating this, we give ourselves a way of moving forward. Educators must collaborate with students to locate, unpack, and provide alternatives to these restrictive discourses. McLean (1997) urges us to capture, critique, and identify the cost to boys as well as girls of the discourses which inform "the masculine culture of hardness, competition, the obsession with strength and power, emotional distance, and boys' determination at all costs not to be female" (p. 15).

Through disclosing and dislocating gender inequities, ideologies, and assumptions that lock us into limiting life performances, we provide our students with a starting point for moving beyond gender binaries to a more socially just and equitable world. In casting a critical eye over a strategically selected sampling of media texts, we give ourselves a way of disrupting what is so that we can begin to create the conditions for exploring what could be.

CONCLUSION

This chapter contributes to a discourse making transparent media complicity in perpetuating heteropatriarchal gender discourses which in turn work to limit and restrict lives. It puts forward a case for educators to make use of such discourses to problematize and disrupt gender binaries which can manifest as a denigration or trivializing of the feminine and a devaluing of formalized schooling. In challenging and resisting dominant hegemonies which have become naturalized, foundations are laid for the emergence of alternative, less restrictive ways of thinking about and, ultimately, performing gender. Whilst moving forward will be a challenge, to do nothing will, ultimately, be even more of a challenge.

NOTES

1. Any research that exposes and/or questions community values and belief systems is, by nature, sensitive. Therefore, all data have been anonymized. All sensitive citations, including those to articles cited from the local newspaper used as data, have been omitted. The editorial team has verified the accuracy of the original data.
2. It is quite possible that the reporting journalist identified the discriminatory nature of these statements and deliberately inserted them into her articles to provoke and disrupt community thinking. Indeed, the following week, one of the males quoted wrote a letter to the editor defending his opinion and complaining that his words had been taken out of context.

3. Bachelor and Spinsters' balls are events unique to rural Australia. They are usually held in isolated paddocks or sheds and require all attendees to be single. They are often associated with binge drinking and risk-taking driving exhibitions commonly referred to as "circle work." In recent years insurance restrictions have limited their number and some of their activities. A proportion of the funds raised at these events is donated to charities.

REFERENCES

Alloway, N., Freebody, P., Gilbert, P., & Muspratt, S. (2002). *Boys, literacy and schooling: Expanding the repertoires of practice.* Retrieved from http://www.dest.gov.au/schools/publications/2002/index.htm

Beckett, L. (2001). Challenging boys: Addressing issues of masculinity within a gender equity framework. In W. Martino & B. Meyenn (Eds.), *What about the boys? Issues of masculinity in schools* (pp. 66–81). Philadelphia, PA: Open University Press.

Butler, M. (2009, August 10). Melbourne Storm star Greg Inglis arrested over assault over girlfriend. *The Australian.*

Casamento, J. (2003, June 29). Bring back real men. *The Sunday Telegraph,* p. 131.

Change attitudes towards women or get out: Gallop (2009, May 13). *Australian Associated Press (AAP).*

Charlton, E., Mills, M., Martino, W., & Beckett, L. (2005). Sacrificial girls: A case study of the impact of streaming and setting on gender reform. *British Educational Research Journal, 33*(4), 459–478.

Chilcott, T., & Johnstone, C. (2009, May 5). Girls pip boys in student scores. *Courier-Mail,* p. 16.

Connell, R. (1995). *Masculinities.* Sydney, Australia: Allen & Unwin.

Connolly, P. (2004). *Boys and schooling in the early years.* London: Routledge Falmer.

Davies, B. (2005). The subject of post-structuralism: A reply to Alison Jones. In C. Skelton & B. Francis (Eds.), *A feminist critique of education: 15 years of gender education* (pp. 96–109). London: Routledge.

Dillabough, J., McLeod, J., & Mills, M. (2008). In search of allies and others: 'Troubling' gender and education. *Discourse: Studies in the Cultural Politics of Education, 29*(3), 301–310.

Fairclough, N. (1989). *Language and power.* London: Longman.

Fairclough, N. (1995). *Critical Discourse Analysis: The critical study of language.* London: Longman.

Fairclough, N. (2003). *Analysing discourse: Textual analysis for social research.* New York: Routledge.

Fitzclarence, L., Hickey, C., & Matthews, R. (1997). Getting changed for football: Challenging communities of practice In J. Kenway (Ed.), *Will boys be boys? Boys' education in the context of gender reform* (pp. 22–26). Deakin West, Australia: Australian Curriculum Studies Association.

Francis, B. (2008, July 23). *Deconstructing meritocracy: Social identity and educational achievement.* Paper presented at the Winter Seminar on Gender, Social Identities and Education, University of Queensland, Australia.

Francis, B., & Skelton, C. (2008). 'The self-made self': Analysing the potential contribution to the field of gender and education of theories that disembed selfhood. *Discourse: Studies in the Cultural Politics of Education, 29*(3), 311–323.

Hammerschmidt, C. (2003, July 13). The basics of being a bloke. *Sunday Life: The Sun-Herald Magazine,* pp. 10–14.

Henderson, R. (2005). A Faircloughian approach to CDA: Principled eclecticism or a method searching for a theory? *Melbourne Studies in Education, 46*(2), 9–24.

How to be a man. (2003, July 13). *Sunday Life:.The Sun-Herald Magazine*, p. 1.

Howard, J. (2004). Govt facing resistance to teacher plan [radio program]. *National News*. South East Queensland, Australia: ABC.

Jones, A. (1997). Teaching post-structuralist feminist theory in education: Student resistances. *Gender and Education, 9*(3), 261–269.

Keddie, A. (2003). Little boys: Tomorrow's macho lads. *Discourse: Studies in the Cultural Politics of Education, 24*(3), 289–305.

Keddie, A. (2004). Working with boys' peer cultures: Productive pedagogies . . . productive boys. *Curriculum Perspectives, 24*(1), 20–29.

Keddie, A. (2007). Games of subversion and sabotage: Issues of power, masculinity, class, rurality and schooling. *British Journal of Sociology of Education, 28*(2), 181–194.

Keddie, A., & Mills, M. (2007). *Teaching boys: Developing classroom practices that work.* Crows Nest, Australia: Allen & Unwin.

Keddie, A., & Mills, M. (2009). Disrupting masculinised spaces: Teachers working for gender justice. *Research Papers in Education, 24*(1), 29–43.

Kenway, J. (1995). Masculinities in schools: Under siege, on the defensive and under reconstruction? *Discourse: Studies in the Cultural Politics of Education, 16*(1), 59–70.

Kenway, J. (1997). Boys' education, masculinity and gender reform: Some introductory remarks. In J. Kenway (Ed.), *Will boys be boys? Boys' education in the context of gender reform* (pp. 3–7). Deakin West, Australia: Australian Curriculum Studies Association.

Kenway, J., & Fitzclarence, L. (2005). Masculinity, violence and schooling: Challenging 'poisonous pedagogies.' In C. Skelton & B. Francis (Eds.), *A feminist critique of education: 15 years of gender education* (pp. 38–54). London: Routledge.

Kincheloe, J., & Berry, K. (2004). *Rigour and complexity in educational research: Conceptualizing the bricolage.* Maidenhead, UK: Open University Press.

Kincheloe, J., & McLaren, P. (2005). Rethinking critical theory and qualitative research. In N. Denzin & S. Lincoln (Eds.), *The Sage handbook of qualitative research* (3rd ed., pp. 303–342). London: Sage.

Livingstone, T. (2006, April 3). Top marks go to the girls. *The Courier-Mail*, pp. 8–9.

Martino, W., & Meyenn, B. (2001). Preface. In W. Martino & B. Meyenn (Eds.), *What about the boys? Issues of masculinity in schools* (pp. x–xii). Philadelphia, PA: Open University Press.

McLean, C. (1996). Boys and education in Australia. In C. McLean, M. Carey, & C. White (Eds.), *Men's ways of being* (pp. 65–83, 239–245). Boulder, CO: Westview Press.

McLean, C. (1997). *Engaging with boys' experiences of masculinity: Implications for gender reform in schools.* Deakin West, Australia: Australian Curriculum Studies Association.

Mills, M. (2004). The media, marketing, and single sex schooling. *Journal of Education Policy, 19*(3), 343–360.

Mills, M., Martino, W., & Lingard, B. (2007). Getting boys' education 'right': The Australian government's parliamentary inquiry report as an exemplary instance of recuperative masculinity politics. *British Journal of Sociology of Education, 28*(1), 5–21.

Pallotta-Chiarolli, M. (1997). We want to address boys' education but . . . In J. Kenway (Ed.), *Will boys be boys? Boys' education in the context of gender reform* (pp. 65–68). Deakin West, Australia: Australian Curriculum Studies Association.

Reay, D. (2001). 'Spice Girls', 'Nice Girls', 'Girlies', 'Tomboys': Gender discourses, girls' cultures and femininities in the primary classroom. *Gender and Education*, *13*(2), 153–166.

Robinson, G. (2009, May 14). Sex scandal: All players should apologise, says Sharks chief. *The Sydney Morning Herald*.

Walkerdine, V. (1990). *Schoolgirl fictions*. London: Verso.

Wodak, R. (2004). Critical discourse analysis. In C. Seale, G. Gobo, J. F. Gubrium, & D. Silverman (Eds.), *Qualitative research practice* (pp. 197–213). London: Sage.

Zyngier, D. (2009). Doing it to (for) boys (again): Do we really need more books telling us there is a problem with boys' underachievement in education? *Gender and Education*, *21*(1), 111–118.

15 Expectations of Ability and Disability at University
The Fine Art of Managing Lives, Perceptions, and Curricula

Sara Hammer, Shalene Werth, Peter Dunn, Kym Lawson, and Danielle d'Abadie

ABSTRACT

The impact of a disability or chronic illness plays a major role in decision making regarding many life choices including education options. Studying with chronic illness or disability is about making choices and decisions. It is also about negotiating the reactions of others to what is a rather personal condition. Research has shown that outward manifestations of chronic illness or disability are often viewed differently by others from how they are experienced by those who experience it. The experiences of a student with disability or chronic illness at university are influenced by the perceptions of others such as friends' support, academic, and administrative staff members. This in turn complicates the binary, examined in this chapter, of the appearances and expectations of ability or disability.

This chapter discusses the findings of the first year of a three-year study currently underway at the University of Southern Queensland, Australia. It focuses on the learning journeys of students with chronic illness or disability and the impact of the appearances and expectations of ability and disability on these students. Thirty-three students have been surveyed and interviewed to assess these research questions. The preliminary findings have uncovered two major themes that resonate with students' positioning in relation to the ability/disability binary. Firstly, students in the study regularly transcend the ability/disability binary by actively managing their needs as part of their individual learning journeys. Despite their activism, student responses highlight the inherent difficulty of managing simultaneously their studies, the perceptions of others, and a sometimes unpredictable condition. Unexpected calls for assistance against a background of unproblematic achievement can lead to academic and support staff questions about the veracity and validity of their needs. The second theme relates to academic standards. From their responses, it is clear that students in this study operated within the confines of the ability/disability binary where their perceptions of meeting academic standards were concerned.

The chapter concludes by briefly examining two possible strategies to support students in transcending the ability/disability binary. The first is to offer students greater choice in terms of both pathways through curricula and the curricula themselves. The second related strategy is to provide academic staff with greater support to design curriculum and assessment alternatives that provide students with greater choice without undermining desired learning objectives and standards.

INTRODUCTION

People with a chronic illness or disability have been historically defined in opposition to the able: those with ability. As such, those with chronic illness or disability often experience this as a stigmatizing condition or life event that they wish to keep hidden. Students beginning higher education often wrestle with this stereotype whilst simultaneously learning to negotiate the many challenges their conditions pose. Tertiary institutions must now comply with national disability legislation, such as Australia's Disability Discrimination Act (1992), and there is a growing awareness about inclusive teaching amongst education providers which has addressed key barriers faced by affected students. However, disability continues to impact on every aspect of students' learning experiences in higher education (Goode, 2007; Konur, 2002; Oakes, 2005). This chapter discusses the preliminary findings of a research project at a regional Australian university which examines the experiences of students with a chronic illness or disability. The findings arguably highlight the existence of an ability/disability binary, which frames the experience of students in the study. It begins with a brief exploration of this binary and the student learning experience within existing research. The chapter then examines relevant themes emerging from the preliminary study data. The first theme shows that students actually straddle the ability/disability binary by engaging in strategies to manage needs arising from their condition. However, this process of management is made more complex by the unpredictability of their conditions, and the reactions of others. The second theme relates to students' perceived ability to meet desired academic standards—a theme that appears to reinforce this binary, because students within this study tended to position themselves as less than or potentially falling outside the academic norm. The chapter concludes by briefly outlining possible avenues for change that may assist students with a chronic illness or disability to move beyond the ability/disability binary.

BACKGROUND

Recent literature has sought to dissolve the ability/disability binary by framing chronic illness or disability as a sociopolitical issue (Rizvi & Lingard, 1996; Ryan & Struhs, 2004; Vickers, 1997). Authors conceptualize *disability* as a product of social and environmental attitudes rather than as a problem to be solved. Within the context of higher education, therefore, the sociopolitical model of disability tends to focus on how teaching and curriculum practices disadvantage some students (Fuller, Healey, Bradley, & Hall, 2004; Konur, 2002). Despite this shift away from a deficit view, some argue that university students with a disability or chronic illness continue to be framed as a problem (Ryan & Struhs, 2004) in need of remediation. Others also cite recent trends within higher education such as massification (Nunan, Rigmor, & McCauseland, 2000), bureaucratic categorization and labeling (Prowse, 2009), and internationalization (McClean, Heagney, & Gardner, 2003) as factors that tend to reinforce rather than reduce challenges for students with a chronic illness or disability.

Massification, internationalization, and the increasing emphasis on bureaucratic systems and labeling are by-products of increased participation levels of both Australian and international students in universities (Marginson & Considine, 2000). Greater numbers of students have meant less student–lecturer contact. Fewer students now believe that lecturers know their name (James, Krause, & Jennings, 2010). However, greater numbers of students have also led to greater student diversity, and a greater range of student needs. Added to this paradoxical scenario, there is pressure from government for universities to ensure equity for these diverse student groups (Coombs, 2010). Such phenomena provide a likely explanation for increasing bureaucratic systems in which labeling of students is provided. Combined with other issues emerging from these trends, such as increasing student anonymity, this labeling is something that may reinforce the ability/disability binary.

Consequently, a key decision for students with a disability or chronic illness is whether to disclose their condition to relevant university service providers, because they do so within a normative context that continues to measure them against normal or average students (Link & Phelan, 2001; Ryan & Struhs, 2004). This context sets up an able/disabled binary where students' decision to disclose can have a significant, stigmatizing effect on their identity. Indeed, stigma has been acknowledged as one of the single most influential factors in the decision of students to disclose completely an illness or disability to others (Link & Phelan, 2001; Prowse, 2009). Students appear particularly concerned that they will be judged as potentially incompetent if their lecturers or other university staff become aware of their illness or disability (Jung, 2002; Prowse, 2009). However, without such disclosure, students are unable to qualify for valuable assistance and benefits, and there is some evidence to suggest that students who disclose tend to be more successful in their studies (Rizvi & Lingard, 1996).

Whether to disclose or not can be a vexing issue for those with a chronic illness or disability that is largely invisible to others. This is because in such cases there are times when appearance can be, at least to some extent, controlled by the individual (Vickers, 2001), and they can pass as able rather than disabled. This is an important variation because the appearance of wellness or capability tends to be uppermost in the mind of a student who is trying to fit in with a culture of academic competition and excellence (Nunan et al., 2000). From this perspective, the attitudes of institutions, lecturers, and other staff can also have a significant effect on the student's ultimate decision to disclose.

For students with a chronic illness or disability, the act of disclosure can significantly change their relationship with others (Olney & Brockelman, 2003). Expectations of what constitutes ability and disability in an academic environment will vary between lecturers and other staff members and are influenced by their own personal experiences of illness and disability (Goffman, 1976; Myers, 2004). Despite such variation, there is some evidence that individuals within a university setting experience difficulty in accepting that students with a chronic illness or disability might be both able and in need of some assistance (Olney & Brockelman 2003). Because of the tendency of some staff and students to equate disability with inability, some students are willing to struggle on without revealing their circumstances, because doing so allows them to maintain their ability in terms of capability and competency. Research shows that expectations of academic staff can be based broadly on a limited understanding of illness or disability (Fuller et al., 2004). More specifically, disability can be seen as a condition that is predictable and constant (Olney & Brockelman, 2003), while illness can be seen as something to recover from quickly (Goffman, 1976; Levine & Kozloff, 1978; Parsons, 1970). Yet existing research on students with a chronic illness or disability shows that these conditions function in a context-dependent way (Olney & Brockelman, 2003).

THE STUDY

A three-year longitudinal project is being undertaken within a regional Australian university to delve into the learning experiences of students with chronic illness and disability and to develop greater understandings of what it means to study for these students. This chapter examines student experiences as represented in preliminary data from thirty-three students in their first year of study. For this phase of the project participants were recruited from students newly registered with Disability Resources: voluntary participants filled in a survey that detailed the nature of their illness and its impact on any previous study experiences. Later, respondents were interviewed by telephone to obtain a more detailed qualitative assessment of potential barriers and issues faced by participants during their studies throughout the year. The data examined in the chapter are drawn from both survey forms and telephone interviews. The nature of the data examined in the chapter and the effect of binary, normative constructs on individuals in this study—and elsewhere—have led us to adopt a constructivist paradigm (Guba, 1990; Schwandt, 1994). This paradigm allows the exploration of the way study participants are both framed by, and respond to, the ability/disability binary as part of negotiating and constructing their individual contexts and identities.

DISCUSSION

Straddling the Binary: Managing Disability, Managing the Perceptions of Others

The experiences of students in our study affirm existing research, which refers to a paradox where students with a chronic illness or disability can be both able and in need. This view conceptualizes students as effectively straddling the ability/disability binary by making choices and engaging in active strategies to manage needs relating to their condition. According to our preliminary study, students actively manage the impact of their disability by choosing particular programs, courses, and modes of study. For example, many students in our preliminary sample chose to study externally as one means of managing their disability. Students also referred to the issue of management in relation to their capacity to balance work—life priorities along with their chronic illness or disability:

> My biggest concern was my ability to manage time—manage my studies with my disability. Rheumatoid Arthritis can impact on my ability to concentrate as some days I need to rest more than others.

This form of active management of a condition is echoed by other research about students with a chronic illness or disability (Rizvi & Lingard, 1996; Vickers, 2005; Werth, 2008).

For students with a chronic illness or disability, one factor that worked counter to their ability to manage their condition was sometimes its sheer unpredictability. A relapse or another critical incident can have a negative impact on students' ability to complete their studies successfully. For one participant, fear of the unknown extent of their illness and the possible severity of the symptoms is reflected here:

> I fear a major flare up and surgery again. This would have an extreme impact, possibly causing me to drop out. This is my first semester and as I write I am recovering from a serious operation. This is making my semester exceptionally difficult.

Not surprisingly, the capacity to manage their condition has a direct correlation with some students' ability to engage successfully with their studies:

I worry that I may have underestimated the work/study load and that I may not have the "stickability" to see it through due to my illness.

However, for some students in this study perceptions of personal ability as influenced by their condition can also impact at the general level of identity, including how they appear to others. For example, it may appear to others that they do not have what it takes to succeed in a particular discipline or field.

The issue of difference was a recurring theme in many student responses within the study. In this context, fitting in might express a general desire to be like other students, such as in this statement from one student who expressed the wish of "fitting in and meeting new people [and] not having people find out about my condition." Fitting in could also refer to relative performance. Here one student expressed the desire to "keep up with other students." Within such statements students appear to acknowledge the power and desirability of the norm, expressed in their concern to appear as able instead of disabled. This position is powerfully reflected in the following student's comment: "I don't like to use my illness as an excuse for not achieving—this embarrasses me." On one level this comment demonstrates a sense of agency and strength. However, it also, arguably, expresses a desire to meet what this student considers normal standards of academic performance.

TRAPPED WITHIN THE BINARY: MEETING ACADEMIC STANDARDS

In many student comments, there were references to their ability to meet desired academic standards. As students in this study were all enrolled in their first year of study, these comments must also be seen within the broader context of students' transition to university. This is because existing research shows that the transition to university presents all students with significant challenges, including the ability to understand and meet often tacit expectations of lecturers (see, e.g., Kift, 2008). Such challenges are inevitably compounded when first-year students, such as those in our study, have an illness or disability. Such a condition adds an element of contingency to what is already a process of significant normative and behavioral adaptation. One student referred directly to standards:

> The ability to cope with the standards required; left school at 14, which was a naval school with an emphasis upon subjects to prepare for induction into the Navy—royal or merchant; not being able to use cursive writing.

Others referred to specific academic qualities of their program of study:

[I didn't know] if I would be up to the intellectual task of studying law and having to let people know occasionally (every 6 or more months) [that I] suffer from a very painful illness.

One other student referred indirectly to standards through their statement about passing:

Not passing [is my concern]. . . . Wasting my time and time of lecturers. Ending up in a less satisfying job than the one I'm in now.

In each of these comments the students positioned themselves as potentially deficient, or as a potential problem. In each case the students considered whether they would be good enough to meet various performance benchmarks that they will encounter as part of their learning journeys in higher education.

HOW TO SUPPORT STUDENTS FURTHER WITH A CHRONIC ILLNESS OR DISABILITY?

The first theme explored in this chapter highlights the importance of choice in assisting students in this study to move beyond the ability/disability binary. In the current context, student choice is often limited to accommodations and modes of study. Accommodations can include changes in assessment format, timing, access to resources, the allocation of note takers, sign language interpreters, and readers (Konur, 2002). Such accommodations tend to work best for students with fairly static or physical disabilities. For others, particular forms of curriculum design and assessment practice may be inherently inequitable (Hammer, Werth, & Dunn, 2009). There is also evidence (Searle, 2006) to suggest that barriers can exist for students with a chronic illness or disability in relation to online education. Neither of these options on their own offers a neat solution to students with a chronic illness or disability.

Core higher education activities such as curriculum and assessment design arguably offer the possibility of further support for students with a chronic illness or disability. Nunan, Rigmor, and McCauseland (2000) argue that for universities to be more inclusive they need to focus on desired outcomes rather than inputs, as well as the relationship between exclusion and the design of curricula and assessment:

To focus upon the site (curriculum decision making) where compromise, adjustment and preference is writ large in choice of content and methodologies is the fundamental way of addressing issues of inclusivity. (p. 69)

For example, particular forms of assessment were inherently difficult for some students in this study—in particular, those forms of assessment which included some physical requirement, such as sitting for long periods or some kind of performance. In this context, an inclusive curriculum would offer all students alternative types of assessment, where possible, that enable them to demonstrate the same learning objectives and the same level of performance. In order to implement such changes, however, a greater understanding of the relationship among curriculum, assessment, and academic standards is required.

The emphasis on standards is unsurprising given that universities are known to value excellence, and to value individuals based on their proven academic ability. Indeed, the practice of applying accommodations for students with a chronic illness or disability is often concerned with negating any ill effect of a student's condition without undermining academic standards. Yet there are few resources currently available to assist academic staff in designing curricula and assessment tasks that offer students some element of choice, and which also uphold academic standards (Hammer et al., 2009). This is a significant issue in an educational context where, anecdotally at least, academic staff tend to conflate examinations with standards. A more inclusive curriculum requires greater support for staff so that students are provided with greater choice and, ultimately, a greater capacity to transcend the ability/disability binary.

These suggested strategies are brief, and they reflect the early stages of the research project itself. Further research will provide greater direction on more finely-grained strategies to enable students with a chronic illness or disability to manage their tertiary learning experience more effectively.

CONCLUSION

Preliminary results from the study examined here indicate a need to move beyond a conceptual binary that problematizes and, often unwittingly, stigmatizes students with a chronic illness or disability. Comments from students participating in the study show that many make specific choices relating to their enrolment and their work–life–learning balance that enable them to manage their condition. In this case, enabling students to transcend the ability/disability binary may require offering students increased choice, where practicable, not just in terms of their learning pathway but also in relations to assessment and different ways in which they might legitimately demonstrate desired learning objectives. The vexing question for students in this study, and for practicing academic staff, is whether institutions can meet the requirements of those with a chronic illness or disability without undermining academic standards. It has been suggested that any movement toward an inclusive curriculum requires an investigation of the relationship among desired learning objectives, academic standards, curriculum design, assessment practices, and exclusion. In particular, greater support for academic staff is required to assist them in designing legitimate curricular and assessment alternatives that maintain necessary academic standards, but that also enable affected students to transcend the ability/disability binary.

REFERENCES

Coombs, J. (2010, April 7). Student equity front and centre. *The Australian.* Retrieved from http://www.theaustralian.com.au

Disability Discrimination Act. (1992). Commonwealth Consolidated Acts. Retrieved from http://www.austlii.edu.au/au/legis/cth/consol_act/dda1992264/

Fuller, M., Healey, M., Bradley, A., & Hall, T. (2004). Barriers to learning: A systematic study of the experience of disabled students in one university. *Studies in Higher Education, 29*(3), 303–318.

Goffman, E. (1976). *Stigma: Notes on the management of spoiled identity.* Harmondsworth, UK: Penguin.

Goode, J. (2007). Managing disability: Early experiences of university students with disabilities. *Disability and Society, 22*(1), 35–48.

Guba, E. (1990). The alternative paradigm dialog. In E. Guba (Ed.), *The paradigm dialog* (pp. 17–30). Newbury Park, CA: Sage.

Hammer, S., Werth, S., & Dunn, P. (2009). *Tertiary students with a disability or chronic illness: Stigma and study.* Paper presented at the 3rd National Conference of Enabling Educators, University of Southern Queensland, Australia.

James, R., Krause, K., & Jennings, C. (2010). *The first year experience in Australian universities: Findings from 1994 to 2009.* Melbourne, Australia: Centre for the Study of Higher Education, University of Melbourne.

Jung, K. E. (2002). Chronic illness and educational equity: The politics of visibility. *NWSA Journal, 14*(3), 178–200.

Kift, S. (2008). *First year curriculum principles: Articulating a transition pedagogy.* Retrieved from http://www.fyecd2009.qut.edu.au/index.jsp

Konur, O. (2002). Assessment of disabled students in higher education: Current policy issues. *Assessment and Evaluation in Higher Education, 27*(2), 132–152.

Levine, S., & Kozloff, M. A. (1978). The sick role: Assessment and overview. *Annual Review of Sociology, 4*, 317–343.

Link, B., & Phelan, J. (2001). *On stigma and its public health implications, stigma and global health: Developing a research agenda.* Retrieved from http://www.stigmaconference.nih.gov/LinkPaper.htm

Marginson, S., & Considine, M. (2000). *The enterprise university: Power, governance and reinvention in Australia.* Cambridge, UK: Cambridge University Press.

McClean, P., Heagney, M., & Gardner, K. (2003). Going global: The implications for students with a disability, *Higher Education Research and Development, 22*(2), 217–228.

Myers, K. R. (2004). Coming out: Considering the closet of illness. *Journal of Medical Humanities, 25*(4), 255–270.

Nunan, T., Rigmor, G., & McCauseland, H. (2000). Inclusive education in universities: Why it is important and how it might be achieved. *International Journal of Inclusive Education, 4*(1), 63–88.

Oakes, W. T., (2005). *Perspectives on disability, discrimination, accommodations, and law: A comparison of the Canadian and American experience.* New York: Scholarly.

Olney, M. F., & Brockelman, K. F. (2003). Out of the disability closet: Strategic use of perception management by select university students with disabilities. *Disability and Society, 18*(1), 35–50.

Parsons, T. (1970). *The social system*. London: Routledge.

Prowse, S. (2009). Institutional construction of disabled students. *Journal of Higher Education Policy and Management, 31*(1), 89–96.

Rizvi, F., & Lingard, B. (1996). Disability, education and the discourses of justice. In C. Christensen & F. Rizvi (Eds.), *Disability and the dilemmas of education and justice* (pp. 9–16). Buckingham, UK: Open University Press.

Ryan, J., & Struhs, J. (2004). University education for all? Barriers to full inclusion of students with disabilities in Australian universities. *International Journal of Inclusive Education, 8*(1), 73–90.

Schwandt, T. (1994). Constructivist, interpretivist approaches to human inquiry. In N. Denzin & Y. Lincoln (Eds.), *Handbook of qualitative research* (pp. 118–137). Thousand Oaks, CA: Sage.

Searle, J. (2006). *E-Learning and disability in higher education: Accessibility, research and practice*. London: Routledge.

Vickers, M. H. (1997). Life at work with 'invisible' chronic illness (ICI): The 'unseen', unspoken, unrecognised dilemma of disclosure. *Journal of Workplace Learning, 9*(7), 240–252.

Vickers, M. H. (2001). Unseen chronic illness and work: Authentic stories from 'women in-between.' *Women in Management Review, 16*(2), 62–74.

Vickers, M. H. (2005). Illness, work and organisation: Postmodern perspectives, antenarratives and chaos narratives for the reinstatement of voice. *Journal of Critical Postmodern Organisation Science, 3*(2), 74–88.

Werth, S. (2008). Putting chronically ill university students into the research limelight. In R. Henderson & P. A. Danaher (Eds.), *Troubling terrains: Tactics for traversing and transforming contemporary educational research* (pp. 67–76). Teneriffe, Australia: Post Pressed.

16 Formal, Informal, and Incidental Learning

How Recreational-Diving Instructors Achieve Competency

Keith Cardwell

ABSTRACT

Scholarly, commercial, and anecdotal argument around the tensions between formal and informal learning have produced perplexing perspectives on the validation of workplace competencies and qualifications. This chapter explores one site where these complexities produce various tales and notions of work readiness regarding instructors within the recreational-diving industry. The chapter begins with voices that extoll the virtues of formal learning through a set curriculum being pitted against those that highlight the value inherent in informal learning. It positions informal learning as the means through which gaps in the diving curriculum might be filled, and promotes raising the diving industry's consciousness on the use of incidental learning experiences as important activities that enable the production of all-round competent diving instructors.

Data gained from interviews and observational studies indicate that in this context there is a presumption that informal and incidental learning processes work together more effectively to attain instructor competence as opposed to prior formal training. Although the informal processes are not entirely unpredictable, little recognition is given to their importance or the fact that improved leadership in this regard can create greater opportunity for both instructor development and organizational growth.

INTRODUCTION

The training of scuba divers moved rapidly from its early beginnings in the military to the civilian population. With what became a burgeoning demand for involvement in the sport, there was, and remains, a directly proportional demand for instructors to teach diving. Yet, whereas the early divers gained much and varied experience prior to becoming instructors, today's generation becomes certified much more quickly and often with questionable experience levels. From this is an ever-present argument of which is better: learning from the school of hard knocks through varied and unregulated experiences or education in a formal framework of learning that focuses on what should be done, attempting to avoid mistakes often made by unregulated practice and within a more abbreviated time frame.

This chapter discusses the binary question of informal versus formal training and reflects on the manner in which recreational-diving instructors are presently trained and the experience levels necessary but arguably absent from that training. It looks in particular at the value of incidental learning within the entire learning process and how this contributes to the ultimate objective of instructor training: workplace competence and a recreational-diving instructor who is capable of doing their job effectively.

This chapter is therefore composed of the following sections:

- A brief history of recreational diver training
- Time for a change
- Workplace competence
- Formal versus informal learning
- Incidental learning

Many of the observations and quotations used in this discussion are from an unpublished doctoral research study on the topic of what it takes to become a workplace competent recreational-diving instructor. Pseudonyms have been used to protect the identity of the instructors cited.

> The early divers were mostly water people. . . . Water experience was important because there were no classes in the beginning. People would buy equipment from surplus stores or fabricate it in their home workshops. If there were instructions they would read them; if not they went diving anyway. (Hanauer, 1994, p. 11)

A BRIEF HISTORY

Diver training evolved from the (naval) military and consequently many of those divers thus trained became the first civilian instructors. This was reflected in many of the skills incorporated into the early beginner-diver programs. One skill, for instance, labeled a bailout, was considered by some as an essential and final test of how familiar a diver has become with her dive equipment. The diver is expected to stand on the edge of the deep end of a swimming pool and, holding all dive equipment, fall in (usually pushed), and sink to the bottom. Successful completion of this skill was when the diver arrived back at the surface correctly dressed and wearing all of the scuba equipment she descended with. If one were to consider what a navy diver was to do when shot at by enemy fire, this would be an appropriate skill to be master of, but in civilian terms, it doesn't really make much sense. This is typical of many of the skills once taught.

In other words, many subjects and skills taught in the earlier days of recreational diver training were derived from what was previously thought to be relevant but with little reflection on the altered contexts of demographics (civilian versus military) and technology (crude and makeshift equipment versus specifically designed equipment). Things had to change. With the increasing popularity of recreational diving, there was a directly proportional increase in the demand for training and for the production of instructors to fulfill this need. It was in response to this increased need that greater thought was given to what skills and knowledge should be taught to both beginner diver and instructor alike.

TIME FOR A CHANGE

In the mid to late 1960s, organizations such as the Professional Association of Diving Instructors (PADI) and Scuba Schools International (SSI) became established and commenced using a systems-oriented approach to diver training where skill requirements are immediately relevant to the course being taught. This approach obligates the trained divers to dive within the limits and conditions in which they have been trained. This change brought more efficiently achievable steps required to gain instructor status whilst still requiring formal attendance of classes for knowledge and skills development. This situation has become even more streamlined over the last decade with less demand for classroom attendance by providing more opportunity for home study instead. Even so, little change has been made to either skill requirements or prerequisite dive experience levels for the respective courses leading up to and including instructor training. This creates situations where instructors are certified but are possibly missing the real experience and skills necessary for many diver-training situations. In turn, this leads to statements such as the following from recently trained instructors:

> I think that there should be more of an [sic], well induction is probably the wrong word, but real life experiences. I'm not sure what instructors go through now but I know when I went through the instructor course [it] didn't prepare you at all for what was out there. (Geoff)

> It's [IDC—Instructor Development Course] a very brief quick course for the responsibility you are ultimately given. I think also as far as going from OW [open-water diver is the first certification step] to Instructor in one shot is silly. (Leila)

Well, I wouldn't think that that would be it. Some of the people who come out of the IDC and IE [instructor examination] are pretty raw, aren't they? They come into the industry; they've done their open water course with someone. They've maybe got a job on the boat as an intern and do their advanced, rescue, divemasters—okay, that may have happened within five weeks or six weeks. So they say "Oh, now I'm a divemaster I'm going to be an instructor." So next month they're off to do their instructor course, they do their IDC, they do their IE, they get awarded an instructor ticket and then a week later on they're out on the boat and teaching people, maybe twice their age, how to dive, with little or no experience actually in the real world. (Jeremy)

This indicates the apparent gap between what should be learned prior to certification and what may eventually have to be further learned informally to ensure competence in performing the job for which certification has already been achieved. Certification, as it appears in this context, is certainly not qualification. A certificate indicates that a person should be qualified to do something, but just how genuinely workplace competent are they?

WORKPLACE COMPETENCE

Boyatzis (1982) defines competence as "an underlying characteristic of a person, which results in effective and/or superior performance in a job" (p. 21). But there are many variations on this definition, some of which have been outlined by Hoffmann (1999) reflecting on the work of Sternberg and Kolligian (1990), Burgoyne (1993), and Bowden and Masters (1993), who propose meanings that fall in line with their own specialist activities of psychology, management theory, human resources, politics, and education respectively. Although all of these definitions may have some bearing on the competence required of recreational-diving instructors, a more clearly defined description of the skill sets necessary for workplace competence in this context is desired. This section looks at how experience is gained and how prior and ongoing learning reflects on this experience in achieving workplace competence.

The recreational-diving industry is an important sector of the tourism industry in many tropical destinations such as Far North Queensland, Australia. With the existing systems of instructor training offering relatively easy access to involvement within the diving industry, there is an obvious financial advantage to be gained from having more instructors to train, and being as expeditious in that training as possible. On the other hand, there is the possible future disadvantage of producing instructors who are not yet workplace competent and who may be accidents waiting to happen.

Specific competency standards are listed in the relevant texts and guides that are issued by the major diver-training agencies. One such diver-training agency (PADI) in Australia has been granted a Registered Training Organisation status, which enables the delivery of nationally recognized training. According to this organization, "PADI programs are performance based, not time based" (Professional Association of Diving Instructors, 2001, pp. 2–3).

Time, however, is when we gain experience, and, according to Harris, Guthrie, Hobart, and Lundberg (1995), "competency and experience are inextricably linked" (p. 99). In an attempt to define competency, the Australian National Training Board in 1992 maintained that these standards should relate to workplace practices, be expressed in outcomes, and be understood by trainers, supervisors, and prospective employers. The board also believed that these standards should acknowledge workplace reform requirements and an industry's needs. These needs should include the ability to apply skills in varying situations, rather than just perform current tasks (Harris et al., 1995, p. 94). This means it is important not only that the training received gives the student a structured set of immediate objectives to achieve, but also that achievement of those objectives will enable performance under changing conditions. A good example is a diving instructor who is capable of dealing with students in a calm, clear, confined water area but should also be able to deal with those same students when the conditions are not so tranquil or so clear. Current instructor-training programs discuss these changing situations but rarely, if ever, give the opportunity to experience them.

It is this type of situation as described above that prompted Garrick (1998) to comment: "The pre-defined nature of competencies can remove elements of professional judgment" (p. 157). Workplace competence is thus a result of learning processes that involve conformity to a set of predefined standards applied in a working environment. Yet that environment often changes and exposure to these variables, with time and experience, will enable good judgment and yield positive outcomes. With regard to the above example, this would then indicate a knowledge of industry standards limiting maximum student numbers to have in the water at any one time given ideal conditions, but experience would be the factor defining what this number should be reduced to in this specific situation. It appears that the only available way of improving this ability is through practical involvement with the communities of practice located in the immediate workplace in which more informal learning takes place.

FORMAL VERSUS INFORMAL LEARNING

It is an emerging realization that informal learning has more validity in the workplace than the quantum of information learned in less contextualized settings (Boud, 2005; Cross, 2007; Garrick, 1998; Hager & Halliday, 2009; Marsick & Watkins, 1990; Rowden, 2007; Senge, 1993). Cross's (2007) comment that "Workers learn more in the coffee room than the classroom" (p. 235) is particularly telling, and the value in this may well be reflected by dive instructors' daily reflections when informally discussing their problems on site during breaks in the day.

If informal learning is then seen to be of such significance to the development of appropriate training in the workplace environment, it requires more research to answer the question as to how the training of recreational-diving instructors could, or should, be modified to enable workplace competence.

Much of the formal training in the IDC process is objective oriented with more or less standard responses required to set questions and skill demands. These conform well to the present-day competency-based training design. However, criticism of formal competency-based training is provided by Cooper (1992), who observes that "in the assessment process no question could be asked of a participant for which the answer was not provided in the modules; and that no materials were presented as problems to be engaged with, or situations to be investigated" (p. 20). This agrees with Bone, Harris, and Simons's (2000) findings indicating that trainer competency standards do not match the actions involved in formal training.

Present diving instructor development processes are composed of a set of short-term learning activities grouped to teach the trainee instructor how to teach in the classroom, swimming pool, and open-water environments. This is followed by a cluster of knowledge-development sessions explaining the standards, procedures of conduct, and marketing of various programs available for the instructor trainee to teach. After a two-day summative assessment phase, the successful trainee instructor is deemed capable of entering the workforce as a productive unit. There is little reference to any developmental learning such as reflective activity (Schön, 1983) to "bridge the gap between academic theory and professional practice by integrating the two into a cycle of learning" (Johnston, 1995, p. 76). The gap between traditional schooling and professional practice requires consideration of complex problems and new professional images to deal with them (Schön, 1983).

As well as technical competencies such as diving-skill performance, other attributes ascribed to competent trainers are well-developed human interaction skills such as those of questioning, listening, and providing considered feedback. Florian, a recently certified instructor, gives a typically echoed comment of the formal training he did for his instructor's course:

> There was no training in terms of dealing with people. That's 90% of the job—the ability of being nice, friendly, and offering some kind of service. I keep going back to that one because for me personally it's the main thing. (Florian)

The theory supporting the value of human interaction skills and feedback goes back a long way (Boyatzis, 1982; DeVito 1993; Lewin, 1951) and may suggest at least one area of the present curriculum that requires greater scrutiny. Lave and Wenger (1991) maintain that human interaction skills are an important part of the development phase of technical competencies.

They consider that apprentices learn much from their peers, noting the effectiveness of the circulation of information. This suggests that engaging in practice (rather than being its object) may be a condition for the effectiveness of learners.

This consideration is supported by Cross (2007), who writes that there is another factor at work which makes learning informally often more memorable than formal education methods. He believes that repetition spread over intervals is more likely to be retained in long-term memory than repetition taking place within a relatively shorter time frame. In other words, regular and constant exposure to certain methods and practices is better than reading and memorizing detail about a process and perhaps considering it only once or twice. In the former instance, the learning can become an embedded capability learned through practice; in the latter instance it is less likely to be embedded. Furthermore, this may breed the belief that, because a subject has been examined once, sufficient learning has taken place; therefore it does not need revisiting until such time as it may be needed. This could produce a very dangerous situation if the learner who had a brief and cursory practice of lifesaving techniques in the classroom or confined water were called on to attempt resuscitation in a real-life situation. Less dramatically, and with absent leadership, learning from peers with equally poor interpersonal communication skills could produce negative outcomes such as customers rejecting opportunities to participate in an introductory dive or customers failing to return.

Informal learning within the workplace in the company of communities of practitioners is thus asserted to be of greater importance to job performance than formal training in classroom settings. This is a likely reflection of the manner in which recreational dive-instructor training occurs in practice. However, this does not in itself entirely negate the value of formal learning processes. The question remains now as to the boundaries of the formal and informal learning processes that take place in this context and whether these can be modified, if at all, to enable and maximize more effective and efficient workplace competency.

Whilst informal learning thus far has been discussed in contrast to formal, structured programs of instruction, it is becoming identified as separate also from nonformal learning, defined by Smith and Clayton (2009) as "not intentionally accessed by the learner, and thus is neither structured nor institutionalized" (p. 6). This description reflects the many definitions given to *incidental learning*, which, although interconnected, is not necessarily the same as informal learning (Rowden, 2007).

INCIDENTAL LEARNING

Incidental learning is defined variously as "a by-product of some other activity, such as task accomplishment, interpersonal interaction" (Marsick & Watkins, 1990, p. 121); "a spontaneous action or transaction, the intention of which is task accomplishment, but which serendipitously increases particular knowledge, skills, or understanding" (Ross-Gordon & Dowling, 1995, p. 315); "unintentional or unplanned learning that results from other activities" (Kerka, 2000, p. 1); and occurring as "an unintended by-product of some activity such as trial-and-error experimentation or interpersonal interaction" (Rowden, 2007, p. 7).

From these four particular definitions it would be fair to say that incidental learning is a spontaneous, unplanned by-product of another activity. This is diametrically opposed to formally planned processes. Whichever view is taken, this form of learning is not planned; it just happens. Owing to its spontaneous nature, it defies the idea of control and subordination to deliberate generation and subsequent rules and guidelines.

However, in preparation for such learning being realized, Lankard (1995) states, "Awareness of opportunities and the value of such learning may be brought to the learners' attention by emphasizing the outcomes they might anticipate through incidental learning" (p. 2). Mealman (1993) indicates that these opportunities can include increased competence, increased self-knowledge, value for lifelong learning, improved life skills, and development of self-confidence. These opportunities are certainly of great value to an individual but may also be of similar benefit to an organization, community, or industry.

From a recent interview with Stewart, reflecting on why he is so successful with introductory diving:

> My thing on the boat is I'm really fussy about masks. I hate it if a diver has a foggy mask, even slightly foggy, or if the mask doesn't fit properly, if it's too tight or loose because I found that that was the main reason that people would spit [out] their regulator . . . and I just put two and two together. (Stewart)

Stewart realized that, if he were more deliberate about ensuring a properly fitting mask, as opposed to a mask that was barely adequate, he virtually eliminated the problem of introductory divers becoming overstressed by water leakage and blurred vision and, as a result of this, rushing to the surface and ending what could have become a great experience.

An early example from this writer's experience of the significance of incidental learning in the recreational-diving industry was a by-product of reflecting on what was inspirational and what was not. After only a short period of using the traditional method of diver training during the latter part of 1979, concern was given to two issues: why student diver trainees were canceling courses; and what excited others enough to continue. On reflection, both were tied together. In the first instance, students were being put off by the then relatively difficult prerequisite exercises of swimming and snorkeling before they were allowed to use a self-contained underwater breathing apparatus (SCUBA). In the second instance, for those who fulfilled those prerequisites, nothing provided greater excitement than actually breathing underwater. This provoked a change in marketing and training. Free introductory courses (two hours in duration) were offered as an enticement to try diving, and, when potential customers signed up for the courses, the first element of training in the course was breathing on SCUBA, changing places with the more rigorous activities traditionally required. This quadrupled the annual number of student divers trained within the first year. It is important to note that this writer does not claim credit for this innovation. Even though I was ignorant of other actors, from subsequent research it is clear that this realization was occurring worldwide at that time.

Today this introductory course is a stand-alone program that enjoys a significant part of what the recreational-diving industry offers by way of diving experiences. The unpublished "2008 Diver Certification Statistics for QLD" as produced by one major diver-training agency (J. Hutchinson, personal communication, September 10, 2009) indicates that this form of diving experience represents 78% of all registered diving experiences resulting in some form of certification.

In the incidental learning example detailed above, the solution to that problem now reflects a significant proportion of present-day diving activities. Further, as can be seen in the data collected in this study, the enjoyment that can be experienced by the customer is reflected in the continuing pleasure and breadth of human interaction skills developed by instructors in providing this particular training. This regular and varied interaction with customers begins also to define the value of social capital brought to, and often developed in, the workplace situation by both the instructor and the company to which he or she belongs. But that is another story altogether!

CONCLUSION

Recreational diving is with little doubt a very stimulating sport and reflects a significant sector of the potential income in particular areas such as the far north of Queensland. With this comes a demand for competent instruction to ensure the safety of those visitors wishing to experience diving at the Great Barrier Reef. It is hoped that these visitors will give both a positive testimonial to that experience and add to the future potential growth of the recreational-diving industry by continuation of their diver training and/or by becoming return customers. It is thus how recreational-diving instructors learn to become workplace competent and capable of producing this type of positive response that is brought into question. The formal processes of training are arguably inadequate and require complementing by further informal learning processes. Much data exist to suggest that this binary situation of both formal and informal learning processes is out of balance and must be modified to ensure improved instructor training through more negotiation and involvement with all stakeholders and in particular the communities of practice presently found in the workplace.

REFERENCES

Bone, J., Harris, R., & Simons, M. (2000). *More than meets the eye? Rethinking the role of the workplace trainer.* Leabrook, Australia: National Centre for Vocational Education Research.

Boud, D. (2005). *Productive perspectives for research in workplace learning.* Paper presented at the Australian Vocational Education and Training Researchers Association conference, Brisbane, Australia.

Bowden, J. A., & Masters, G. N. (1993). *Implications for higher education of a competency-based approach to education and training.* Canberra, Australia: Australian Government Publishing Service.

Boyatzis, R. (1982). *The competent manager: A model for effective performance.* New York: John Wiley & Sons.

Burgoyne, J. (1993). The competence movement: Issues, stakeholders and prospects. *Personnel Review, 22*(6), 6–13.

Cooper, T. (1992). Qualified for the job: The new vocationalism. *Education Links, 42,* 18–22.

Cross, J. (2007). *Informal learning: Rediscovering the natural pathways that inspire innovation and performance.* San Francisco, CA: Pfeiffer.

DeVito, J. A. (1993). *Messages: Building interpersonal communication skills.* New York: HarperCollins College.

Garrick, J. (1998). *Informal learning in the workplace: Unmasking human resource development.* London: Routledge.

Hager, P., & Halliday, J. (2009). *Recovering informal learning: Wisdom, judgement and community.* Dordrecht, The Netherlands: Springer.

Hanauer, E. (1994). *Diving pioneers: An oral history of diving in America.* San Diego, CA: Watersport.

Harris, R., Guthrie, H., Hobart. B., & Lundberg, D. (1995). *Competency based education and training: Between a rock and a whirlpool.* Melbourne, Australia: Macmillan.

Hoffmann, T. (1999). The meanings of competency. *Journal of European Industrial Training, 23*(6), 275–285.

Johnston, R. (1995). Two cheers for the reflective practitioner. *Journal of Further and Higher Education, 19*(3), 74–83.

Kerka, S. (2000). *Incidental learning.* Retrieved from http://library.nald.ca/purchase/item/1243

Lankard, B. A. (1995). *New ways of learning in the workplace: ERIC Digest 161.* Columbus, OH: ERIC Clearinghouse.

Lave, J., & Wenger, E. (1991). *Situated learning: Legitimate peripheral participation.* Cambridge, UK: Cambridge University Press.

Lewin, K. (1951). *Field theory in social science: Selected theoretical papers.* New York: Harper & Row.

Marsick, V. J., & Watkins, K. (1990). *Informal and incidental learning in the workplace.* London: Routledge.

Mealman, C. A. (1993). *Incidental learning by adults in a nontraditional degree program: A case study.* Paper presented at the 12th Annual Midwest Research-to-Practice Conference, Columbus, OH.

Professional Association of Diving Instructors. (2001). *Professional Association of Diving Instructors instructor candidate workbook.* Rancho Santa Margarita, CA: Author.

Ross-Gordon, J. M., & Dowling, W. D. (1995). Adult learning in the context of African-American women's voluntary organisations. *International Journal of Lifelong Education, 14*(4), 306–319.

Rowden, R. W. (2007). *Workplace learning: Principles and practice.* Malabar, FL: Krieger.

Schön, D. A. (1983). *The reflective practitioner: How professionals think in action.* London: Temple Smith.

Senge, P. M. (1993). *The fifth discipline: The art and practice of the learning organization.* Milsons Point, Australia: Random House.

Smith, L., & Clayton, B. (2009). *Recognising formal and informal learning: Participant insights and perspectives.* Adelaide, Australia: National Centre for Vocational Education Research.

Sternberg, R. J., & Kolligian, J. (Eds.). (1990). *Competence considered.* New Haven, CT: Yale University Press.

17 Limited-Term Contracts and Tenure

The Case of Foreign-Language Teachers in a Japanese University

Sean Mehmet

ABSTRACT

This chapter examines the binary relationship between foreign language teachers on limited-term employment contracts in Japan and their tenured Japanese colleagues. The dualism here can be viewed as an insider–outsider one. The chapter focuses on the practice of limiting non-Japanese academic employees to such contracts, in the context of one Japanese university, which has been shown to impact negatively on foreign-language instruction. The primary question under consideration is: "What conceptual model could help transcend the insider–outsider binary that seems to inform this employment arrangement?" The chapter advocates a framework based on a hybrid of Limerick, Cunnington, and Crowther's (2002) Fourth Blueprint paradigm, infused with intercultural communications (ICC) theory.

INTRODUCTION

This chapter argues that restricting foreign-language teachers to limited-term contracts negatively impacts on foreign-language instruction and learning. Such contracts penalize not only the foreign teaching staff but also their Japanese clientele—that is to say, the student body. A reworked, interculturally competent hybrid of Limerick, Cunnington, and Crowther's (2002) Fourth Blueprint is presented as a conceptual model to help transcend the permanent employee/limited-term employee binary. The chapter is a conceptual, rather than an empirical, one. Thus, it focuses on existing research. It is argued that a hybridized Fourth Blueprint can serve as a model for solving the pedagogical problem that seems to arise from this binary.

LIMITED-TERM CONTRACTS AND THE QUALITY OF PEDAGOGY

Japanese higher education institutions have systematically employed foreign faculty members since the Meiji period (Rivers, 2010). In most cases, such non-Japanese faculty members have been employed on limited-term contracts. Until very recently there has been a paucity of research examining the pedagogical implications of such contracts. However, a pioneering study has recently concluded that limited-term contracts, *sentaku ninkisei*, have contributed to a decline in the standard of language instruction (Burrows, 2007). This is because such contracts have caused some faculty members to pander to student expectations, which are often influenced by their previous English as a Foreign Language (EFL) experiences. These EFL experiences have very often focused on the passive, receptive language-acquisition skills of reading and listening at the expense of the more active, productive skills of writing and speaking. The reduction in the quality of educational delivery would appear to counter the current Ministry of Education, Culture, Sports, Science, and Technology (MEXT) directive for universities to improve both their accountability and the quality of education (MEXT, 2004).

Many full-time Japanese faculty members are in tenured positions, while most full-time non-Japanese are in contracted, nontenure track positions, despite the fact that Article 3 of the Japanese Labor Standards Law prohibits any kind of discrimination based on nationality (Johnston, 2004). Theoretically, at least, contract employees are protected under Japanese labor law even if the employer chooses not to renew the contract once it has expired. Employees who want to continue are legally entitled to expect their contract to be renewed, as the law does not allow for dismissal owing to contract expiry once renewal has occurred. Sugeno (1992) explains that, "after such a contract has been repeatedly renewed, it will resemble a contract without a fixed period" (p. 389). However, this legislation does not specify how many times a contract must be renewed before an employee can legally expect his/her contract to be automatically renewed.

Regardless of this legislation, Burrows (2007) has noted that "[faculty members on contracts] will be more inclined to ingratiate themselves with the university to reduce the prospect of contract non-renewal. It is this ingratiation which is most likely to influence how they behave in the classroom" (p. 32). This fear of nonrenewal makes teachers highly cognizant of how they are perceived by their students, as these perceptions will directly influence course evaluations.

Japanese university students use different criteria when evaluating Japanese and non-Japanese teachers. As Burrows (2007) has noted, this difference in assessment criteria could result in evaluations which may, or may not, be based on criteria related to the pedagogical merits of the class. In other words, foreign teachers who excell in their classrooms, at least as far as their own cultural conditioning is concerned, are not necessarily conforming to their Japanese students' culturally informed image of what constitutes a good teacher. Pre-tertiary foreign language learning in Japan tends to be teacher-centered, wherein learners usually develop a reliance on the teacher. This can lead to student confusion when non-Japanese, post-secondary educators require them to perform independent, creative, active learning. Western teacher training programs typically ascribe only minimal, or negative, value to both rote learning and didactic learning (Burrows, 2007).

In a study conducted by Shimizu (1995), Japanese learners indicated that the two most important criteria for evaluating non-Japanese language educators were: (1) how easy they were to get acquainted with (28%); and (2) how entertaining they were (26%). Hadley and Yoshioka (1996) listed other attributes that Japanese university learners believed non-Japanese English teachers should have: kindness, friendliness, cheerfulness, fun, enthusiasm, and humor. This contrasts markedly with the criteria Japanese learners used to evaluate ethnically Japanese university EFL educators: (1) knowledge of the subject area (34%); and (2) pronunciation (33%) (Hadley & Yoshioka Hadley, 1996). Attributes that Japanese students believed ethnically Japanese educators should possess included being demanding and professional, items which were not listed for non-Japanese educators.

What cultural explanations could account for these differences in university student perceptions about appropriate criteria for evaluating language teachers? One possible explanation is that Japan has historically been a homogeneous nation. As with similar cultures, there has been a strong national identity, and therefore a tendency to view anyone outside the group as different (Najita & Harootunian, 1988).

A CONCEPTUAL MODEL FOR POTENTIALLY TRANSCENDING THIS BINARY

The *Third Blueprint* and *Fourth Blueprint* concepts of Limerick et al. (2002) are useful conceptual frameworks to consider. Third Blueprint organizations are generally characterized by corporate citizenship. In the West, this Third Blueprint was often found in organizations prior to 1980. These organizations had stable structures with defined, stable roles, and with predictable career paths. For individuals in such a system, self-identity and role were synonymous: the individual was simply what he or she did. Identity was provided by the continuity of the role. This was reinforced by an expectation of lifelong employment. For people in such a system, a long-service award was not trivial; it represented the successful completion of reciprocal rights and obligations. Those in these organizations valued a group of behaviors that could be broadly termed as citizenship behavior: altruism, conscientiousness, loyalty, teamwork, good relationships with others, and general contributions to the system.

The heart of the organizations of the Third Blueprint was an unwavering connection between the individual and the structure. People within such organizations found that changes in organizational structure were often personally devastating because they led to a redefinition of self (Limerick et al., 2002). Part of the psychological contract was for employees to give high levels of commitment to the organization in return for security, mentorship, growth, and development. Responsibility for the development of an individual's career rested with the organization itself and its human resource planning systems. In a very real sense, employees belonged to the organization. They and their careers were essentially owned by it. The Japanese university that is the focus of this chapter typifies these characteristics, so it is clearly a Third Blueprint organization.

In marked contrast, Fourth Blueprint organizations are characterized by what its three originators have termed *collaborative individualism* (Limerick et al., 2002). Individuals within such loosely coupled network organizations cannot use structure and role as a definition of identity. Such individuals move in and out of a series of systems or contracts, many of them temporary, which demand different role definitions. Under these conditions, individuals define their identities in terms of the unique set of factors. For these individuals, the ability to tolerate the uncertainties of engaging in multiple temporary systems of action demands a mature understanding of self. People in network or collaborative organizations therefore become concerned with self-mapping, which involves getting to know and understand the self, in addition to developing a mature self-acceptance. However, Limerick et al. explicitly state that this focus on the self is not to be confused with facile selfishness.

Individuals in Fourth Blueprint organizations do not develop allegiance to the organization; rather, they develop a commitment to the issue, the mission, and the vision of the shared enterprise (Limerick et al., 2002). These individuals develop a process of what Tucker (as cited in Limerick et al., 2002) has called *mentally incorporating* themselves. Thus, each individual becomes *You, Inc.*, networking and collaborating with others toward shared projects. Fourth Blueprint organizations allow their employees to accept self-responsibility for their own career development, and for the overall achievement of the organizational mission. In return, these employees expect sufficient autonomy and empowerment to realize the collaborative goals. Fourth Blueprint employees create alliances with organizations; they do not become owned by them. This rejection of being the property of an organization is expressed by a movement toward establishing real contracts with the organization, or to becoming a consultant. Fourth Blueprint employees have the freedom to set their own hours, to exercise their own values, and to make as much money as their talents will allow.

Given that this Fourth Blueprint is premised on a fundamentally Western worldview (Limerick et al., 2002), one might well question its level of suitability for a change-resistant Japanese university. The formerly national university that is the focus of this chapter conforms to the Third Blueprint organizational model, as evidenced by lifetime employment, an ethos of loyalty to one's academic department, minimal contact with colleagues from other faculties, and its vertical hierarchy.

While Limerick et al. (2002) astutely acknowledge that hybrids of their four blueprints are both feasible and effective, the argument could be made that, when such hybrids are to be applied outside a Western context, steps must be taken to ensure that such a framework conforms to the local culture. In order to develop a hybrid Fourth Blueprint that may be suitable for a university in Japan, the following discussion applies Bennett's (1999) assumptions for cross-cultural effectiveness, Gudykunst and Kim's (1984) characteristics of intercultural persons, Hall's (1985) distinction between high context and low context societies, and his five suggestions for educators.

Intercultural Communication (ICC) theorist Bennett (1999) has defined intercultural competence as the ability to interpret intentional communications, such as language, signs, and gestures; unconscious cues, such as body language; and interpersonal customs that are different from those one is normally exposed to. The two dominant tenets of intercultural competence are empathy and communication. How could this definition help contextualize Limerick et al.'s (2002) Fourth Blueprint to the Japanese university in this chapter? While the authors do not write extensively about being open to customs that are different from one's own, they do assert that empathy is a required component of the Fourth Blueprint. When observing how collaborative individuals are characterized by empathy, they note that empathy is favorably equated with love. Although Bennett (1999) refrains from using the word *love*, the theoretical common ground here is unequivocal.

Bennett (1999) postulated five propositions regarding cross-cultural effectiveness: language is the heart of culture and cognition; intercultural competence is enhanced by development of the ability to recognize cultural influences on one's own cognition; there are modes of human communication which transcend cultural barriers; there are some facets of the diverse cultures within a larger society that can be identified, defined, and taught; and people can achieve a psychological balance between cultural pride and identity on the one hand and an appreciation for different cultures on the other. Many of these five propositions are based on what have traditionally been regarded as female values: language and interpersonal communication, introspection, self-reflection, and/or having an appreciation for difference (Limerick et al., 2002).

Gudykunst and Kim (1984) postulated five characteristics of interculturally competent people. Such people have lived through experiences that challenge their own cultural assumptions, such as culture shock, and have had experiences that give insight into how their world has been formed by their culture. Secondly, they can serve as facilitators for contacts between cultures. A third characteristic is that they have come to terms with the origins of their own ethnocentrism, and have thus achieved objectivity in viewing other cultures. Fourthly, they have developed a *third place*, or third space, mentality which allows them to evaluate intercultural encounters more accurately, while the fifth attribute that Gudykunst and Kim note centers upon their ability to manifest cultural empathy.

Hall (1985) defined two kinds of culture: low context and high context. In low context culture, meaning is assembled from parts, such as words, which by themselves hold great meaning. The meaning of these parts changes with their selection and arrangement (Hall, 1985, p. 164). For example, in *Developing Teacher Leaders: How Teacher Leadership Enhances School Success*, Crowther, Kaagan, Ferguson, and Hann (2002), list typical expressions and vocabulary associated with four leadership theories, and present a T-chart for what is referred to as the *language of leadership*. The authors of this text argue that analyzing leadership language can reveal the degree to which a school's culture is amenable to teacher leadership, and whether the school in question is an environment where such *parallel leadership* can occur. According to Hall (1985), such a predilection for spoken or written language is typical of low context societies. Low context cultures include North America, Australia, and Western Europe. High context cultures include the Pueblo people of the United States, many Indigenous African cultures, the Russians, and the Japanese (Hall, 1985).

At the Japanese university with which this chapter is concerned, the staff members on limited-term contracts generally come from low context cultures, unlike their native Japanese colleagues. This can be seen as another differentiating factor between the two groups. One potentially useful conceptual resource for engaging with and helping to move beyond these differences is parallel leadership, which has three main qualities: mutualism; a sense of shared purpose; and an allowance for individual expression (Crowther et al., 2002). These qualities are now individually examined.

Mutualism has to do with the sharing of trust and respect between administrator leaders and teacher leaders (Crowther et al., 2002). Given the Third Blueprint character of the Japanese university being discussed in this chapter, there is an absence of mutualism in key aspects of the institution's operations. A sense of shared purpose has to do with a common commitment to values such as the integrity of teaching, or the need for social justice (Crowther et al., 2002). This perception of shared purpose thrives in workplaces characterized by transparent decision-making processes, collaborative problem solving, and positive communications. Once again, given the Third Blueprint character of the university under discussion here, it does not exhibit a strong sense of shared purpose. Indeed, there is evidence that the institution demonstrates *nemawashi*, the Japanese organizational tradition of behind the scenes, private, consensus building in advance of formal, and public, decision making. On the other hand, the teachers in this university are for the most part dedicated professionals who strive to offer students the best possible instruction. Seen from this angle, there is a definite sense of shared purpose: namely, to offer learners the best possible education.

The third facet of parallel leadership, individual expression and action, provides for both administrator leaders and teacher leaders to engage in unilateral expression and behaviors (Crowther et al., 2002). Crowther et al. acknowledge that this flies in the face of teamwork, collegiality, and consensual decision making. Nevertheless, they assert that each of the North

American and Australian cohorts of parallel leaders that their research team studied manifested strong convictions and assertive capabilities, as well as a capacity to accommodate the values of coleaders and work collaboratively with them. This characteristic does not easily translate into a high context, group-oriented organization, such as the university featured in this chapter. However, this fact serves to emphasize the rationale for advocating and promoting a hybridized Fourth Blueprint paradigm, one that takes into account such intercultural considerations.

According to Hall (1985), meaning in high context cultures is not so much assembled by the selection of component parts as it is extracted from the *specific environment* that surrounds one. High context cultures inhabit a "sea of culture" (p. 164) that is collectively shared. All or most of the component parts of meaning join to make the environment meaningful. From this perspective, the contracted, native English-speaking teachers in this study are almost all low context Westerners, whereas their Japanese colleagues, not to mention the working *milieu*, are high context. The proposed solution to this situation involves superimposing a low context leadership theory, namely, a hybrid of the Fourth Blueprint (Limerick et al., 2002), onto this high context environment. Accordingly, care will need to be taken when implementing this paradigm to ensure that the various parts, or the lexical set, of the hybridized Fourth Blueprint do not override the primacy of the group-oriented focus of the workplace at the center of this study.

This could present a substantial test, given that theories are usually defined as a collection of meaningful, abstract parts (that is, suppositions, hypotheses, and presumptions), and are not often regarded as a collectively experienced environment. Specifically, this Western theory would need to be implemented in a way that maximizes an awareness of the workplace setting, as well as the worldviews, opinions, and perceptions of the authority figures in it. The degree to which this can be accomplished will determine its chances for success.

Hall (1985) also compiled a list of five recommendations specifically designed for those involved in cross-cultural education: (1) pedagogy should emphasize the commonalties or "interfaces" shared by all human cultures; (2) Indigenous education systems should be encouraged and increased, and should build on past successes; (3) outstanding educators should be rewarded; (4) cross-cultural educators must be highly aware of different learning styles; and (5) effective intercultural pedagogy should be used to promote a wider recognition of the importance of "the microculture of education."

In terms of the university that this chapter is concerned with, the first of these recommendations is highly applicable. This is because the non-Japanese staff members who receive short-term contracts have to interact on a daily basis with their tenured colleagues, and focusing on that which is not divisive helps to ensure a harmonious, amicable, professional *milieu*.

As for Hall's (1985) second suggestion, the idea of encouraging and upholding Indigenous education systems does not necessarily fit easily within the organization's formally top-down hierarchy.

It is doubtful that Hall's (1985) recommendation concerned with rewarding exceptional educators would be accepted in the university under discussion here because Japanese workplaces tend to be group-oriented, and being distinguished from the group, for reasons either positive or negative, is not normally desirable. Regrettably, the time-honored Japanese proverb *"The nail which stands up gets hammered down"* still resonates loudly within the institution.

Hall's (1985) recommendation about prizing different learning styles also needs to be considered. Since all humans, regardless of their cultural backgrounds, have individual traits, the adoption of a hybridized Fourth Blueprint (Limerick et al., 2002) will need to account for different styles of learning. Although two of the principal theorists in this field, Kolb and Gardner, are firmly ensconced in the Western mind-set, their research clearly crosses cultural and ethnic boundaries. More specifically, the Kolb Learning Style Inventory is premised on the idea that learning preferences can be described using just two archetypes: active experimentation–reflective observation, and abstract conceptualization–concrete experience (Kolb & Fry, 1975). Perhaps not surprisingly, Kolb's research has determined that some learners have more than one strong learning preference. Gardner's (1983) theory of multiple intelligences also supports educators who cater to different learning styles. The work of both Kolb and Gardner has been well-received in the university in question, so this particular facet of ICC would most likely stand a strong chance for success if a hybridized Fourth Blueprint (Limerick et al., 2002) were to be established there.

CONCLUSION

This chapter has focused on the issue of foreign EFL teachers working on limited-term contracts in Japan, and the negative impact that this employment arrangement may have on the effectiveness of their pedagogy. The chapter has posed the question: "What conceptual model could help transcend the insider–outsider binary that seems to inform this employment arrangement?" One specific leadership theory has been advocated—an ICC-informed, hybridized Fourth Blueprint (Limerick et al., 2002). It has been seen, however, that not all aspects of this Fourth Blueprint are appropriate to the Japanese university at the center of this discussion. More specifically, two of the three main attributes of parallel leadership—mutualism, and individual expression and actions—would be difficult to implement at the university in question. In terms of ICC, encouraging and upholding Indigenous education might well prove problematic, as would Hall's (1985) exhortation to reward exceptional educators.

Considerably less problematic is this blueprint's (Limerick et al., 2002) utility in helping to solve the reduction in the quality of EFL delivery. Being relegated to contracts has caused some non-Japanese tertiary educators to cater to student expectations, which are not always based on strictly academic criteria. Implementing a hybridized Fourth Blueprint would do away with such insider–outsider hiring practices. In addition, the Fourth Blueprint's espousal of female values was seen to share much common ground with Bennett's (1999) five propositions about cross-cultural effectiveness. Clearly, the enactment of these propositions would go a long way to reducing any sort of us-versus-them dichotomy.

Finally, and as discussed at the beginning of this chapter, non-Japanese educators who believe they are excelling in their classrooms are not necessarily perceived as being excellent by their Japanese students. Although this issue initially appears to have little relevance to the dualism that would be transcended by a modified Fourth Blueprint (Limerick et al., 2002), the ICC component of such a blueprint could certainly empower students with the knowledge that empathy and communication are crucial when dealing with intercultural transactions. Hopefully, the high esteem reserved for empathy and communication in intercultural competence (Bennett, 1999) might help such language learners, and their teachers, become more cognizant of such differences in perception.

REFERENCES

Bennett, C. I. (1999). *Comprehensive multicultural education: Theory and practice.* Boston, MA: Allyn & Bacon.
Burrows, C. (2007). The effect of limited-term contracts on teaching standards at tertiary-level education in Japan. *OnCUE Journal, 1*(1), 64–73.
Crowther, F., Kaagan, S., Ferguson, M., & Hann, L. (2002). *Developing teacher leaders: How teacher leadership enhances school success.* Thousand Oaks, CA: Corwin Press.
Gardner, H. (1983). *Frames of mind: The theory of multiple intelligences.* Boston, MA: Basic Books.
Gudykunst, W. B., & Kim, Y. Y. (1984). *Communicating with strangers: An approach to intercultural communication.* Reading, MA: Addison-Wesley.
Hadley, G., & Yoshioka Hadley, H. (1996). The culture of learning and the good teacher in Japan: An analysis of student views. *The Language Teacher, 20*(9), 53–55.
Hall, E. T. (1985). Unstated features of the cultural context of learning. In A. Thomas & E. W. Ploman (Eds.), *Learning and development in a global perspective* (pp. 157–176). Toronto, Canada: OISE Press.
Johnston, E. (2004, December 12). Limited-term foreign professors seen cornering workload but not benefits. *Japan Times.*
Kolb, D. A., & Fry, R. (1975). Toward an applied theory of experiential learning. In C. Cooper (Ed.), *Theories of group process* (pp. 27–56). London: John Wiley & Sons.
Limerick, D., Cunnington, B., & Crowther, F. (2002). *Managing the new organisation* (2nd ed.). Chatswood, Australia: Business & Professional Publishing.

MEXT. (2004). *A new image of university corporations.* Tokyo: Government of Japan.

Najita, T., & Harootunian, H. D. (1988). Japanese revolt against the west: Political and cultural criticism in the twentieth century. In P. Duus (Ed.), *The twentieth century: The Cambridge history of Japan* (Vol. 6, pp. 711–774). Cambridge, UK: Cambridge University Press.

Rivers, D. J. (2010). *The internationalization of Japanese higher education institutions: Implications for 2012 and beyond.* Retrieved from http://relc.org.sg

Shimizu, K. (1995). Japanese college student attitudes towards English teachers: A survey. *The Language Teacher, 19*(10), 5–8.

Sugeno, K. (1992). *Japanese labor law.* Tokyo: University of Tokyo Press.

18 Beyond Educator/ Practitioner Binaries

Overcoming Barriers to Cooperation Using Professional Cultural Axes

R. Todd Hartle, Rosemary J. Smith, Stephen Adkison, DJ Williams, and Paul Beardsley

ABSTRACT

Although partnerships between discipline-based practitioners and educators are a powerful means of creating learning and teaching connections, these partnerships can easily suffer from professional culture differences that are often perceived as binary states. Based on the results of a previous study using the United States National Science Foundation (NSF) GK-12 program at Idaho State University (ISU GK12), this chapter describes how perceived stereotypical binaries between educators and practitioners were identified and negotiated in the ISU GK12 example. Professional culture differences in other educator–practitioner partnerships can be identified by focusing on instances where educators or practitioners use binary statements about personality quirks, experience levels, and stereotypes. By modeling these differences as continuous axes of professional values rather than binary stereotypes, the participants in or administrators of partnerships can move beyond the binaries and into effective conflict prevention and negotiation through a process of metacognition, cultural relativism, and communication.

INTRODUCTION

Science education has become increasingly important in our everyday modern lives (Lagemann, 2000). The Trends in International Mathematics and Science Study (TIMSS) reports have shown that United States and Australian students do not understand science as well as students from other countries (Martin, Mullis, Foy, Olson, Erberber, Preuscho, et al., 2008; Mullis, Martin, Foy, Olson, Preuschoff, Erberber, et al., 2008), and American studies have shown that scientific literacy within the United States does not meet desired criteria (Lederman, 1998; NRC, 2002). The increasing need for scientific literacy and the evidence that scientific literacy may not be as advanced as desired have prompted several major calls for greater emphasis on science education by the popular press (Begley, 2004a, 2004b; Broad, 2004; Shapiro, 2004), nongovernmental organizations (ACT, 2004; BHEF-ACE, 2005; Sanders, 2004), the United States National Science Foundation (NSF) (National Science Board, 1999; Suter, 1996; Suter & Frechtling, 1998), the United States National Research Council (NRC) (Donovan, Bransford, & Pellegrino, 1999; NRC, 2002), the Australian Council for Educational Research (Tytler, 2007), and the Australian Department of Education, Science, and Training (Goodrum & Rennie, 2007).

In addition to calls for more extensive science education to be presented to a broader audience, the focus of science education has shifted toward understanding of the nature of science. Although the need for greater understanding of the nature of science has been articulated for many years (Jacobs, 2000; Lagemann, 2000; Robinson, 1998a, 1965/1998b), the concept has been increasingly emphasized in the literature (Eick, 2000; Elfin, Glennan, & Reisch, 1999; McComas, Almazroa, & Clough, 1998; NRC, 2002). Several studies have also been published demonstrating that teaching the nature of science both to students (Lederman, 1998; Lederman, Wade, & Bell, 1998; Schwartz & Lederman, 2002; Schwartz, Lederman, Khishfe, Lederman, Matthews, Liu, et al., 2002) and to teachers (Abd-El-Khalick & Lederman, 2000; Lederman, 1999; Schwartz & Lederman, 2002) has not been adequate. The need for a critical understanding of the scientific process has led to the promotion of inquiry-based science education (Anderson, 2002; DePriest & Shirk, 2003; Olson & Loucks-Horsley, 2000). Inquiry was chosen as the primary method not only because it is supported by currently accepted learning theories like constructivism (Anderson, 2002; DePriest & Shirk, 2003; Olson & Loucks-Horsley, 2000) but also because it most closely resembles the processes used by scientific researchers themselves.

All of the recent changes in the goals of K–12 science education suggest that science educators need a broader and more comprehensive understanding of scientific principles and of the nature of science including the methods and activities used by scientists and researchers (Abd-El-Khalick & Lederman, 2000; Lederman, 1999; Lederman et al., 1998; Luft & Patterson, 2002; Melear, Goodlaxson, Warne, & Hickok, 2000; Schwartz & Lederman, 2002; Schwartz et al., 2002; Westerlund, Garcia, Koke, Taylor, & Mason, 2002; Zeidler, 2002). In addition, science educators need hands-on experiences and the laboratory equipment necessary to present scientific knowledge in an inquiry-based context. Research scientists are the natural partners in this endeavor, and thus enabling partnerships may enhance science education.

James Spradley (1980) characterizes culture by saying, "When ethnographers study other cultures, they must deal with three fundamental aspects of human experience: 1) what people do, 2) what people know and 3) the things people make and use. When each of these aspects are learned and shared by members of some group, we speak of them as cultural behavior, cultural knowledge, and cultural artifacts" (p. 5). Although the word *culture* is traditionally used to describe groups of different nationality or ethnicity, it can be applied to any distinct group of people. A distinct group of people defined by their profession can be said to belong to a professional culture.

This chapter is based on the results of a research project (Hartle, 2007) that examined the partnerships between two such professional cultures, namely: scientific researchers, represented by graduate students (primarily biology and geology), and middle and high school science educators (grades 4–12). Specifically, the research project analyzed the professional culture differences which caused conflicts in researcher partnerships formed through the Idaho State University (ISU) grant from the U.S. National Science Foundation (NSF) program called the Graduate-K-12 Fellowship Project (ISU GK12) (NSF, 2005, 2007). The results of this study were used here to develop a system for identifying and negotiating the conflicts that can arise between people from different professional cultures. Although the reference study (Hartle, 2007) used scientific researchers and science educators as a model, the principles and general concepts should be applicable to any situation involving partners from other practitioner and educator professional cultures. Although no evidence of applying these principles to other professional cultures has been analyzed and published to date, the authors have been involved in a variety of academic training and program evaluation projects involving practitioners and educators from a variety of disciplines. Anecdotal evidence suggest that, while the actual professional culture differences are unique to the professions, the methods for discovering and negotiating these differences appear to be transferable.

BEYOND CATEGORICAL BINARIES TO POSITIONS ON CRITICAL AXES FROM THE ISU GK12 STUDY

In the ISU GK12 study (Hartle, 2007), the most important and pervasive factors identified in the partnerships' interactions had to do with differences between the professional culture values of the educators and the practitioners. These factors each defined a continuum or spectrum of attitudes, values, and perspectives called *axes*. Each axis can be defined by two opposite extremes, or stereotypes, as well as all the different variations between them. The axes from the ISU GK12 study represent the values, topics, assumptions, and perspectives that led, in these partnerships, to conflict. While these axes actually represent a continuum of values and assumptions, the fact that each end of an axis can be represented by a stereotype led people to perceive the axes to be a binary relationship where all educators are in one category, and all practitioners are in an opposing category. Many miscommunications and frustrations can be avoided by moving beyond this binary perception when participating in or administrating educator–practitioner partnerships.

In order to give an example of how professional culture differences could be identified in a partnership, how they can cause conflict, and how that conflict might be resolved, a fictional example from the ISU GK12 study can be examined. This example does not reflect any specific partnership from the study, but all the elements were present to some degree in the data across the different partnerships. A selection of the critical axes found in the study is illustrated using a fictional partnership between Sally, a biology graduate student in an NSF GK-12 program (practitioner), and her partner, Bill, a high school science teacher (educator), and then techniques for identifying and negotiating similar axes in other partnerships are presented.

Axis 1: The Task Dictates the Context versus the Context Dictates the Task

In the most important and ubiquitous axis, the participants frequently approach most tasks from different perspectives. In the practice of scientific research, the experiment, study, or task itself is paramount to almost everything else. If the researcher needs a quiet lab with specific equipment for a 12-hour stretch of time, then she or he arranges her or his context to obtain 12 hours in a quiet, equipped lab. The school context where teachers educate is another matter. Many variables remain out of the control of educators. Standards are set by government agencies, school years are set by the local board, the bell rings in 47 minutes whether the educator is done or not, and students' moods cannot be standardized. Educators are successful when they know how to adapt their teaching techniques and styles to fit the lesson, the time frame, the students, and all the other contextual variables in their lives. If Sally, the practitioner, and Bill, the educator, are working together to teach a class, Sally might design lessons that require significant equipment, time, and focused, detailed work from the students. If the students are not cooperative, for example, she might expect Bill to keep them focused at all times. Bill might come in with a loose plan for an activity, notice that the students are in a talkative mood and change the activity to a discussion, or he might constantly revise Sally's plans because they will not help meet the standards, will take more than 50 minutes, or will require the students to use skills they do not have yet.

Axis 2: Prior Planning versus Implementation Flexibility

Another axis is the belief that success comes primarily from prior planning or from being flexible during implementation. A researcher can run into trouble if experiments, field work, or research proposals are not properly planned. Likewise, an educator who cannot read students and adjust lessons to fit their needs will run into problems. If Bill plans a whole lesson based on covalent bonds, and the students start class by asking what an electron is, it would be ridiculous to continue the planned lesson. Likewise, if his students start asking about molecular polarity, he will likely need to jump ahead of his plan. Sally, on the other hand, cannot change her methods in the middle of an experiment or get her study subjects to stop flowering because she is not ready to collect data. When working together, Sally may want to plan out every detail and contingency of a lesson plan in great detail, whereas Bill may go into a lesson with a list of objectives and a brief description of a lab procedure. If they do not negotiate their relative values in planning and flexibility, Sally could see Bill as being lazy and every problem as a call for more preparation while Bill could see Sally as inflexible and insensitive to the needs of the students.

Axis 3: Flexible versus Rigid Time Sense

This axis looks at the partners' values surrounding time, especially whether they believe that schedules and timing exist to frame tasks or whether tasks must be molded to fit rigid schedules. Educators live by the bell. Bill can tell you exactly which minute of the day his lunch period starts and which minute it ends. As he plans new lessons, he is always conscious of the time factor, including what he is going to do if things go fast, or if they go slow. Researchers frequently have idiosyncratic work schedules. Sally might do all of her data collection during fieldwork trips over a couple of months working 14 hours a day. If a chemical experiment that was planned to take 10 hours really takes 16, she will stay the whole time and maybe take the next day off. Consequently, Sally might be fairly relaxed about meeting times with Bill, designing a lesson that takes longer than the class period, or about taking a week off to go to a conference. Bill might cut Sally off if he thinks she is taking too long while planning a lesson, or he might be more insistent about not meeting during nights or weekends.

Axis 4: Focused Time versus Multitasking

Research tasks often require a distraction-free time devoted only to that task. Writing, analyzing, even most data collection cannot be done while simultaneously working on something else. Educators' schedules are dictated to them, and, if they waited until they had a quiet empty room with no distractions before they graded papers, met individual students, or planned lessons, they would be working 90 hours a week. If Sally wants to devote a two-hour session exclusively to planning, and they meet in Bill's classroom, Bill might be frequently interrupted by students, other teachers, and announcements. Bill will also likely be facing a large stack of papers that need to be graded before school the next day.

If we consider these four differences between Bill and Sally's professional cultures, it is easy to see how conflicts might arise. Bill and Sally agree to design a lab experience together for their students. Sally assumes that they will plan the lab out in great detail prior to the lesson day, so she asks Bill if they can meet. Bill assumes they need to get a list of materials and review the general goals and learning objectives of the lesson, so he tells her to meet him during his prep period. Sally comes in with a lab description, list of materials, and a model of the lab so they can walk through the procedure together in their planning session. Bill has pulled out a premade lesson plan and has been thinking about how to get the key ideas across if the experiment does not work for the students. During their meeting several students come in for help, and Bill is entering grades into his grade book. Sally feels that they are unprepared, so she suggests that they go through the lab even if they have to stay later that evening, and Bill suggests that they each think about the lesson on their own and come prepared to the lesson the next day. During the actual lesson, Sally keeps trying to get the students and the equipment to work as planned, and Bill keeps trying to follow promising learning opportunities. In the end, Sally thinks that Bill is scatterbrained and disorganized. She thinks that he does not really care about the lesson and is not committed to teaching. She is frustrated and feels the lesson was a failure that could have been avoided with a little better preparation. She sees Bill as fitting one stereotypical category of a binary relationship, and herself as fitting an opposing binary category. Bill thinks Sally is too self-centered and inflexible. He thinks that she does not really care about the students and cares only about her experiment. He is frustrated and feels the lesson was a failure that could have been avoided if they could have better responded to the students. He also sees Sally as fitting the opposite binary category to his own. Both Bill and Sally believe that the other has a personal character flaw based on a perceived binary position, which makes her or him impossible to deal with. Because they see their partner as fitting an opposing binary category, they assume they must: (a) completely cross over to the opposite of what they view as important; (b) drag their partner completely over to their own beliefs; or (c) live with the dissonance of being such opposite people.

In reality, the differences between two professional cultures cause friction in the relationship not because the partners are in separate binary categories but because the partners are not closer to each other along some important professional culture axis. The only way to resolve the conflict is to move closer to each other along the axis, which requires one or both partners to be more flexible than a binary perspective will allow. This flexibility starts with metacognition, which allows the participants to realize that they are not inherently opposites in a binary relationship, but rather that they are at different places along a continuum of professional culture values. Likewise, recognizing that differences may have a cultural source doesn't help if the participants consider their professional cultures to be

248 R. Todd Hartle, et al.

binarily opposed. Therefore, a certain level of cultural relativism is necessary not only to recognize that the differences fall along a continuous axis but also to accept that these differences are functional in their own cultural context. Finally, negotiation-friendly communication is necessary to convey these ideas and ultimately to decide cooperatively how to resolve the conflict.

HOW TO SEE THE AXES BEYOND THE BINARIES ARISING FROM PROFESSIONAL CULTURE DIFFERENCES

The most insidious difficulty in working with someone from a different professional culture is that the differences that have the greatest impact are rarely the obvious ones. In preparing for the ISU GK12 study, it was predicted that differences in vocabulary, jargon, or communication language would cause difficulties. However, both educators and researchers seemed comfortable defining the terms they used and explaining what they meant in different ways, and none of the partnerships mentioned any difficulty in communication owing to language differences. Likewise, it was predicted that problems would arise because researchers know a lot about a narrow topic and educators know a little bit about a wide range of topics. While the participants all agreed that this generalization was usually accurate, all partners either saw no difficulty with this difference, or they saw it as a benefit to the partnership.

The differences that had the greatest impact on the ISU GK12 partnerships were usually seen by the participants as personality quirks in their partner owing to a binary difference between themselves. Sally's insistence on planning and practicing every lesson was seen by Bill to be Sally's fastidiousness and anal-retentive compulsions. At the same time, Sally saw Bill as being lazy and flippant. In working in or with partnerships of people from different professional cultures, it is important to watch for binary personality quirks, especially if they seem to be incongruent with the partner's success in her or his profession. It is unlikely that researchers could be successful if they were as compulsive as Bill's impression of Sally. Likewise, an educator who was as lazy and uncaring as Sally perceived Bill to be, would not be likely to volunteer for a partnership program with a researcher. Of course some perceived "personality quirks" really are personality quirks, but maybe that particular quirk is either not a detriment to the individual's profession, or it may even be valued. No easy litmus test exists that can determine whether a behavioral or attitudinal difference is rooted in a professional culture axis or is unique to that person. However, if Bill assumes Sally's differences are personality quirks, he dismisses her as having a completely internal and likely unalterable trait that defines her in a binary position to him. Professional culture differences exist beyond any single individual and are not binary, but rather subject to identification, negotiation, and modification. Therefore it is usually more productive to assume a strong and persistent difference in behavior or attitude is a cultural difference until you are sure it is a personality trait of the individual.

Similar indicators of possible professional culture differences are dismissals of naiveté or entrenchment. Just as labeling a behavioral or attitudinal difference as a personality quirk dismisses it as external and unalterable, so too does saying that individuals are either too inexperienced or that they are stuck in a rut from being in their profession too long. In fact, these judgments may be a measurement of how acculturated the person is into a given professional culture. If Bill decides he cannot work with Sally because she is too inexperienced in teaching, or that she is too entrenched in research, he is admitting that the conflict is due to a difference in professional cultures, but he is also implying that these values are binary and can be changed only by making a complete shift in profession. In Bill's mind Sally is just like that. He might try to work around her culture, but he is not likely to address it in a direct fashion. After all, she comes from the binary opposite profession. If, however, Bill were to attribute their conflict to differences in their cultural values, then those values can be negotiated regardless of how entrenched individuals are in their own profession, or how naive they are in the other's profession.

A final, seemingly paradoxical, cue for recognizing professional culture differences is the participants' use of binary stereotyping. In gathering and analyzing the data in the original study (Hartle, 2007), we were confused over how to find themes in stereotypical statements. The participants frequently made comments about how "all researchers are like . . ." or "all teachers always do . . . ," implying that the professions of practitioner and educator lock their members into fixed roles in binary opposition. At first we assumed they were too simplistic to represent traits of either profession, and in fact the statements did not follow any discernable pattern. They were regularly contradictory even within a single partnership. They did not seem to be correlated with one profession or the other. While the stereotypical statements appeared to follow loose themes, they were almost as likely to be used to describe why the partners felt they were working well together as they were to describe the sources of conflict. Most importantly, the stereotypes were very poor predictors of what the members of each profession thought or what they did. In other words, "not all researchers really were . . ." and "not all teachers really did . . ."

Eventually we discovered that stereotypes were an informal and often unconscious qualitative analysis of the professional cultures. Interestingly, these stereotypes provided an excellent representation of how the stereotyping participants positioned their partners along the cultural axes relative to themselves. Sally might make several comments about how teachers are lazy or they do not think their lessons through properly. If she were asked to clarify or give examples, eventually we would see a pattern that Sally was valuing prior planning much more than Bill. If he were interviewed, he might comment about how scientists are too rigid and do not have any people skills. Further analysis would show that Bill valued the ability to read students and the flexibility to adapt to their immediate needs.

Stereotypes may not be consistent with common assumptions. Frequently a researcher would be described as fitting the educator side of a binary stereotype, and the teacher would be on the researcher side. While these participants would be more likely to use a personality quirk or experience level as explanations for their relative positions, they would occasionally use stereotypes and would describe researchers or teachers as being something opposite of the general conception. For example, Bill might value a flexible time perception more than Sally. He might make a statement about how scientists are so rigid in their thinking that they have to plan out every minute and stick to it. Sally might likewise comment on how teachers get caught up in their teaching and cannot keep an eye on the clock. Even if stereotypes do not match the general consensus, they are still excellent indicators of value perceptions and can point to actual differences along a professional culture axis.

Stereotypes can also be positive, and might be indicators of either shared or negotiated values. The researchers would often comment on the people skills of educators, and how teachers are *people* people. On further investigation, the researcher might be indicating that both partners share the same position on the context-dictates-task axis. Or the researcher might be admiring the ability of the teacher to match her or his tasks or actions to the contextual needs of her or his students, and was indicating a desire to move along the task-versus-context axis herself or himself. Regardless of whether the stereotypes are positive or negative, they are key indicators of relative cultural positions.

HOW TO APPROACH A PERCEIVED BINARY
DIFFERENCE ALONG PROFESSIONAL CULTURE AXES

Metacognition and careful examination of the perceived binary quirks, relative experiences, and stereotypes will identify differences between two professional culture-based values; however, negotiating a successful compromise will require, firstly, the realization that these differences are actually continuous, not binary; secondly, the understanding that the differences come from different professional culture values; and thirdly, a respect, if not acceptance, for the other's values. The traditionally anthropological concept of cultural relativism is a very handy tool for negotiating cultural differences (Boas, 1896; Heyer, 1948). Tilley (2000) discusses the merits of cultural relativism from the point of view of ethical and moral philosophy rather than the practical perspective of anthropology. Tilley's moral philosophy arguments are not relevant to professional culture differences whose values tend to address much more pragmatic topics; however, in distinguishing his arguments he defines two aspects of anthropological cultural relativism extremely well:

- *Methodological Contextualism*: Every custom, belief, or action must be studied in the context of the culture in which it occurs. . . . Otherwise, we will gain little insight into other cultures.
- *Methodological Neutralism*: To understand other cultures, social scientists must suppress their moral convictions when studying those cultures. Although they cannot entirely free themselves from such convictions, they should try to put the convictions aside in the interest of accurate research. (Tilley, 2000, p. 508)

The concept of cultural relativism as defined by contextualism and neutralism can be as practically applicable to an educator or practitioner involved in a cross-professional culture partnership as it is for an anthropologist studying a foreign society. In fact, the metaphor of the anthropologist has been extremely useful in helping practitioner–educator partnerships negotiate their differences. Many of the exercises used by the authors in workshops or consultations have asked the participants to consider their partners' (or their own) behaviors from the perspective of an objective social scientist.

Contextualism essentially says that it is neither useful nor meaningful to isolate a specific value from the context which helped to create it. If Sally views Bill's rigid time sense as an isolated action or value and compares it to the complex requirements of her own researcher culture, she is perceiving him in a binary position to herself, and will be extremely limited in how well she can understand his perspective. She may then miss several key arguments that might convince her to change her time sense for the good of the partnership. Even if she still believes that her propositions are the best, she will usually be unable to see any way of approaching Bill to negotiate a change in his position. If, on the other hand, Sally can see that his rigid time sense comes from both the external exigencies of the school bell and the need to model punctual and organized behaviors to the students, she might decide that, while working in the school, she needs to be more rigid herself. If she still sees the need to be flexible with her time sense while planning, she might approach Bill with the compromise of staying after school until their setup is complete, so that they will be able to finish on time during the lesson the next day. Understanding how Bill's need for a rigid time sense fits into his professional cultural context will reveal options for negotiation through the cultural differences inherent in their conflict.

Neutralism, in moving beyond perceived professional culture binaries, can be described as judging the decisions, not the person. If Sally insists that Bill not grade papers while they prepare a lesson together, she is likely to be communicating her values of focused work over that of multitasking. If Bill judges Sally by thinking that she is just a compulsive science geek who cannot do more than one thing at a time, he will

252 R. Todd Hartle, et al.

discount any opportunity to negotiate a better working condition. Also, his actions, however veiled, will send subtle hints to Sally that he sees her in binary opposition to, and consequently of less value than, himself and consequently does not respect or trust her. If, instead, Bill can judge the decision rather than the person, he will find it easier to see that Sally's work habits are effective and meaningful ways to conduct research in her own professional culture. Bill is then able to decide whether Sally sees something about their current situation that makes focused work a better approach, or if she is simply using her professional culture value without considering the benefits of multitasking while lesson planning. If Bill still judges the decision to be less practical, he can approach Sally with arguments that respect her professional cultural position while still pointing out the benefits of multitasking in this instance.

HOW TO NEGOTIATE PROFESSIONAL
CULTURE DIFFERENCES SUCCESSFULLY

If you are able to use metacognition to recognize a professional culture axis rather than a binary in a relationship, and have managed to maintain a sense of cultural relativism about your own and your partner's positions along this axis, the actual negotiation of a shared position still requires communication and an honest desire for collaboration. Almost every instance of professional culture differences that the authors have worked with were successfully negotiated either without assistance or by helping the participants to use their metacognition and cultural relativism skills. However, some differences were simply tolerated, usually by one member acquiescing to the other's actions, while maintaining her or his own position. The most influential factor in locking a participant into a specific position without attempting to negotiate was a feeling that these positions were nonnegotiable binaries. Sally might still believe that the lessons are failing because they have not been properly planned, even though she has given in to Bill's style of preparation. If Sally believes that Bill is dead set against preparation, and she is dead set herself against trying to be flexible in the classroom, then she is likely either to prepare by herself, or simply to show up and quietly consider the exercise a failure if it doesn't go as she expected. While these compromises could often avoid open confrontation, and sometimes were the easiest way to move beyond a temporary conflict, the participants were rarely satisfied with the outcomes.

Likewise, the factor that was most likely to help the participants want to collaborate was constant and insightful communication. Even if Sally believes that Bill is unlikely to change, but she attempts to understand his position anyway, the rigid barriers of the binary perception are likely to soften into more continuous professional culture differences. The more

Sally asks about what Bill is doing and why, the more both of them will start to see the subtle nuances of their positions and ways that they might find a compromise. In addition, asking questions about a person's values and decisions will encourage her or him to ask questions about yours. Finally, the decision to be flexible with your own professional culture values will go a long way to encouraging your partner to be flexible with her or his.

CONCLUSION

Moving beyond the perceived stereotypical binaries and instead using the model of professional culture axes can be a useful tool for reducing conflict and increasing the effectiveness of partnerships between educators and practitioners. The differences between the professional cultures of educators and practitioners can be both influential and difficult to identify at the same time. By identifying the significant binary perceptions and discovering the underlying professional culture axes, fostering cultural relativism, and actively negotiating differences, conflicts can be resolved quickly and in a mutually beneficial way.

If you are a participant in a cross-professional partnership, several best practices can help you to move beyond your own professional culture binaries. Firstly, prevention is always better than cure. The more that you can find out about your partner's professional culture before you address a difference or conflict, the easier the resolution is likely to be. For example, if you are an educator and your partnership will be working primarily in your school, be sure to spend a day or more in your partner's work setting and try to identify the most important influences or values in her or his work. Secondly, self-reflection is the easiest entry into metacognition. Writing, or even simply thinking, about what your professional values are and why you have them can give you key clues to discovering the values of your partner. Thirdly, remember that questions will always get you further than announcements. If you sense a professional culture difference, the best way to approach the topic with your partner is to ask her or him for her or his experiences or perspectives. If you announce what your professional values are without recognizing your partner's, she or he is more likely to see your values as binary personality quirks than professional values. Finally, if it is possible, try communicate with others in similar partnerships, or possibly others in your partner's profession. Failing that, communication with an administrator or social scientist might yield useful insights. Having objective feedback, especially from someone who has been there, can be a real comfort, if not an essential tool.

If you are an administrator of a partnership program, the way you structure your partnerships and the interactions you encourage can support your participants to move beyond their professional culture binaries. Firstly, make sure that you allow plenty of room for reflection and communication around professional culture differences. Orientation programs and regular meetings are excellent opportunities for encouraging and modeling metacognition, cultural relativism, and negotiation. Frequently these exercises can easily be integrated into other necessary tasks. If you will be requesting writing from your participants for evaluations or training, you can ask for an essay or journal entry on their professional values, or what each of the professions can bringing to the partnership. Also, administrative meetings can be a chance to split into educator and practitioner groups to allow corroboration with peers. Secondly, try to balance the professional cultures that you are working with in your program. If you have social science educators who are partnering with lawyers to do work in a law firm, make sure that you structure in opportunities for the educators to demonstrate their professions and the lawyers to learn about teaching and schools. Finally, use the professional culture axes model to help identify partnerships that may be experiencing conflict. If the participants seem unaware of their partners' professions, if they tend to use a lot of stereotypes, or complain about personality quirks, and especially if one partner constantly follows the other partner's lead without seeming to engage in the tasks, you can then start probing for professional culture differences. Catching a conflict early and intervening with a few well-placed questions or exercises can often keep the conflict from escalating to a point where neither participant is willing to negotiate.

ACKNOWLEDGMENTS

The authors would like to thank Noah Anderson, Erin Naegle, and Jill Petrisko for all of their help in analyzing and interpreting these data, as well as their general academic support. This study is based upon work supported by the United States National Science Foundation (NSF) under grant #DGE-0338184 to R. Smith. Any opinions, findings, and conclusions or recommendations expressed in this material are those of the authors and do not necessarily reflect the views of the NSF. The study was also based on work supported by the Idaho State University (ISU) Graduate Student Research and Scholarship Committee (GSRSC) under grant #S06–109 to R. Todd Hartle. Finally, R. Todd Hartle was partially supported throughout the duration of this study by a Doctor of Arts Fellowship awarded by the Department of Biological Sciences at ISU. As the original study involved human subjects, it was overseen by the ISU Human Subjects Committee. The initial proposal was submitted and approved on November 16, 2004. A renewal proposal was submitted and approved on November 9, 2005. All data collection was completed by July 1, 2006, and the termination was reported in a yearly status report. The final report was submitted and approved by May 30, 2007.

REFERENCES

Abd-El-Khalick, F., & Lederman, N. G. (2000). Improving science teachers' conceptions of nature of science: A critical review of the literature. *International Journal of Scientific Education, 22*(7), 665–701.

ACT (American College Testing Program). (2004). *Crisis at the core: Preparing all students for college and work.* Iowa City, IA: American College Testing Program (ACT).

Anderson, R. (2002). Reforming science teaching: What research says about inquiry. *Journal of Science Teacher Education, 13*(1), 1–12.

Begley, S. (2004a, December 4). The best ways to make schoolchildren learn? We just don't know. *Wall Street Journal.*

Begley, S. (2004b, December 17). To improve education, we need clinical trials to show what works. *Wall Street Journal.*

BHEF-ACE, Business and Higher Education Forum—American Council on Education. (2005). *A commitment to America's future: Responding to the crisis in mathematics and science education.* Washington, DC: Business and Higher Education Forum (BHEF).

Boas, F. (1896). The limitations of the comparative method of anthropology. *Science, 4*(103), 901–908.

Broad, W. J. (2004, May 3). U.S. is losing its dominance in the sciences. *New York Times.*

DePriest, T., & Shirk, J. (2003). *Authentic science learning and inquiry-based learning.* Paper presented at the 76th annual conference of the National Association for Research in Science Teaching. Retrieved from http://csip.cornell.edu/Publications/Depriest_NARST_03.asp

Donovan, M., Bransford, J., & Pellegrino, J. (Eds.). (1999). *How people learn: Bridging research and practice.* Washington, DC: National Academy Press.

Eick, C. (2000). Inquiry, nature of science, and evolution: The need for more complex pedagogical content knowledge in science teaching. *Electronic Journal of Science Education, 4*(3). Retrieved from http://ejse.southwestern.edu/

Elfin, J., Glennan, S., & Reisch, G. (1999). The nature of science: A perspective from the philosophy of science. *Journal of Research in Science Teaching, 36*(1), 107–116.

Goodrum, D., & Rennie, L. (2007). *Australian school science education: National action plan, 2008–2012 (volumes 1 & 2)* (Report No. ISBN: 0 642 77688 1). Canberra, Australia: Australian Department of Education, Science, and Training.

Hartle, R. T. (2007). *A collection of research reporting, theoretical analysis, and practical applications in science education: Examining qualitative research methods, action research, educator–researcher partnerships, and constructivist learning theory* (unpublished doctoral dissertation). Idaho State University, Pocatello, ID.

Heyer, V. (1948). In reply to Elgin Williams. *American Anthropologist, 50*(1), 163–166.

Jacobs, S. (2000). Michael Polanyi on the education and knowledge of scientists. *Science and Education, 9,* 309–320.

Lagemann, E. (2000). *An elusive science: The troubling history of education research.* Chicago, IL: University of Chicago Press.

Lederman, N. G. (1998). The state of science education: Subject matter without context. (guest editorial). *Electronic Journal of Science Education, 3*(2).

Lederman, N. G. (1999). Teachers' understanding of the nature of science and classroom practice: Factors that facilitate or impede the relationship. *Journal of Research in Science Teaching, 36*(8), 916–929.

Lederman, N. G., Wade, P., & Bell, R. (1998). Assessing the nature of science: What is the nature of our assessments? *Science and Education*, 7, 595–615.

Luft, J., & Patterson, N. (2002). Bridging the gap: Supporting beginning science teachers. *Journal of Science Teacher Education*, 13(4), 267–282.

Martin, M. O., Mullis, I. V. S., Foy, P., Olson, J. F., Erberber, E., Preuscho, C., et al. (2008). *TIMSS 2007 International science report: Findings from IEA's trends in international mathematics and science study at the fourth and eighth grades.* Chestnut Hill, MA: TIMSS & PIRLS International Study Center, Boston College.

McComas, W., Almazroa, H., & Clough, M. (1998). The nature of science education: An introduction. *Science and Education*, 7, 511–532.

Melear, C., Goodlaxson, J., Warne, T., & Hickok, L. (2000). Teaching preservice science teachers how to do science: Responses to the research experience. *Journal of Science Teacher Education*, 11(1), 77–90.

Mullis, I. V. S., Martin, M. O., Foy, P., Olson, J. F., Preuschoff, C., Erberber, E., et al. (2008). *TIMSS 2007 International mathematics report: Findings from IEA's trends in international mathematics and science study at the fourth and eighth grades.* Chestnut Hill, MA: TIMSS & PIRLS International Study Center, Boston College.

National Science Board. (1999). *Preparing our children: Math and science education in the national interest.* Retrieved from http://www.nsf.gov

NRC (National Research Council). (2002). *Learning and understanding: Improving advanced study of mathematics and science in U.S. high schools: Report of the content panel for biology.* Washington, DC: Author.

NSF (National Science Foundation). (2005). *Graduate teaching fellows in K–12 education.* Arlington, VA: Author. Retrieved from http://www.nsf.gov

NSF (National Science Foundation). (2007). *NSF graduate teaching fellows in K–12 education (GK-12).* Retrieved from http://www.nsf.gov/funding/

Olson, S., & Loucks-Horsley, S. (Eds.). (2000). *Inquiry and the national science education standards.* Washington, DC: National Academy Press.

Robinson, J. (1998a). Reflections on "Science teaching and the nature of science." *Science and Education*, 7, 635–642.

Robinson, J. (1965/1998b). Science teaching and the nature of science. *Science and Education*, 7, 617–634.

Sanders, T. (2004). *No time to waste: The vital role of college and university leaders in improving science and mathematics education.* Retrieved from http://www.ecs.org

Schwartz, R., & Lederman, N. G. (2002). "It's the nature of the beast": The influence of knowledge and intentions on learning and teaching nature of science. *Journal of Research in Science Teaching*, 39(3), 205–236.

Schwartz, R., Lederman, N. G., Khishfe, R., Lederman, J., Matthews, L., & Liu, S. (2002). *Explicit/reflective instructional attention to nature of science and scientific inquiry: Impact on student learning.* Paper presented in the Proceeding of the 2002 annual international conference of the Association for the Education of Teachers in Science. Retrieved from http://www.ed.psu.edu/CI/journals/2002aets/02file1.asp

Shapiro, S. R. (2004, August 16). A blunt view of the cutting edge. Sarah R. Shapiro interviews Shirley Ann Jackson (AAAS president). *BusinessWeek*.

Spradley, J. (1980). *Participant observation.* Orlando, FL: Holt, Rinehart, & Winston.

Suter, L. E. (Ed.). (1996). *The learning curve: What we are discovering about U.S. science and mathematics education* (No. NSF 96–53). Washington, DC: National Science Foundation.

Suter, L. E., & Frechtling, J. (1998, November). *Guiding principles for mathematics and science education research methods: Report of a workshop.* Paper presented at the Guiding Principles for Mathematics and Science Education Research Methods Conference, Arlington, VA.

Tilley, J. J. (2000). Cultural relativism. *Human Rights Quarterly, 22*(2), 501–547.

Tytler, R. (2007). *Re-imagining science education: Engaging students in science for Australia's future.* Camberwell, Australia: ACER Press.

Westerlund, J., Garcia, D., Koke, J., Taylor, T., & Mason, D. (2002). Summer scientific research for teachers: The experience and its effect. *Journal of Science Teacher Education, 13*(1), 63–83.

Zeidler, D. (2002). Dancing with maggots and saints: Visions for subject matter knowledge, pedagogical knowledge, and pedagogical content knowledge in science teacher education reform. *Journal of Science Teacher Education, 13*(1), 27–42.

Respondent's Text

Máirín Kenny

We all probably remember Stephen Leacock's knight who, hastening to rescue his princess, jumped on his horse and galloped off in all directions. I want to avoid giving a similarly useless response to the range and complexity of issues, topics, and themes discussed in the 18 chapters of this challenging and thought-provoking book. The binaries considered here are multiple and intersecting—a sort of intellectual spaghetti junction. Pity the poor knight if he had to shoot off simultaneously along such a knot of possible pathways.[1]

Fortunately, in the Introduction the editors have neatly summarized the themes. In this response, I will try to identify a few of the connections that sang out for me. I hope this will serve to spark off your awareness of the connections that registered with you as you engaged with this book. My focus reflects my current position as an independent scholar working outside the university system and my history of teaching in a marginal education sector serving a marginal people.[2]

A strong common thread linking all the chapters in this text is the emphasis on the fluidity of binary pairs. Such pairs, instead of being two extremes linked by often hostile *othering*, become a continuum along which identities and perspectives enrich each other. Obviously, the move toward dialogical relationships runs counter to the inflexible institutional desire to fix anything fluid.

The book rightly opens with considerations of how we go about doing research. We are warned against "vanity ethnography" (Walford, 1998, as cited by Midgley); globalization, and its attendant weals and woes, demand that we become sensitized to how we engage with others in and out of the research context. Ethnic and gender issues shape relations between researcher and research participant; institutionalized cultural values become increasingly contradictory, as some new practices are seamlessly absorbed and others queried (Saito). Cultural immersion brings a whole new set of insights and challenges (Dovona–Ope).

But we need caution. As we are told, binary pairs are unequal in power, which leads the *marginal* to assert their identity and to resist assimilation. Even in collaboration with the minority who are seeking to be heard, the *dominant* can choose a strategy that backfires. Perhaps this is indicative of lack of skill or insight, or perhaps it should be read as the dominant sector's desire to domesticate strategies of resistance. Several instances are given in this book; I will comment on two: distance learning and children's voices. Distance learning for migrant and nomadic learners, initiated to increase their engagement in education, can serve assimilation rather than self-determination (Danaher & Henderson). Kinash and Kinash highlight how children's voices have been silenced, not only by the dominant society's concern for them but also by that society's preference for reading over oracy in education. This silencing is endorsed by cultural values regarding knowledge transmission (literacy is valued over oracy), and unequal adult/child power relations. So "We made the shift from orality to literacy and then froze, failing to notice that the children have left us behind" (Kinash & Kinash)—but we still have the power to leave their voices out of the frame in education planning. How can we avoid this waste and redress the power imbalance? Kocher and Pacini-Ketchabaw, and Hawkins, show that the process can start in the pedagogic practices of preschool teachers, and in recognition of children's competence and capacity for reflection. Thus, reflective methodology is intimately linked with participant engagement.

Particularly in the central section of the book (*Privileging Participants*), one can feel the energy that is released when them-and-us distancing is challenged and overcome. People who would formerly have seen universities as alien are empowered when they discover that they can bring their life experience into play with their college learning, to the enrichment of both (Henderson & Noble). Likewise, the divide between teachers' necessary spontaneity and researchers' elaborate organization is well described (Abawi; Hartle, Smith, Adkison, Williams, & Beardsley). Teachers rightfully, perhaps, viewed researchers as aliens using a language of inaccessible loftiness; researchers, with some justification, perhaps, saw teachers as unreflective and careless. Happily, joint engagement in achieving a common goal transformed the way they judged each other. Everyone was enriched and energized as a result of careful documentation of pedagogic exploration. Changing a hierarchical relation into a dialogical one blended what Ted Fleming (2003) calls common knowledge and college knowledge. The common/college binary catches the power inequalities between child and adult, student and institution, and practitioner and theorist. The unequal relation is caught in language differentials, Bernsteinian or other. Reflective and engaged dialogue generates "a hybrid language . . . vibrant and alive in its continued evolution" (Abawi).

Then there are the more overt cultural imbalances: the dominant ideology of *new vocationalism* and other corporatist orientations can frustrate a teacher's desire to respond sensitively to a learner's perspective. Predictably, the huge increase in student numbers has led to increased bureaucratization; commitment to broadening access has not been accompanied by necessary resources (Hammer, Werth, Dunn, Lawson, & d'Abadie). Context and ideology intersect. But policy and resource constraints have the effect of raising teachers' awareness of their own values—the seeds of resistance are sown in this binary struggle. This is true of almost all teachers, ranging from nursing tutors in TAFE (Tyler) to scuba diving instructors (Cardwell). The evidence of teacher resilience is inspiring. However, we would do well to remember Kocher and Pacini-Ketchabaw's observation that "some reflexive practices, although presented as tools for destabilizing binaries, have become part of neoliberal strategies of government."

In the opening chapter of the final section in this book, Hammer, Lawrence, and Huijser highlight the effects of globalization. Worldwide, we are in conflict-fraught transitions relating to the binary of national identity and global citizenship. These authors call for reflection in, on, and before action to promote cultural flexibility and sensitivity. In his introduction to the *Report on the Future of Multi-Ethnic Britain* (2000), Bhikhu Parekh warns that England, Scotland, and Wales "could become narrow and inward-looking, with rifts between themselves and among their regions and communities." He advocates building a "community of citizens and communities" and states what this will involve:

- rethinking the national story and national identity
- understanding that all identities are in a process of transition
- developing a balance between cohesion, difference, and equality
- addressing and eliminating all forms of racism
- reducing material inequalities
- building a human rights culture

Each element in this list suggests the need to move from binary oppositions to positions of connectivity and flexibility. Parekh's (2000) words could be applied to any divide, and his warning is echoed in the introduction to this book: the editors say that "the continuing operation of deeply embedded sociocultural binaries constitutes one of the most serious obstacles to new and more transformative experiences of human relationships within communities, in nation states, and globally."

The various cases which highlight international binaries are interesting: Saudi students in Australia (Midgley); English-language teachers in Japan (Mehmet); East/West education values meeting—or not (Saito; Zhou & Pedersen). When trying to engage in dialogue, we must be sensitive to cross-cultural communication issues. Cultural value differences can conspire to endorse denigration of teachers. The professional status of English-language teachers in Japan, for example, founders on the institutional structures in Japanese universities. The teachers' professional culture is mismatched with the values of the dominant culture. Cultural and systemic values conspire, and the pedagogic style of the teachers of English is accorded a lightweight status that matches their employment contracts. Although the writers here did touch on the need to be open to *mutual* benefits, there is little discussion of what Western philosophy and practice of education could learn from other traditions, such as Confucianism. That would be fascinating. In that most international of binaries—gender—the influence of context is clear. Context includes the regressive impact of media stereotypes (Lennon), the much quieter persistence of gender inequality in universities, and the persistent sexism in any society you care to mention. This binary is alive and well, but alternative discourses are developing.

The last chapter in this book (Hartle et al.) offers us a timely reminder that binaries are never neat. They are a "potentially inconsistent cluster of expectations and associations"[3] which we draw on as the moment requires. Danaher and Henderson cite McVeigh's comment that opposing images of Travellers—romantic/deviant—"simultaneously inform contemporary ideas about . . . all nomadic peoples." How should we respond when a less powerful group's identity becomes a metaphor for something in the dominant sector's world—"Gypsy" fashions on catwalks, the QashQai car (model named after the Qashqai nomads of Iran, because the designers "believe that the car's typical buyer would also be itinerant in nature" (Wikipedia, 2010)? Such metaphors trivialize marginalized populations. And trivialized, the nomads lose their freedom to be themselves. Today, nomadism is almost an impossibility for nomadic peoples. One Traveller pithily summed up this outcome of antinomadic public hostility and state policy: "Travelling is dying as a way of living" (in Kenny & Mc Neela, 2005, p. 42).

What do we mean when we call an intellectual enquiry a "nomadic act"? I like the validation of the nomadic tradition implicit in this metaphor, but I am concerned that it endorses romantic academic assumptions regarding nomadism. Might not this new metaphor actually bury the nomads' experience of oppression? Even at this linguistic level, it is difficult to keep a balance (or to recognize the many imbalances) when moving from binaries as oppositional to binaries as continuities.

Finally, how can research contribute to changing the world? In this book there is evidence that, when researchers engage with those who are being studied, the research results are grounded and linguistically accessible. Wherever we are located in the academic research community, we cannot change the world if people don't know what we're saying. Nor do we have much hope of effectiveness if our theories and propositions don't sound doable to our research participants (and, like it or not, to policymakers). To return to the researcher/researched binary: Martin Collins (1994), a Traveller activist, summed up what the melting of this binary meant for him and for Travellers generally:

> For too long Travellers have been unaware of the theories that have been constructed about them. . . . More Travellers are rejecting the sub-

culture of poverty theory . . . [W]e see ourselves as an ethnic group. This enables us to put into words and to have concepts which explain our experiences and what has been happening to us. (pp. 130, 132)

We must hope that, in such dialogue, we can play our small part in changing the world.

1. The princess might be relieved.
2. The Irish Travellers.
3. A discourse-analysis "category." See Potter and Wetherell (1987, p. 133).

REFERENCES

Collins, M. (1994). The sub-culture of poverty: A response to McCarthy. In M. McCann, S. Ó Síocháin, & J. Ruane (Eds.), *Irish Travellers: Culture and ethnicity* (pp. 130–133). Belfast, Ireland: Institute of Irish Studies, Queen's University.

Fleming, T. (2003). College knowledge and common knowledge: What learning are we leading? *American Adult Higher Education Alliance Newsletter, 14*(1), 2–3.

Kenny, M., & Mc Neela, E. (2005). *Assimilation policies and outcomes: Travellers' experience.* Report on a research project commissioned by Pavee Point Travellers' Centre. Dublin, Ireland: Pavee Point Publications. Retrieved from http://www.paveepoint.ie/pdf/AssimilationPolicies.pdf

Parekh, B. (2000). Introduction. *Commission report on the future of multi-ethnic Britain.* London: Runnymede Trust. Online summary retrieved from http://www.runnymedetrust.org/projects/meb/report.html

Potter, J., & Wetherell, M. (1989). *Discourse and social psychology.* London: Sage.

Walford, G. (1998). *Doing research in education.* London: Falmer Press.

Wikipedia. (2010). http://en.wikipedia.org/wiki/Nissan_Qashqai last modified on 18 September 2010.

Contributors

Ms. Lindy Abawi is a lecturer in curriculum and pedagogy in the Faculty of Education at the Toowoomba campus of the University of Southern Queensland, Australia. Over the years Lindy has taught secondary art and English, primary music, and English as a second language. She is involved in the implementation of the Innovative Designs for Enhancing Achievement in Schools (IDEAS) project and has been a facilitator of the process at school, state, and interstate levels. Her doctoral dissertation topic is linked to the use of a common language to facilitate pedagogical development and meaning making.

Dr. Stephen Adkison is currently the provost and senior vice-president of Eastern Oregon University, USA. His academic interests are in English/rhetoric and composition, tertiary teaching and learning, and academic administration. During the development of the chapter in this book, he was serving as the interim director of the Center for Teaching and Learning, faculty coordinator for Assessment and Program Review, and associate professor of English at Idaho State University, USA.

Dr. Paul Beardsley is an evolutionary biologist/science educator. His research interests include evolution education, plant evolution and genetics, and rare plants. He has been involved in science education from kindergarten to PhD supervision. He is currently a science educator for the Biological Sciences Curriculum Study (BSCS), USA. During the development of the chapter in this book, he was an assistant professor of biological sciences at Idaho State University, USA.

Mr. Keith Cardwell is qualified as a mechanical and production engineer and also has a diploma in sport and recreation, a diploma in business and industrial administration, and a master of education in lifelong learning. He is currently a PhD candidate in the Faculty of Education at the Toowoomba campus of the University of Southern Queensland, Australia. His research involves looking at the competencies learned and necessary for recreational diving instructors.

Ms. Danielle d'Abadie is a counselor with an interest in the learning experiences of students with disabilities. Danielle graduated with a bachelor of science (honors) in psychology in 2006. Her research interests include supporting students with disabilities through their programs of study and she is also interested in the wider impacts of life on the student experience. At the time of writing the chapter in this book, Danielle was the research assistant in the project.

Professor Patrick Alan Danaher is professor in education (education research) in the Faculty of Education at the Toowoomba campus of the University of Southern Queensland, Australia. He is coauthor of two research books and sole or coeditor of nine edited books, four refereed conference proceedings, and 31 academic journal theme issues. His research and writing interests include educational mobilities; educational research ethics, methods, and politics; the work and identities of academics, educators, and researchers; lifelong education; open and distance education; rural education; and vocational education and training.

Ms. Samantha Dean holds an undergraduate degree in journalism from Griffith University, Australia and a masters degree in international relations. She has had her work published in the *Koori Mail* and the *Courier-Mail*, and, in her current position as Communications and Media Officer at Eidos Institute, Brisbane, Australia, runs a series of seminars aimed at encouraging a democratic debate around key issues of public policy within the wider community. Sam is committed to the Eidos ethos of closing the growing gap among individuals and groups in our knowledge economy and firmly believes in the power of collaborative research in innovative networking.

Dr. Dinah R. Dovona-Ope contributed to this book whilst undergoing PhD study in the Faculty of Education at the Toowoomba campus of the University of Southern Queensland, Australia. She recently graduated as the first Papua New Guinean with a PhD from USQ. Upon her return to her country she was appointed the head of department and senior lecturer in educational psychology, guidance, and counseling at the University of Goroka in Papua New Guinea. She hails from Bougainville Island.

Associate Professor Peter Dunn is a biostatistician at the University of the Sunshine Coast, Australia. He has broad expertise in the application of statistics to a variety of applications, including publications in the areas of teaching, technology, health, ecology, and agriculture. He has a strong background in mathematical statistics, and especially generalized linear models. He is a world leader in research to understand the Tweedie class of distributions, where his research has developed methods for the accurate numerical evaluation of the densities of the Tweedie distributions. He has presented numerous conference papers (winning a prize at the 16th International Workshop on Statistical Modeling in Odense, Denmark, in 2001, and the E. J. Pitman Prize at the Australian Statistics Conference in 2002), and he has broad experience in the application of statistics in applied settings.

Dr. Sara Hammer is a learning and teaching designer at the Toowoomba campus of the University of Southern Queensland, Australia. Sara has a PhD in applied ethics and social policy. Her current research interests include the learning experiences of students with disabilities, graduate attributes, lifelong learning, criterion-referenced assessment, and critical thinking.

Dr. R. Todd Hartle is an educator/researcher with an eclectic range of interests and experiences. He holds degrees in anthropology, psychology, ecology, and tertiary biology education. He has lived in several countries around the world and is currently at the Toowoomba campus of the University of Southern Queensland, Australia, performing tertiary education research, academic learning support, and research program evaluation. The chapter in this book is an extension of his dissertation research from Idaho State University, USA.

Dr. Karen Hawkins is currently the program coordinator for the bachelor of education (early childhood) program in the School of Education, Southern Cross University, Tweed/Gold Coast campus, Australia. As well as her first teaching degree she holds a graduate diploma in special needs education, a master of education, and a doctor of philosophy (the latter from the Faculty of Education at the Toowoomba campus of the University of Southern Queensland, Australia). Through participatory action research, Karen's doctorate examined specific pedagogical strategies that assisted early childhood educators to teach for social justice. Karen's research interests gravitate toward early childhood education, social justice, literacy, "wholeness," and well-being.

Associate Professor Robyn Henderson is an associate professor (literacies education) in the Faculty of Education at the Toowoomba campus of the University of Southern Queensland, Australia. She teaches undergraduate and postgraduate students in courses that relate to literacy curriculum and pedagogy. Most of her research is also in the literacy area, and she is particularly interested in the education of mobile school students and finding ways that education systems might better cater for students with mobile lifestyles.

Dr. Henk Huijser is a curriculum development specialist (problem based learning) at Bahrain Polytechnic in the Arabian Gulf. Prior to that he was a lecturer in the Learning and Teaching Support Unit at the Toowoomba campus of the University of Southern Queensland, Australia. His research interests include technology-enhanced learning and teaching, cross-cultural communication, and cultural studies, and he has published widely in all three areas. His current interests include mobile learning and social networking technology, and their potential applications in higher education.

Dr. Máirín Kenny, former principal of a primary school for Irish Traveller children, is an independent academic in Dublin, Ireland. Her main focus is on marginalization in education. Topics she has researched include: sectarianism in infant classes; ethnicity and racism in Irish schools; young people with disabilities in primary and secondary schools; and engagements between education and nomadism, with specific focus on Roma and Travellers. She is the author of *The Routes of Resistance: Travellers and Second Level Schooling* (Ashgate, 1997), and coeditor of *Traveller, Nomadic and Migrant Education* (Routledge, 2009).

Miss Kirsten Kinash is a 12-year-old girl in Year 7 at Clover Hill State School, Australia, where she is the School Captain. Kirsten lives in the hinterland on the Gold Coast. She is passionate about wildlife and the environment. She is a synchronized swimmer with the Gold Coast Mermaids and plays the flute.

Dr. Shelley Kinash is the director of quality, teaching, and learning at Bond University on the Gold Coast, Australia. Shelley has been a university academic for 16 years, teaching previously at the University of Calgary in Canada and the University of Southern Queensland in Australia. Shelley's PhD is in educational technology and her dissertation topic was blind online learners. Shelley is an active researcher and her current inquiries are into measuring the impact of mobile technologies on learning.

Dr. Laurie Kocher is a lecturer in the Faculty of Child, Family, and Community Studies at Douglas College near Vancouver, British Columbia, Canada. She has taught in a variety of settings, from kindergarten to university. Her doctoral research, undertaken in the Faculty of Education at the Toowoomba campus of the University of Southern Queensland, Australia, focused on how and where hermeneutic phenomenology intersects with the practice of pedagogical documentation that emerges from the early childhood educational project of Reggio Emilia, Italy.

Associate Professor Jill Lawrence is associate dean (learning and teaching) in the Faculty of Arts at the Toowoomba campus of the University of

Southern Queensland, Australia. Her research interests include higher education, the first-year experience, cross-cultural communication, and critical discourse theory. Her PhD looked at how first-year students made their transition to an unfamiliar university culture.

Ms. Kym Lawson is experienced in the field of disability and at the time of writing the chapter in this book was coordinator of disability resources at the Toowoomba campus of the University of Southern Queensland, Australia. After graduating as an occupational therapist, she worked in the disability field for 11 years, initially in early intervention and services for adults with intellectual disabilities. Kym has an interest in investigating the experiences of students to assist in improving services and ensuring that students reach their full potential in their studies.

Ms. Sherilyn Lennon is a part-time head of department at a rural Queensland high school and a full-time PhD student in the Faculty of Education at the Toowoomba campus of the University of Southern Queensland, Australia. She is also a mother of three, farmer's wife, and avid gardener. Her research explores the link between sociocultural influences within and beyond the school gate and students' schooling and life performances.

Ms. Alison Mander is a lecturer (teaching and learning studies) in the Faculty of Education at the Toowoomba campus of the University of Southern Queensland, Australia. She has research interests in teachers' work and professionalism, professional practice, education policy, and curriculum and practice. She was the coauthor of a paper that won an Outstanding Paper Award at the 2006 annual conference of the Society for Information Technology and Teacher Education.

Mr. Sean Mehmet teaches at Shinshu University's School of General Education, located in Matsumoto City, Nagano prefecture, Japan. He is concurrently a doctoral candidate in the Faculty of Education at the Toowoomba campus of the University of Southern Queensland, Australia. His doctoral research involves examining the extent to which the Developmental Model of Intercultural Sensitivity can be used to uncover potential connections between foreign-language learners' intercultural sensitivity and their achievement on language-proficiency tests. He lives with his lovely spouse Reiko and their two children, Tara and Duncan.

Dr. Warren Midgley is a lecturer in curriculum and pedagogy in the Faculty of Education at the Toowoomba campus of the University of Southern Queensland, Australia. His doctor of philosophy study explored the experiences of Saudi students at an Australian university, and his research interests include second-language acquisition and use, culturally and linguistically diverse students' experiences, diversity and social justice in education, and the methodology and ethics of cross-cultural research. Warren is coeditor of and contributor to the research book *Sustaining Synergies: Collaborative Research and Researching Collaboration* (Post Pressed, 2010).

Professor Bruce Muirhead is the founding Chief Executive Officer and Professor of the Eidos Institute, Brisbane, Australia. Prior to joining Eidos, he was the founding Director of the University of Queensland's "Boilerhouse" Research Centre. He has more than 25 years of experience in building partnerships between the public and private sectors, focusing on the connections among economic, public, and social innovation in the development of community capacity at local and global levels. He writes and travels extensively and over the past few years has been invited to speak about collaborative innovation at conferences in Europe, South Africa, the United Kingdom, and the United States of America.

Dr. Karen Noble has held roles in the university sector for the past nine years and prior to that a number of teaching positions in a broad range of contexts. Karen is currently the associate dean (teaching and learning) and the early childhood program coordinator in the Faculty of Education at the Toowoomba campus of the University of Southern Queensland, Australia. Her expertise in education and capacity building is evident in the quality of her academic teaching and learning, and she has been chief investigator for education and community development research projects in Queensland and internationally.

Associate Professor Veronica Pacini-Ketchabaw is associate professor and coordinator of the early years specialization in the School of Child and Youth Care at the University of Victoria, Canada. She has worked professionally in the field of early childhood education for over 15 years and taught at different levels in a variety of educational settings in Argentina and Canada. She teaches and conducts research on issues related to poststructuralist, feminist, and postcolonial theory–practice in early childhood education.

Mr. Cec Pedersen is a senior lecturer (management and organizational behavior) in the Faculty of Business and Law at the Toowoomba campus of the University of Southern Queensland, Australia. Previously he was the Queensland administrator for the Royal Australian College of General Practitioners Training Program and prior to that he spent over 14 years in general management and consulting positions in small- and medium-sized organizations. His current research and educational interests are leadership in tertiary education, human resource development, and Eastern business education.

Mr. Akihiro Saito is a PhD candidate in the Faculty of Education at the Too-woomba campus of the University of Southern Queensland, Australia. The topic of his dissertation is language attitudes of Japanese sojourners studying English overseas. His research interests cover a range of issues in the broad area of applied linguistics, including language attitudes, motivation, identity, and their implications for language pedagogy. While his methodological interests straddle both positivist and postpositivist paradigms, he is currently keen on applying postmodernist theories to this fascinating field.

Professor Michael Singh directs the "Knowledge Work Democracy" research program, Centre for Educational Research, University of Western Sydney, Australia. He undertakes curriculum research focusing on internationalizing education through transnational knowledge exchange; work-related education, training, and learning; the links among education policy, people, and place; and embedded international research education. Strategic partnerships involving transnational and interorganizational collaborations to effect knowledge flows through capacity building are key elements of his research.

Dr. Rosemary J. Smith's research includes behavioral ecology and science education. The focus of her biological research is on the behavior, ecology, and evolution of burying beetles, particularly population dynamics and reproductive strategies. In biology education, she studies the effectiveness of a variety of teaching methods, including methods to enhance teacher training and inquiry-based activities. She is currently a tenured professor of biological sciences at Idaho State University, USA.

Dr. Mark A. Tyler is a lecturer in the Faculty of Education at the Toowoomba campus of the University of Southern Queensland, Australia. Mark has a background in human services and technical and further education teaching. His expertise lies in learning and teaching within the workplace and distance education. His academic interests are critical spirit, criticality, teacher identities, mentoring, teaching and learning in vocational and technical education, lifelong learning, and workplace learning.

Ms. Shalene Werth is a lecturer in employment relations in the Faculty of Business and Law at the Toowoomba campus of the University of Southern Queensland, Australia. Her PhD study is on the topic of the workforce outcomes of women with chronic illness. Her research interests include the impost that chronic illness has on the lives of sufferers, and ways that collective action can improve outcomes for both workers and students. The ways that employers accommodate chronic illness with a specific focus on gender and related industrial relations theories are also of interest.

Dr. DJ Williams is a leading expert on deviant leisure, including gambling behavior in correctional settings, and critical issues in sexology, forensic social work, and criminology. His research frameworks range from statistics to postmodern autoethnography. He is currently an assistant professor of sociology, social work, and criminal justice at Idaho State University, USA.

Dr. Peng Zhou is a lecturer in the Faculty of Business and Law at the Toowoomba campus of the University of Southern Queensland, Australia. Before coming to Australia in 1998, Dr. Zhou was a business lecturer at a Chinese regional university. After completing his PhD in 2002, Dr. Zhou was employed to coordinate a Mandarin MBA program jointly operated by the University of Southern Queensland and its Chinese partners. His current research interests are in cross-cultural issues in business education, international marketing of higher education services, and Chinese consumer behavior.

Index

A

ability 53, 122, 124, 156, 167, 181,
    183, 201, 211–212, 214–216,
    218, 225–226, 235, 236, 250
academic standards 211–212, 216, 218
adaptability 182–183
advocacy 29–31, 100, 103, 185
age xxii, 53, 101, 120, 123, 125–126,
    155–156, 201, 204, 224
agency (sociocultural) 24, 69, 74, 85,
    90, 97, 121, 149, 216
assimilation 66, 71–72, 171, 259–260
assumptions, unexamined 60
Australia 3, 9, 15, 19, 34, 38, 42, 49,
    60–61, 67, 71–73, 81, 83, 86,
    90, 97, 102, 112, 119–121, 133,
    135, 149, 161–162, 166–168,
    170, 172–173, 182, 184–185,
    188, 191, 195–197, 200, 208,
    211–214, 224–225, 237–238,
    242–243, 261
authorship 100, 102–103, 105,
    108–109, 111–114
autoethnography 18, 24, 35, 111, 272

B

binaries: ability/disability xxi, 9, 179,
    211–213, 215, 217–219
abstract/practical 163, 165, 169–170,
    172
academia/pop culture xxi
academic/vocational xxi
acculturation/cultural persistence 70
active/passive 162, 164–168, 172,
    233
adult/child xxi, 9, 54, 100, 102–103,
    260
analytic/holistic 135, 162, 164–166,
    172

Australian/international 182, 185,
    191
boy/girl 54, 67, 195–197, 200–202,
    204, 206–207
center/margin 7, 62–63
citizen/non-citizen 70
conceptualization/interpretation 3
corporeality/sociality 3
deep/surface 162–165, 168, 172
dominant/deficit 185
educator/practitioner xvii, 9, 242,
    244, 249, 253
elite/mass 182
empowered/disempowered 48
experience/reflection 4
expert/novice 126
formal/informal learning 221–222
    225, 227, 229–230
gazer/gazed at 18
global/local 2–3, 183, 185
good/evil xxi
'good mother'/'working mother' 3
home/abroad 3, 5–6
homeland/new land 70
host/visitor 182, 185, 191
included/excluded 48
individualism/collectivism 164–165
individualized learning/cooperative
    learning 54
insider/outsider 182, 232, 239–240
learners/situations 4
learning/play 54
liberal democracy/bureaucratic
    authoritarianism 164–165, 167
majority/minority 182–183, 185, 191
male/female xxi–xxii, 198, 200–201,
    203–204, 206–207
me/you vii, 36–38
migrant/nonmigrant 70

mind/body 46
nature/culture 46
new vocationalism/professional
    identities 9, 83–85, 89, 92, 95,
    97, 260
objectivity/subjectivity 48, 51,
    147–148, 150–151, 169, 197
observer/observed 9, 22, 34, 43
ordered/unordered 48
permanent employee/limited-term
    employee 232–233, 237
policy/practice 3
positive/negative xxii, 8, 63
production/consumption 3
public/private xxi, 3, 46, 237
quantitative/qualitative 28–29, 69–70
rational/irrational 48, 54, 165–166,
    197
representation/practice 3
research/practice 18–23, 46–47, 49, 56
researcher/researched 33, 138, 147–
    150, 153–154, 157, 159, 262
researcher/teacher xvii, 9, 81, 131, 134,
    139–141, 145, 156, 250, 260
scientific exploration/spiritual perfec-
    tion 164–165
self/other 4–7, 17–18, 20, 22, 36, 38,
    85, 144, 185
settled/itinerant 9, 61–62, 64–69, 71,
    73–75
settled/unsettled 65
successful/unsuccessful 119–120,
    122–126, 128–129
theory/practice xvii, 52–54, 87, 136,
    139, 142, 164, 170, 226, 260,
    270
voice/voiceless 48
West/East xxi, 3, 21, 23, 161, 172,
    261
West/non-West 3, 17–18, 22, 41
Western/Confucian 161–173, 262
work/family 3
work/home 4–5
worker/mother 4–5

C

capability 141, 156, 169, 171, 185,
    214, 227
case method (methods—case study) 83,
    97, 123, 195, 197, 206, 219
centrifugal forces 36
centripetal forces 36
certification 98, 179, 224, 229
children publishing 101–102, 109–111

class (as in class of students) 113, 136,
    233, 246
class (as in position in society) 47, 156
collaborative individualism 235
community of learners 50
competency 188, 214, 221, 224–225,
    227
Confucian-heritage learners 169–170,
    172
contextualism 251
critical approach 6, 49
Critical Discourse Analysis (CDA)
    199–200
critical reflection 50, 56, 149
critical spirit 84–89, 93–95, 97
cross-cultural communication 183
cultural competence 29
cultural maintenance 181–184, 191
cultural relativism 242, 248, 250–254
cultural sustainability 181–186,
    188–191
curriculum 83–84, 90–93, 95–96, 112,
    114, 142, 148, 190–191, 212,
    217–218, 221, 226

D

data ownership 41–43
deconstruction xviii, xxi, 1–2, 5, 52, 68
deconstructive talks 52–53
demystification 68–69
developmental psychology 51, 53
dialogic engagement 36, 39, 43
dialogism 36
dichotomy xvii, 2, 64, 67, 70, 91, 140,
    167, 240
disability 30, 179, 211, 213–218, 236
Disability Discrimination Act
    (Australia, 1992) 219
discourse 3, 17–18, 22–23, 48, 51,
    53, 55, 63, 83, 85, 87, 89–90,
    92–95, 97, 98, 179, 182–183,
    188–189, 195, 199, 204,
    206–207, 263
Discourse, Gee 85, 119–122, 128
discursive concealment 21
discursive constructions 65, 184
discursive objects 20
discursive position 20
discursive representation 21–22, 206
dominant discourse 18, 51

E

early childhood education 15, 46–49,
    51–53, 56–57

epistemology 100, 102, 151
equitable practice 49
essentialization 55, 65
ethics of resistance 52
ethnicity 4, 47, 66, 244
etiology 61, 64–65, 74

F
female students 30, 195, 202
first year student experience 121–126,
  128, 211, 214, 229
forgetting 21
Fourth Blueprint Paradigm 232, 238

G
gender xxii, 3–4, 47, 52, 67, 109,
  156, 179, 195–199, 202–204,
  206–207, 259, 262, 271
global citizenship 182–183, 185, 191,
  261
globalization 161, 163, 171–172, 181,
  183, 259, 261

H
hermeneutic phenomenology 131–132,
  144–145, 268
heteropatriarchy 199, 205–207
higher education 112, 115, 162,
  171–172, 179, 181, 184, 191,
  212–213, 217, 232, 268–269,
  272
homogenization 63, 65
hyper-masculine discourse 199,
  205–206

I
identity: formation, (trans)formation
  81, 83–85, 87–92, 97, 107, 109,
  181, 185, 203, 213, 216, 222,
  234–236, 261–262
ideology 6, 200, 260–261
inability 66, 86, 98, 201, 214
incidental learning 179, 221–222,
  227–229
informal learning 221–222, 225–227,
  229
Innovative Designs for Enhancing
  Achievements in Schools
  (IDEAS) 131–133, 136–137,
  139–145
integration 55, 71–72, 121
interconnectivity 69
intercultural communication 190, 232,
  236

Intercultural Communications Theory
  190
interdependence 53, 62, 232, 236
internationalization 162, 171–172, 191,
  213
interview 86, 88–89, 91–96, 122–125,
  128, 144, 196, 211, 214, 221,
  228, 249
introspective depiction 18
itinerancy 60

J
Japan 9, 15, 19–22, 40, 180, 232–240,
  261, 269

K
knowledge xvii–xix, xxi–xxii, 2–3,
  5, 10, 35–36, 41–43, 48–49,
  51–52, 56–57, 65–66, 69, 84,
  86–87, 90, 101–103, 108–109,
  116, 120–122, 126, 132, 134,
  137–138, 140–143, 149–151,
  157, 164–167, 169, 171–172,
  181, 184, 186–187, 197, 199,
  223, 225–226, 228, 234, 240,
  243–244, 260, 266, 271

L
language as a meaning-filled practice 48
learner differences 166–167, 179
learning traditions 162, 164, 167, 172
life choices 211
lived experience 18, 131–132, 134–135,
  139, 143–145
lobbying 71–72

M
make visible 49, 52, 54, 189, 196
male hegemony 204
marginalization xvii–xviii, 3, 30, 60,
  69, 74, 81, 84, 185, 191, 262,
  268
massification of higher education 119,
  182, 213
master narrative 18
matrilineal: cultures; kinships systems
  27, 31–32
media; texts, discourse 4, 63, 101, 115,
  179, 181, 195–199, 201–203,
  205–207, 262
member checking 42
memory of the nation 20
mixed methods research 27–30, 32–33
mobile learners 60–61, 65, 71–75

mobile show people, Australian 61
multiculturalism 3, 183, 185, 191
multiliteracies 131–133, 136, 142
multiple perspectives 50–51

N
naming 63
narrative 10, 17–18, 20–21, 23, 39,
    50–51, 86–88, 90, 93, 97,
    103–104, 107
neutralism 251
nomadic act 55, 262
norm 51, 60–61, 63, 182, 199, 202,
    212, 216

O
omissions 49
ontology; of becoming, of being 55,
    202
ordinary moments 50
othering 62, 203, 259
otherness xviii, 4–6

P
Papua New Guinea 9, 15, 28–31, 266
paradigm/s 6–7, 18, 30, 43, 50, 65,
    143–145, 147, 162–164, 171–
    172, 183, 215, 232, 238, 271
participant/s 8–9, 15, 23, 31, 34,
    38–39, 41–44, 51–52, 73, 79,
    81, 104, 139, 141, 143, 147–
    154, 156, 158, 203, 214–215,
    226, 242, 245, 247–254,
    259–260, 262
Participatory Action Research (PAR)
    147, 149, 151
pathologization 64–65
patrilineal: cultures; kinship systems 31
pedagogical documentation 15, 46–47,
    49–53, 55–57
performativity 17, 21–22
personality 242, 248–250, 253–254
polarization xvii, 62
positioning 62–63, 81, 88, 91, 97, 113,
    198, 206, 211
postcolonialism 5, 41, 270
postmodernism 9, 10, 21
poststructuralism xxi, 21–22, 46–49,
    51, 56, 68, 197–198, 200, 270
power, exercise of 1–2, 4–6, 8, 30–32,
    48–49, 54–55, 57, 62, 69, 95,
    102, 104–105, 111–113, 115,
    126, 136, 143, 147, 149–150,
    152–154, 156–159, 189–190,

    197–199, 204, 206–207, 216,
    235, 240, 259, 260
practices, cultural 3–5, 18, 30, 33, 46,
    48–52, 54–56, 61–62, 64, 71,
    92, 116, 128, 133, 144, 149,
    156–158, 181–182, 184–191,
    195–200, 205–207, 213, 218,
    225, 227, 240, 253, 259–261
pre-school 52, 148, 150, 153, 155–160
professional culture 180, 242, 244,
    247–254, 261

Q
qualitative research 28–29, 42–44, 144,
    150, 159
quality standards in research 43, 157

R
race 47, 156
race-based policies 60–61
recreational diving 179, 221–226,
    228–229, 261, 265
reflective practice 56, 186
reflexive analysis 35, 39
reifying 20
reimagining 49, 56
reinventing 49
representation 1, 4, 6, 21–22, 32, 42,
    48, 53, 63, 68–69, 81, 141, 149,
    189, 195, 199, 202–206, 249
research methodology 15, 17, 23, 40
researcher/s xvii–xix, xxii, 5, 8–9,
    13, 15, 17–18, 21–23, 27–36,
    41–43, 47, 49–51, 54, 56,
    69–70, 72, 75, 81, 84, 102,
    104, 108, 112, 131, 133–134,
    137–145, 147–150, 153–159,
    243–244, 245–246, 248–251,
    259–260, 262, 266–268
resilience of binaries 60, 62, 261
resources, denial of 62, 90
retrospective depiction 18
Roma 60, 65, 67, 72, 268

S
Sami 66
Saudi 34, 38–44, 261, 269
schools 46, 66–68, 72, 107, 111–112,
    116, 131–133, 139–141, 144,
    166, 196, 197, 200–201, 206,
    223, 254, 265, 268
seasonal workers, Australian 60–61
sedentarism xxii, 60–61, 64–65, 68–71,
    73, 75

sedimentation 21–22
semiotic reading 53
sense-making 47, 144
serendipity 39, 40–41, 43
sexuality 3, 156
silences 49, 134
social justice 8, 74, 100, 148–152,
    154–158, 237, 267, 270
socioeconomic status 4, 119–120
specialization 71–73, 270
stereotyping 63, 249
structuralism xxi, 2
surplus of seeing 34, 36–37, 43
sustainability 179, 181–186, 188–191
synergy/ies xxii, 8, 15, 138, 141, 145, 161
systems thinking 62, 69, 165

T

teacher xvii, 3, 5, 9, 40, 50–54, 67,
    71–74, 81, 83–89, 91–92,
    94–97, 101, 103, 107, 109–113,
    115–116, 131–145
teacher identity 81, 83–84, 87–88, 92,
    97
teaching xxi, xxii, 7, 52, 67, 83–88,
    91, 93–94, 96–97, 110, 112,
    121, 132–135, 137, 139–140,
    142, 148, 150, 152, 156–158,
    161–164, 166–173, 180, 182,
    190–191, 197, 212–213, 224,
    232, 237, 242–243, 245, 247,
    249–250, 254, 259, 265–271
Technical and Further Education
    (TAFE) college 81, 83–84,
    86–98, 261
tertiary study 119, 121, 124
thinking xviii, xix, 6,8–9, 37, 39,
    48–49, 51–55, 57, 60, 62, 69,
    71, 73, 87, 115, 120–121, 123,
    126, 128, 138, 162, 164–166,
    169–170, 172, 196–197, 200,
    250, 253, 267

transformation, social 69
transgredience 34, 36, 38
transparency 40, 156, 185–186
truthfulness 20

U
United Kingdom 3, 72, 195, 270
United States 72, 195, 237, 242–243,
    254, 270
university students 81, 119–121,
    123–124, 182, 185, 213, 233
urbanization 65

V
values 18, 27–30, 32, 47, 52, 54, 62,
    84, 87, 133, 143–144, 149, 161,
    164–165, 167, 169, 171, 173
verisimilitude 20
vocational education and training
    (VET) 83–84, 87, 90, 97
vocationalism 9, 83–85, 89, 95, 97, 260
voice: active; first-person-plural; imper-
    sonal; passive; personal; trans-
    formative intellectual 28–29, 32

W
Western
    academia 22, 42–43, 163, 166,
        170–171
    culture 161, 163, 165
    intellectual traditions 17, 68
    learners 164, 167–169
    methods 18
worldviews 235
writing 6, 23, 27, 29–30, 32,-34,
    39, 41, 43, 75, 85, 100, 102,
    104–105, 107–116, 119–121,
    132,144, 153, 166–170, 173,
    216, 233, 246, 253–254

Y
you-and-me 36